HARDPRESS.NET
HOME OF HARD-TO-FIND BOOKS

Conversations on English Grammar
by Charles M. Ingersoll

Address:
HardPress
8345 NW 66TH ST #2561
MIAMI FL 33166-2626
USA
Email: info@hardpress.net

CONVERSATIONS

ON

ENGLISH GRAMMAR;

EXPLAINING THE

PRINCIPLES AND RULES OF THE LANGUAGE.

ILLUSTRATED BY

APPROPRIATE EXERCISES;

ABRIDGED AND ADAPTED TO THE USE OF SCHOOLS.

BY CHARLES M. INGERSOLL.

"There is no other method of *teaching* that of which any one is ignorant, than by means of something already known."—*Dr. Johnson.*

FOURTH EDITION.

PORTLAND:

PUBLISHED BY CHARLES GREEN, TEACHER OF ENGLISH GRAMMAR.

TODD AND SMITH,....PRINTERS.

1824.

SOUTHERN DISTRICT OF NEW-YORK; ss.

BE IT REMEMBERED, That on the twenty-seventh day of April, in the forty-fifth year of the Independence of the United States of America, Charles M. Ingersoll, of the said District, hath deposited in this office the title of a Book, the right whereof he claims as author and proprietor, in the words following, to wit :

"Conversations on English Grammar; explaining the Principles and Rules of the Language, illustrated by Appropriate Exercises ; Abridged, and Adapted to the Use of Schools. By Charles M. Ingersoll. "There is no other method of *teaching* that of which any one is ignorant, than by means of something already known."—Dr. Johnson.

In conformity to the Act of the Congress of the United States, entitled "An Act for the encouragement of Learning, by securing the copies of Maps, Charts, and Books, to the authors and proprietors of such copies, during the time therein mentioned." And also to an Act entitled "an Act, supplementary to an Act, entitled an Act for the encouragement of Learning, by securing the copies of Maps, Charts, and Books, to the authors and proprietors of such copies, during the times therein mentioned, and extending the benefits thereof to the arts of designing, engraving, and etching historical and other prints."

G. L. THOMPSON,
Clerk of the Southern District of New-York.

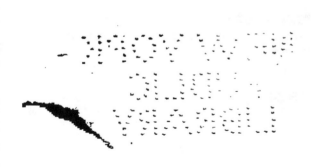

RECOMMENDATIONS.

"Messrs. Todd & Smith:

"Your note, and Ingersoll's Grammar, which accompanied it, have been received. I have examined the book, with some attention, and assure you I am much pleased with it. His arrangement of the work is happily calculated to render it entertaining as well as useful. The author pursues a natural order, and leads the learner on by easy and regular steps, so that what he learns to-day will enable him easily to understand the lesson of to-morrow. There is much plainness and simplicity in his mode of instruction; and the whole is so adapted to the capacity of the pupil as to keep the attention alive in search of new rules and principles, instead of fatiguing it by teaching the rudiments of language by the use of terms before they are understood, and the study and repetition of rules with which he has not been made acquainted. I am of opinion that the book will be highly useful, and I hope it will be extensively circulated.   Yours, &c.   PRENTISS MELLEN."

"October, 1823."

"I have looked through Ingersoll's Grammar, and concur in the opinion which Chief-Justice Mellen has expressed of the merits of the work.
"ASHUR WARE,
Judge United States' District Court for Maine.

"On examination of 'Conversations on English Grammar,' by Mr. Charles M. Ingersoll, I think the work to be an improvement on Murray's excellent Grammar, in many important particulars: 1st, In his natural and systematic arrangement; and hence: 2ndly, The easy gradations by which he conducts the pupil to the knowledge of his subject; 3dly, the appropriateness of the examples, designed to illustrate each part of speech, in succession, by advancing from the simpler parts to the more complex, and from the simple sentence to the compound; and, 4thly, The supplementary distribution of the more difficult rules, which regard rather the construction, than the syntactical parsing of sentences; and which belong as properly to Rhetoric as to elementary Grammar. And it may be further added, in favor of Mr. Ingersoll's system, that it embraces not only all the excellencies of 'Murray's Grammar,' but also his 'Exercises in false syntax,' newly arranged to correspond with the other improvements.   B. CUSHMAN,
Principal of the Classical Academy

Portland, Jan. 1, 1821.

The following remarks by Mr. Walsh are taken from "The National Gazette," of the 7th Sept. 1821.

"Our avocations prevented us from examining, until lately, 'The Conversations on English Grammar,' &c. by Charles M. Ingersoll; a work which was published not long since at New York. It appears to us to be superior in the plan and execution, as regards the purpose for which it is mainly designed,—the use of schools,—to any elementary treatise of English Grammar with which we are acquainted. He has chosen the happiest form and the most efficacious mode of instruction; and would seem, from the sound general views presented in his well written Preface, to have studied, with the greatest care, the kind and degree of assistance which the youthful mind requires in the pursuit of abstract knowledge. In his 'Conversations, the nature, principles, and rules of English Grammar are so unfolded, progressively, that the learner is assisted by each step in every further advance, and all the preliminary ideas necessary to the comprehension of any particular topic, are fixed in his mind as far as is practicable.

"Mr. Ingersoll has, without question, administered important helps, in this volume, to such as are sufficiently ripe in understanding to master the subject. The work is a valuable accession to the list of school manuals, and may be properly consulted by adults in every liberal walk of life."

RECOMMENDATIONS.

Many eminent teachers in New-York have introduced this book into their schools. The following recommendations exhibit the opinions of some of them.

" To Charles M. Ingersoll, Esq.

" Dear Sir—I congratulate you, and every friend of teaching, on the production of your 'Conversations on English Grammar;' such a work was greatly wanted to render the acquisition of Grammar easy and attractive, by removing, in a plain and rational manner, the veil of mystery in which mere rules of the science necessarily leave it enveloped. You have happily succeeded in rendering English Grammar perspicuous and familiar to the juvenile mind, by giving the *rationale* of every rule ; and the judicious arrangement gradually proceeding from the elementary to the most abstruse parts, enables the learner to comprehend, without difficulty, what is presented at every step of his progress. The recapitulations are admirably adapted to this end, while the exercises in parsing, accompanying every new acquisition are calculated to fix them in the mind, and confirm and illustrate the rules.— Such a plan is entirely new ; I admire its ingenuity, and confidently anticipate its universal adoption in our seminaries of learning. Instead of servilely following your predecessors, you have struck out a new path, where every thing is simple, satisfactory, and inviting. Wishing that your work may meet with the encouragement it so well merits, I remain, dear sir, yours sincerely.   A. O. STANSBURY.

" I have examined ' Conversations on English Grammar,' by Charles M. Ingersoll, Esq. and fully concur in the opinion as given above.
                                    " HEZEKIAH G. UFFORD, A. M.

" May 21, 1821."

' I have read ' Conversations on English Grammar, by Charles M. Ingersoll, Esq.' and have no hesitation in saying that, in my opinion, it offers greater advantages to pupils, who are studying English Grammar, than any other book now in use.   JOSEPH HOXIE, Philom. Academy."
" May 14, 1821."

" In the above opinion I fully concur.   JOHN D. HOLBROOK."

" Charles M. Ingersoll, Esq_
" Sir—I have examined ' Conversations on English Grammar,' with care and I am happy to say, that I think it better adapted to the purpose intended than any other with which I am acquainted.
" I have for many years, been accustomed to instruct in that branch, and have found, in all systems, many difficulties and imperfections ; particularly the want of intelligible explanation, of regular gradation, and of just adaptation of the subject, to the progress of the pupil : these you have happily fallen upon the true method of obviating.
" I hope and trust that we shall soon find your book in general use.
            " Yours, &c.   J. W. KELLOGG.

" Messrs. Wiley & Halstead—I have examined with attention, and with pleasure, ' Conversations on English Grammar,' by Charles M. Ingersoll, Esq. and have no hesitation in saying that, in my opinion, it is incomparably the best English Grammar, for the use of schools, that has been laid before the public. I trust that the facilities which it offers to young learners, will induce parents who consult their own interest and that of their children, and teachers who intend to do their duty to both, to unite in giving this book an immediate introduction into all our schools.
                                    " J. PERRY,
            " Teacher of the Classical and Grammar School, No. 142 Fulton-street .
" New-York, May 14, 1821."

RECOMMENDATIONS.

The following, by N. H. Carter, Esq. late Professor of Languages in Dartmouth College, is an extract from the Statesman.

" Mr. Ingersoll has brought to his subject a clear and philosophical mind ; an extensive and accurate knowledge of the principles of universal grammar, and of the English language in particular; much experience in the science on which he has written, and a happy faculty of expressing and illustrating his ideas. It would exceed the limits of a newspaper paragraph to enter into a full explanation of his system. Suffice it to say, that he has in our opinion, introduced many valuable improvements both in matter and manner.— He has reversed many parts of the system of grammar, putting the first, last, and the last, first, and following the order of the understanding, instead of the artificial and unnatural arrangement which his predecessors have adopted.— His investigations have stripped the science of many of its technicalities, and of much of the mystery in which it has been enveloped ; and by relieving the pupil from the severest and most irksome of all tasks—that of committing to memory what he does not comprehend, Mr. Ingersoll has rendered the study of grammar at once easy, pleasing and profitable. Able and experienced instructers have pronounced it to be decidedly the best system which they have met with, and there is a prospect of its coming into general use. On the whole, we fully concur in the favorable opinions which others have expressed, and believe it to be a work highly creditable to its author, and worthy of public patronage."

William Coleman, Esq. editor of the Evening Post, copied the whole article and said, " As an evidence of our acquiescence in the above remarks of Mr Carter, we have republished the above article Mr. Ingersoll, in the course of this work, discovers an extensive and thorough acquaintance with the English grammarians who have preceded him ; sometimes agreeing and sometimes disagreeing with them, and always states his reasons in language at once plain and perspicuous."

" Mr. Charles M. Ingersoll,
" Sir—I have read with much satisfaction your ' Conversations on English Grammar.' The work contains all that is useful in Murray, Lowth, and others, writers on grammar ; and the instruction is conveyed on a plan entirely new, and well adapted to fix it methodically and permanently on the mind. Its introduction into our seminaries of education would facilitate the progress of the pupil, and I certainly hope that you may receive the patronage which the distinguished merits of this work demand.
" I am, sir, your most obedient servant,   J. V. N. YATES,
" Secretary of State, and ex-officio Superintendant of Common Schools
" Albany, Sept. 1, 1821."

Extract of a letter from the Rev. D. Wilkie, Principal of a Classical and English Grammar School at Quebec, to Thomas Cary, Jun. Bookseller.

" Quebec, August 3d. 1821.
" Dear Sir—I have had an opportunity of looking into Mr Ingersoll's Grammar of the English Language, and think it a very judicious work. But I think it would prove a very useful work in families and for private teacher It seems peculiarly calculated for the advantage of those who desire to advance their knowledge of the English Language by private study.
" I am your obedient servant,   D. WILKIE."

Letter from Dr. Abercrombie, to the Author.
" Philadelphia, July 10, 1821.
" Sir—In reply to your favor of the 5th inst. requesting my opinion of your recent publication entitled ' Conversations on English Grammar,' I do not hesitate to express my highest approbation of the mode you have adopted to inculcate that essentially necessary branch of science. Its novelty will induce attention ; and the very lucid and familiar manner in which you have communicated instruction, renders it a work equally well calculated for the school and for the closet. Its merit will, I hope, be justly appreciated, and its use generally adopted. I am, sir, your most humble servant
" JAS. ABERCROMBIE."

ADVERTISEMENT.

TO THE THIRD EDITION.

———————

THOSE who may have occasion to use Conversations on English Grammar, either entire or abridged, are informed, that the Conversations and Sections on *Etymology* and *Syntax*, and the chapters on *Punctuation*, are, word for word, the same in both editions. No confusion, therefore, can arise from using copies of both in the same class, if the Conversations, Sections, &c. be referred to, instead of the *pages*.

The entire work is full-bound, and contains about ninety pages more than the Abridgment. They are filled with remarks on the sounds of the letters, promiscuous exercises in false Orthography, with Prosody, and the Figures of Speech.

Although the difference in the prices of the two editions, is but twenty-five cents a copy, one being a dollar, and the other seventy-five cents, yet, as this has been found to be an object of consideration with many, particularly with those who have large families to supply with grammars, both kinds will be constantly kept in the market.

The demand for a book, how great soever it may be, seldom exceeds that anticipated by its author. In remarking on the favorable reception which has been given to Conversations on English Grammar, however, the author feels himself bound to acknowledge, that the demand which has, in a few months, called into actual use *eight thousand copies* of his book, and which, now, calls for a third edition, *he* certainly did not anticipate.

In preparing an elementary book for children, the principal object of the writer ought to be, the *general* improvement of the mind. That method of teaching which *most* effectually cultivates *all the powers* of the mind, while it gives a thorough knowledge of a *particular* subject, is undoubtedly the best.

To strengthen the memory, therefore, to aid reflection, to call forth the powers of combining and comparing the objects presented, and to sharpen and invigorate the reasoning faculties of those who use it, were the leading objects which the author endeavored to keep in view in preparing this work.

With what success he has labored, a discerning and impartial public will decide.

He hopes, and he believes, that pupils who use this book, will find the subject of which it treats both easy and pleasant ; and, that, in their succeeding studies, they will long feel the happy effects which this method of teaching, must necessarily produce.

January, 1822.

PREFACE.

In presenting this abridgment of CONVERSATIONS ON ENGLISH GRAMMAR to the public, the author deems it proper to give an outline of his arrangement of the subject; to endeavor to support the distinctions which he has advanced respecting the subjunctive mood, by such reasoning, and such authority, as may justify his positions; to make a few remarks on the facilities which it offers to teachers as well as to learners; and to suggest the advantages which may be expected to result from this method of instruction.

There is perhaps no elementary study in which children find more difficulty than in that of English Grammar; nor one which they generally pursue with less interest. This, it is presumed, arises, not so much from any obscurities peculiar to this subject, as from the manner in which it is usually presented to the youthful mind.

A natural and easy gradation in introducing and connecting the different parts of speech, and in explaining the inflections and properties peculiar to each; presenting, progressively, *that only* which the learner is prepared to understand; and illustrating the rules and principles by examples and practical exercises, in a course of familiar Conversations; seemed to the author, to be the method best adapted to remove this difficulty, and to excite attention and curiosity in those who are endeavoring to acquire a knowledge of the English Grammar.

The first two Conversations, therefore, introduce the subject; treat of the number and division of letters, and the rules of orthography, as exemplified in the different modifications of words.

The third Conversation commences with Etymology and Syntax, and explains the Noun, (the only part of speech, except the Interjection, which can be explained without a reference to some other,) with its persons, numbers, genders, and the *nominative* case, together with the active verb, agreeing with its nominative.

The fourth explains the two other cases of nouns, with their proper government, and the distinctions of the transitive and intransitive verbs.

In the fifth, the Articles are introduced; and the pupil is now prepared to understand the distinctions, and appropriate uses of this part of speech.

The Adverb, which always has its grammatical connexions with a verb, adjective, participle, or with another adverb, is explained in the eighth.

In the ninth, the pronouns are given: and the personal and adjective pronouns particularly explained.

The tenth continues the explanation of the Pronouns, in their respective classes, and treats particularly of the relative and interrogative kinds.

Prepositions are introduced in the eleventh; and the twelfth comprises the Conjunctions and Interjections, and prepares the learner for the analysis of compound sentences.

In these twelve Conversations, the pupil is made acquainted with all the parts of speech; their different offices, properties, connexions and dependencies; except the moods and tenses of verbs; and by means of the exercises in parsing, which are annexed to each Conversation, he is enabled, with the exception just mentioned, to parse them with accuracy and despatch. Additional remarks are also subjoined, which each Conversation prepares the learner to read with intelligence and pleasure; because he can understand them. A series of questions referring to the preceding Conversation, immediately follows the remarks; to answer these the learner is compelled to study with attention and to condense the subject-matter, in order to give his own explanations, instead of reciting a confused multitude of words, without annexing corresponding ideas to what he repeats.

The thirteenth and fourteenth Conversations are occupied in explaining several connexions and rules, which could not have been presented before; and a few pages are taken up on the subject of derivation.

The fifteenth Conversation commences with an explanation of the moods and tenses of the verbs; explains the general distinctions of each to a limited extent, and dwells particularly on the *indicative*, as a means of readily comprehending the others.

The sixteenth gives an exposition of the subjunctive mood; and the seventeenth exhibits with appropriate explanations and rules, the potential, infinitive, and imperative moods.

The eighteenth Conversation gives a more extended definition of the verb than was given in the former Conversations; and explains at large the active, passive, and neuter verbs. At this stage of advancement, there is little difficulty in the pupil's understanding the passive and neuter verbs; and the moods and tenses, as applicable to these, are already understood.

Conversation nineteen treats of the auxiliary verbs, and contains all the remarks on the proper use of the different tenses, that are thought to be necessary. These remarks on the tenses are necessarily more difficult to be understood, by a learner, than any others relating to the subject of Grammar; these, therefore, as the reflecting reader must perceive, could not have been introduced sooner, without an obvious departure from the plan which the author has adopted.

The twentieth Conversation explains the principles, and the application of the XXI. XXII. and XXIII. rules, which, with those before given, will be found sufficient for the parsing of any regular construction in the English language.

The twenty-first and last Conversation, contains a few critical and general remarks, and concludes with exercises in parsing.

After this, the form of Conversation is dropped, and the remaining instructions are divided into Sections, in which all the rules are recapitulated, accompanied with general remarks on the structure of the language; and appended to each Section, are appropriate exercises in false syntax, which will serve also as a continued series of exercises in parsing.

The author now invites the attention of the critical reader to a few remarks respecting the subjunctive mood, as it is exhibited in this work. Though he has ventured to deviate from the beaten path of his predecessors, in the conjugation of the verb in this mood, yet he thinks, that it is in perfect accordance, not only with the practice of the best writers, but also in strict conformity to the definition of this mood, as given by the most distinguished grammarians. Mr Lindley Murray, in his remarks on this mood, (page 210, oct. ed.) says — "Some grammarians think it extends only to what is called the present tense of verbs generally, under the circumstances of contingency and futurity; and to the imperfect tense of the verb, *to be*, when it denotes contingency, &c. : because in these tenses only, the form of the verb admits of variation; and they suppose that it is variation merely which constitutes the distinction of moods. It is the opinion of other grammarians, (in which opinion we concur,) that, besides the two cases just mentioned, all verbs in the three past, and the two future tenses, are in the subjunctive mood, when they denote contingency or uncertainty, though they have not any change or termination; and that, when contingency is not signified, the verb, through all these five tenses, belongs to the indicative mood, whatever conjunction may attend it. They think, that the definition and nature of the subjunctive mood, *have no reference to change of termination, but that they refer merely to the manner of the being, action, or passion, signified by the verb; and that the subjunctive mood may as properly exist without a variation of the verb,* as the infinitive mood, which has no terminations different from those of the indicative."

In this opinion the author of this treatise also concurs. But, if "the definition and nature of the subjunctive mood, have no reference to change a termination," how can Mr. Murray, and other grammarians, with whom he "concurs in this opinion," say, that, in the phrase, " If he studies," the verb may not be considered as in the subjunctive mood, with as much propriety, as in the phrase, " If he study?" Or with what reason or consistency can they say, " If thou remainedst there," " If he remained there," are subjunctive ; but, " If thou wast there," " If he was there," cannot be subjunctive, but that they are always indicative?

In presenting the different opinions of grammarians concerning this mood, Mr. Murray further observes, in a note, page 211 : " We may add a *Fourth* opinion; which appears to possess, at least, much plausibility. This opinion admits the arrangement we have given, with one variation, namely, that of assigning to the first tense of the subjunctive, two forms: 1st, that which simply denotes contingency: as, " If he *desires* it, I will perform the operation;" that is, " if he *now* desires it ;" 2dly, that which denotes both contingency and futurity: as, " If he *desire* it, I will perform the operation ;" that is, " If he should *hereafter* desire it." " This last theory of the subjunctive mood, claims the merit of rendering the whole system of the moods consistent and regular ; of being more conformable than any other, to the definition of the subjunctive ; and of not referring to the indicative mood, forms of expression, which ill accord with its simplicity and nature. Perhaps this theory will bear a strict examination." The writer of this book believes it will ; and this is the manner in which he has exhibited the present tense of the subjunctive mood. But he does not think, with Mr. Murray, that this alone will render " the whole system of the moods consistent and regular." But that, to do this, two forms must also be given to the *imperfect* tense of the neuter verb be, and passive verbs, as they may be seen exhibited and explained in the following work, Conversation XVIII. page 126 ; and Section XX. page 263.

It was observed, that the method adopted in this work, offers peculiar facilities to the teacher as well as the learner. The former will here find, that the familiar style of explanation, avoiding uncommon words, and furnishing very easy examples, will save him the necessity of much verbal comment; will diminish his labor, by preventing the necessity of much reiterated definition ; and that it will also prevent much weariness, and many trials of patience on his part, by the clear ideas it will communicate to his scholars.

The arrangement of the parsing lessons offers an accommodation of the teacher, of which grammars in common use only show the want; and in defect of which, many teachers entirely defer the application to principles, till the whole grammar has been repeatedly committed to memory, without any obvious design or utility, in the perception of the learner. But, in this book, he will be under no necessity to exercise his pupil, for the first time, in a maze of intricate constructions. The words and phrases, necessary to exemplify every principle progressively laid down, will be found strictly and exclusively adapted to the illustration of the principles to which they are referred ; without introducing, in examples designed to illustrate a single grammatical relation, long and complicated phrases, which serve only to involve the relation designed to be shown, in such a connexion, that the unpractised learner is unable to discern, in the various dissimilar members of the sentence, which of them illustrates the principle in question. And besides lessening the fatigues of the teacher, this arrangement, and these lessons, give a positive efficacy to his instructions, and conciliate the mind of the pupil to a pursuit in which his efforts are encouraged by easiness, and rewarded by success.

It is sometimes apprehended, that too many flowers may be spread in the path of the learner; that too many helps may enfeeble the energy of his mind: that too short a course may be pointed out to the attainment of knowledge. But no man, who retraces the steps of his ascent to any eminence, either humble or proud, which he may have gained, can fail to perceive, that some assistances quickened, and some obstacles retarded his progress; that some rational volume, or some intelligent mind, cherished his curiosity and aided his diligence; that there may be a direct as well as a circuitous route; and, that he might be urged on in darkness, or guided in light. The author has observed too many students struggling onward in doubt, and in dread; too many, in revolt and despair, not to feel some commiseration for the youthful sufferers; not to inquire why they suffered, and how they might be relieved; not to question whether this reluctance and rebellion of the will, may not be "the struggle of the understanding, starting from that to which it is not by nature adapted, and traveling in search of something on which it may fix with greater satisfaction."* The result of his experience and observation, in respect to the proper mode of cultivating the human mind, in one department of knowledge, is here laid before the public. The writer's views have not been confined to a mere system of grammar: this is only an instrument of the mind. The fitness of the mind to the instrument; the manner in which the theory and the practice might be made the intelligible objects of reason; have long employed his attention; and where his arrangement has deviated from the order which grammarians commonly observe, it has been dictated by reasoning, and much reflection on the subject, and in conformity to the nature of mental acquisitions. He has endeavored always to bear in mind the maxim expressed on the face of this book: that, "There is no other method of *teaching* that of which any one is ignorant, than by means of something already known." He does not, therefore, commence this subject with the first definition in the common grammar, that, *an Article is a word prefixed to a substantive,* &c. before any idea of a *substantive* has been conveyed to the learner's mind; and soon after inform him, that an "*Objective case generally follows a verb active or a preposition,*" before the student has any conception of either. This inverted order has a pernicious tendency. It disheartens and stupifies. But he trusts that, in the progress of instruction, he has never forgotten the fitness of his subject, to the state of the learner's mind; and he has endeavored to make the labor of study not only profitable, but pleasant; by supplying the young student "with easy knowledge, and obviating that despondence which quickly prevails, when nothing appears but a succession of difficulties, and one labor only ceases that another may be imposed."

New-York, May, 1821.

*Dr. Johnson.

DIRECTIONS TO TEACHERS.

As one important object, proposed in this work is, by the peculiar arrangement of the subject-matter, entirely to abolish, wherever it is used, the practice of *stultifying children*, by compelling them to recite, in endless repetition, " words, words, words," *without annexing ideas; it may not be deemed, either impertinent or improper, to present, on the face of the book, some directions to those who may happen to use it. The Author believes it will be found most advantageous for learners in general, *to begin* at the THIRD CONVERSATION, and return to the two preceding, on Orthography, after those on Etymology and Syntax are well understood.

Begin, then, at the *third Conversation*, and explain to the class, or individual, in a familiar lecture or conversation, the noun, with its two persons, its numbers, its genders, and the *nominative* case as an *actor*, illustrating the remarks by familiar examples, and requiring the pupils also to give examples, illustrative of what has been explained; then explain the *active verb*, and its agreement with the *actor*, or nominative, and give Rule I : A verb must agree," &c The learners may then be exercised, a few moments, in parsing such sentences as these : Boys play ; Girls sing ; Men labor ; Man labors ; Rain falls, &c. ; the teacher calling their attention to the distinctive form of the verb, as singular or plural. By spending twenty or thirty minutes in this manner with a class of learners, the teacher may prepare them to read the Conversation, which must be given for the *next day's lesson*, with intelligence and with pleasure ; and they will find no difficulty in preparing themselves to parse accurately the *exercises* in the Conversation, and answer correctly the *questions* annexed. When the learners are called, the next day, their business will *not* be, *to recite a page*, without acquiring *one idea*, but to *parse* the *exercises*, and *answer* the *questions*. The subject-matter of the *fourth* Conversation, should be explained in a similar manner, before the pupils begin to read it ; they will then proceed in this as in the other. After these two are well understood, the pupils will, doubtless, be able to proceed with the other Conversations, and understand them, without previous verbal comment.

***If any one should choose to begin at the *first* Conversation, there can be no great objection ; but what relates to the *sounds of the letters, in the entire work*, it would be well to omit, or to attend to but *partially*, till the pupils thoroughly understand Etymology and Syntax.

CONVERSATIONS

ON

ENGLISH GRAMMAR.

CONVERSATION I.

OF LETTERS.

TUTOR,—GEORGE,—CAROLINE.

Tutor. I HAVE frequently told you, that, as soon as you could read fluently, and understand what you read, I would instruct you in the principles of Grammar. I now find that you read your books for the purpose of understanding them, and that you do not, as many children do, merely pronounce the *words*, without any regard to the *sense*.

Caroline. You have so often cautioned us, against the practice of reading without trying to comprehend the sense of every sentence, that I now find no pleasure in reading, unless I thoroughly understand the meaning of what I read.

Tutor. I believe so, Caroline, and I have no doubt, that your brother George can say the same; and therefore I shall begin to instruct you in English Grammar, this morning. And now, George, what do you think that Grammar is about.

George. I think it is about words, or language; and, that it will teach us to speak and write what we mean, in such a manner, that others may clearly understand us; and, that it will enable us to avoid putting words together so that a sentence will convey two or three different meanings, when it ought to convey but *one*.

Tutor. Very well. Grammar treats of language, and, if you understand it well, it will teach you to write and speak it correctly. Grammar may be divided into two sorts, *Universal*, and *Particular*. Universal Grammar explains the principles which are common to all languages. Particular Grammar applies those general principles to a particular language, modifying them according to the genius of that language, and the established practice of the best speakers and writers by whom it is used. The practice of the best speakers and writers of any language, then, is the standard of the grammar of that language. But before I say more concerning *language*, I must know whether you can give the definition of an *idea*.

George. An *idea* is whatever a person has in his mind, when he thinks.

Tutor. Very well. And now, Caroline, do you remember the definition of *language*?

Caroline. Language is the expression of our ideas and their relations, by certain articulate sounds, which are used as the signs of those ideas and relations.

Tutor. That is right. We must observe now what we have under consideration, viz. first, *things;* secondly, the images of those things, in the mind, when we think of them, which are called *ideas;* and thirdly, *language,* or articulate sounds, used to express, or to convey, to other minds, those ideas which we have in our own. These articulate sounds we call *words,* which are used by common consent, as the signs of our ideas and their relations. So you will perceive, that, unless these words are used in such manner and order, as will represent truly the order and relation of the ideas in our own minds, another person will not be able to comprehend our meaning.

George. I perceive it very clearly. You say that words are used by common consent.

Tutor. That means, that all the people who speak the same language, consent to call things by the same names ; or to express the same ideas by the same signs.

Caroline. I understand it ; and perceive the necessity of it ; for, if the fact were otherwise, we could not comprehend each other ; there would be as many different languages as there are persons. I wish you to say more, if you please, respecting those words that are the signs of the *relations* of ideas. I think I understand how a word is the sign of an idea, for when I think about this book which you gave me, the word *book* is the sign of what I think of, but I do not precisely comprehend how words are the signs of the *relations* of our ideas.

Tutor. When I say that you hold the book *in* your hand ; what word expresses the relation between the book and your hand ?

Caroline. It is *in.* I see now, that the word *in* is not the sign of a *thing* that I think of, but the sign of a *relation* existing between the book and the hand, which are two things that I can think of ; so then, a word that denotes a relation between things, must be the sign of the relation between the *ideas* of those things.

Tutor. Yes ; and you will, by a little reflection, perceive the different uses of words ; that some are used to express ideas or images of things ; some to express ideas of motion ; and others to express ideas of relations merely. As, in the phrase, " *The son of David studies,*" you may readily perceive, that *of* shows the relationship existing between the two persons ; for if we were to leave it out of the sentence, and say, "*The son, David,*" &c. the phrase would indicate, that the two words referred to one, and the same person ; so, you may as readily perceive, that *of* is used to express the relation of the *ideas* in your mind, and the *signs* of those ideas, when put on paper, which are *son* and *David.*

2*

George.   I think we have a clear notion of what has been said ; and that we perceive the importance of preserving the purity and uniformity of each particular language ; and that, in each, there should be a common set of signs which may be known, by *all* who speak that language, as the representatives of particular ideas, and definite relations.

Caroline.   And this, I suppose, is accomplished by diffusing a knowledge of *Grammar.*

Tutor.   Undoubtedly ; for Grammar treats,

First, of *articulate sounds,* which are the sounds of the human voice, formed by the organs of speech, and of the form and sound of letters, which are the representatives of those articulate sounds ; of the combination of letters into syllables, and of syllables into words ;

Secondly, of the different sorts of words, their various modifications, and their derivations ;

Thirdly, of the just arrangement of words in the formation of a sentence ; and

Fourthly, of the proper pronunciation and poetical construction of sentences.   These four parts of Grammar are called,

1. ORTHOGRAPHY,	3. SYNTAX, and
2. ETYMOLOGY,	4. PROSODY.

I will now proceed with these in their order.

ORTHOGRAPHY.

OF THE LETTERS.

ORTHOGRAPHY teaches the nature and powers of letters, and the just method of spelling words.

A letter is the first principle, or least part, of a word.

The letters of the English language, called the English Alphabet, are twenty-six in number.

These letters are the representatives of certain articulate sounds, the elements of the language.   An articulate sound, is the sound of the human voice, formed by the organs of speech.

Letters are divided into Vowels and Consonants.

A Vowel is an articulate sound, that can be perfectly uttered by itself : as, *a, e, o ;* which are formed without the help of any other sound.

A Consonant is an articulate sound, which cannot be perfectly uttered without the help of a vowel: as, *b, d, f, l ;* which require vowels to express them fully.

The vowels are, *a, e, i, o, u,* and sometimes *w* and *y.*

W and *y* are consonants when they begin a word or syllable ; but in every other situation they are vowels.

Consonants are divided into mutes and semi-vowels.

The mutes cannot be sounded *at all,* without the aid of a vowel. They are *b, p, t, d, k,* and *c* and *g* hard.

The semi-vowels have an imperfect sound of themselves. They are *f, l, m, n, r, v, s, z, x,* and *c* and *g* soft.

Four of the semi-vowels, namely, *l, m, n, r,* are also distinguished by the name of *liquids,* from their readily uniting with other consonants, and flowing as it were into their sounds.

A diphthong is the union of two vowels pronounced by a single impulse of the voice : as, *ea* in beat, *ou* in sound.

A triphthong is the union of three vowels, pronounced in like manner : as, *eau* in beau, *iew* in view.

A proper diphthong is that in which both the vowels are sounded : as, *oi* in voice, *ou* in ounce.

An improper diphthong has but one of the vowels sounded : as, *ea* in eagle, *oa* in boat.

QUESTIONS.

What do you understand by the word *idea ?*
What is an articulate sound ?
What is language ?
What is Grammar ?
How may Grammar be divided ?
What does Universal Grammar explain ?
What does Particular Grammar teach ?
What does English Grammar teach ?
What is the standard of English Grammar, by which we must be governed ?
Into how many parts is English Grammar divided?
What are they called ?
Of what does each treat ?
What are letters ?
How many are there in the English language ?
How are letters divided ?
What is a vowel ?
What letters are vowels ?
What is a consonant ?
When are *w* and *y* consonants ?
And when vowels ?
How are consonants divided ?

What is a mute ?
What is a semi-vowel ?
Which four of the semi-vowels are called *liquids* ?
What is a diphthong ?
What is a triphthong ?
What is a *proper* diphthong ?
What is an *improper* diphthong ?

CONVERSATION II.

OF SYLLABLES AND WORDS.

Tutor. You answered the questions annexed to the first conversation so readily, that I perceive you are very attentive, and that you remember what I tell you. I shall, by-and-by, be able to make the subject more interesting to you.

Caroline. We begin already to be interested in it, for we know how necessary it is, that we should understand it ; and we believe that you will explain it to us in such a manner, that it will not be very dry.

Tutor. You will probably find *Orthography* the least interesting part of Grammar. In acquiring a knowledge of this you must be patient and perform the labor yourselves. But when you come to Etymology and Syntax, more illustration will be necessary, and I shall be able to render you more assistance, than I can at present.

George. We know that, in order to understand any art or science well, its first principles must be clearly comprehended ; and, that it then becomes easy.

Caroline. You showed us, the other day, some remarks on this subject, made by Quinctilian, which I remember. " Let no person," says he, " despise, as inconsiderable, the elements of grammar, because it may seem to them a matter of small consequence, to show the distinction between vowels and consonants, and to divide the latter into liquids and mutes.* But they who penetrate into the innermost parts of this temple of science, will there discover such refinement and subtility of matter, as are not only proper to sharpen the understandings of young persons, but sufficient to give exercise for the most profound knowledge and erudition."

Tutor. I shall now proceed with syllables and words.

OF SYLLABLES.

A syllable is a sound, either simple or compounded, pronounced by a single impulse of the voice, and constituting a word, or part of a word : as, a, an, ant.

Spelling is the art of rightly dividing words into their syllables, or of expressing a word by its proper letters.

The following are the general rules for the division of words into syllables :—

1. A single consonant between two vowels, must be joined to the latter syllable : as, de-light, bri-dal, re-source ; except the letter x : as, ex-ist, ex-amine ; and except likewise words compounded : as, up-on, un-even, dis-ease.

2. Two consonants proper to begin a word, must not be separated : as, fa-ble, sti-fle. But when they come between two vowels, and are such as cannot begin a word, they must be divided : as, ut-most, un-der, in-sect, er-ror, cof-fin.

3. When three consonants meet in the middle of a word, if they can begin a word, and the preceding vowel be pronounced long, they are not to be separated : as, de-throne, de-stroy. But when the vowel of the preceding syllable is pronounced short, one of the consonants always belongs to that syllable : as, dis-tract, dis-prove, dis-train.

4. When three or four consonants, which are not proper to begin a syllable, meet between two vowels, such of them as can begin a syllable belong to the latter, the rest to the former syllable : as, ab-stain, com-plete, em-broil, trans-gress, dap-ple, con-strain, hand-some, parch-ment.

5. Two vowels, not being a diphthong, must be divided into separate syllables : as, cru-el, de-ni-al, so-ci-e-ty.

6. Compounded words must be traced into the simple words of which they are composed : as, ice-house, glow-worm, over-power, never-the-less.

7. Grammatical, and other particular terminations are generally separated : as, teach-est, teach-eth, teach-ing,

* For some general observations on the sounds of the letters, the learner is referred to " Conversations on English Grammar," of which this is an Abridgment, page 10 and onward.

teach-er, contend-est, great-er, wretch-ed, good-ness, free-dom, false-hood.

OF WORDS.

Words are articulate sounds, used by common consent, as signs of our ideas.

A word of one syllable is termed a Monosyllable ; a word of two syllables, a Dissyllable ; a word of three syllables, a Trissyllable ; and a word of four or more syllables, a Polysyllable.

All words are either primitive or derivative.

A primitive word is that which cannot be reduced to any simpler word in the language : as, man, good, content.

A derivative word is that which may be reduced to another word in English of greater simplicity : as, manful, goodness, contentment, Yorkshire.*

QUESTIONS.

What is a *syllable* ?
What is *spelling* ?
What are *words* ?
What are words of one syllable called ?
What are words of two syllables ?
What are words of three syllables ?
What are words of four or more syllables called ?
How are words divided ?
What is a primitive word ?
What is a derivative ?

There are many English words which, though compounds in other languages, are to us primitives : thus, circumspect, circumvent, circumstance, delude, concave, complicate, &c. which are primitive words in English, will be found derivatives, when traced in the Latin tongue.

The orthography of the English language is attended with much uncertainty and perplexity. But a considerable part of this inconvenience may be remedied, by attending to the general laws of formation ; and, for this end, you are presented with a view of such general maxims, in spelling primitive and derivative words, as have been almost universally received.

RULE I.

Monosyllables ending with f, l, or s, preceded by a single vowel, double the final consonant : as, staff, mill, pass, &c. The only exceptions are, of, if, as, is, has, was, yes, his, this, us, and thus.

*A compound word is included under the head of derivative words : as pen-knife, tea-cup, looking-glass ; may be reduced to other words of greater simplicity.

It is no great merit to spel properly ; but a great defect to do it incorrectly.

Jacob worshiped his Creator, leaning on the top of his staf.

We may place too little, as well as too much stres upon dreams.

Our manners should be neither gros, nor excessively refined.

RULE II.

Monosyllables ending with any consonant but f, l, or s, and preceded by a single vowel, never double the final consonant ; excepting only, add, ebb, butt, egg, odd, err, inn, bunn, purr, and buzz.

A carr signifies a chariot of war, or a small carriage of burden.

In the names of druggs and plants, the mistake in a word may endanger life.

> Nor undelightful is the ceaseless humm,
> To him who muses through the woods at noon.

The finn of a fish is the limb, by which he balances his body, and moves in the water.

Many a trapp is laid to insnare the feet of youth.

Many thousand families are supported by the simple business of making mats.

RULE III.

Words ending with y, preceded by a consonant, form the plurals of nouns, the persons of verbs, verbal nouns, past participles, comparatives, and superlatives, by changing y into i : as, spy, spies ; I carry, thou carriest ; he carrieth or carries ; carrier, carried ; happy, happier, happiest.

The present participle in ing, retains the y, that i may not be doubled : as, carry, carrying ; bury, burying, &c.

But y, preceded by a vowel, in such instances as the above, is not changed ; as, boy, boys ; I cloy, he cloys, cloyed, &c. ; except in lay, pay, and say ; from which are formed, laid, paid, and said ; and their compounds, unlaid, unpaid, unsaid, &c.

We should subject our fancys to the government of reason.

If thou art seeking for the living among the dead, thou wearyest thyself in vain.

If we have denyed ourselves sinful pleasures, we shall be great gainers in the end.

We shall not be the happyer for possessing talents and affluence, unless we make a right use of them.

The truly good mind is not dismaied by poverty, afflictions, or death.

RULE IV.

Words ending with y, preceded by a consonant, upon assuming an additional syllable beginning with a consonant,

commonly change y into i : as, happy, happily, happiness.
But when y is preceded by a vowel, it is very rarely changed
in the additional syllable : as coy. coyly ; boy, boyish, boy-
hood ; annoy. annoyed, annoyance ; joy, joyless, joyful, &c.

It is a great blessing to have a sound mind, uninfluenced by
fancyful humours.

Common calamities, and common blessings, fall heavyly
npon the envious.

The comelyness of youth are modesty and frankness :
of age, condescension and dignity.

When we act against conscience, we become the destroi-
ers of our own peace.

We may be plaiful, and yet innocent ; grave, and yet corrupt. It is only from general conduct, that our true character
can be portraied.

RULE V.

Monosyllables, and words accented on the last syllable,
ending with a single consonant preceded by a single vowel,
double that consonant, when they take another syllable begin-
ning with a vowel : as, wit, witty ; thin, thinnish ; to abet,
an abettor ; to begin, a beginner.

But if a diphthong precedes, or the accent is on the pre-
ceding syllable, the consonant remains single : as, to toil, toil-
ing · to offer, an offering ; maid, maiden, &c.

When we bring the lawmaker into contempt, we have in
effect annuled his laws.

By defering our repentance, we accumulate our sorrows.

The pupils of a certain ancient philosopher, were not,
during the first years of study, permitted to ask any questions.

We all have many faillings and lapses to lament and re-
cover.

There is no affliction with which we are visitted, that
may not be improved to our advantage.

The Christian Lawgiver has prohibitted many things,
which the heathen philosophers allowed.

RULE VI.

Words ending with any double letter but l, and taking ness,
less, ly. or ful, after them. preserve the letter double ; as,
harmlessness. carelessness. carelessly, stiffly. successful, dis-
tressful, &c. But those words which end with double l, and
take ness, less, ly. or ful, after them, generally omit one l:
as, fulness, skilless, fully, skilful, &c.

Restlesness of mind disqualifies us, both for the enjoyment of peace, and the performance of duty.

The arrows of calumny fall harmlesly at the feet of virtue.

The road to the blisful regions, is as open to the peasant as
to the king.

A chillness, or shivering of the body, generally precedes a fever.

To recommend virtue to others, our lights must shine brightly, not dullly.

The silent stranger stood amaz'd to see
Contempt of wealth, and willful poverty.

RULE VII.

Ness, less, ly, and ful, *added to words ending with silent e, do not cut it off : as, palences, guileness, closely, peaceful ; except in a few words : as, duly, truly, awful.*

The warmth of disputation, destroys that sedatness of mind which is necessary to discover truth.

All these with ceaseless praise his works behold,
Both day and night.

In all our reasonings, our mind should be sincerly employed in the pursuit of truth.

Rude behaviour, and indecent language, are peculiarly disgracful to youth of education.

The true worship of God is an important and aweful service.

Wisdom alone is truely fair : folly only appears so.

RULE VIII.

Ment, added to words ending with silent e, generally preserves the e from elision : as, abatement, chastisement, incitement, &c. The words judgment, abridgment, acknowledgment, are deviations from the rule.

Like other terminations, it changes y into i, when preceded by a consonant ; as, accompany, accompaniment ; merry, merriment.

The study of the English language is making daily advancment.

A judicious arrangment of studies facilitates improvment.

To shun allurments is not hard,
To minds resolv'd, forewarned, and well prepar'd.

RULE IX.

Able and ible, when incorporated into words ending with silent e, almost always cut it off ; as, blame, blamable ; cure, curable ; sense, sensible, &c. but if c or g soft comes before e in the original word, the e, is then preserved in words compounded with able : as, change, chageable ; peace, peaceable, &c.

Every person and thing connected with self, is apt to appear good and desireable in our eyes.

Errors and misconduct are more excuseable in ignorant, than in well-instructed persons.

The divine laws are not reversiable by those of men.

3

Gratitude is a forceible and active principle in good and generous minds.

Our natural and involuntary defects of body are not chargable upon us.

We are made to be servicable to others, as well as to ourselves.

RULE X.

When ing *or* ish *is added to words ending with silent* e, *the* e, *is almost universally omitted ; as, place placing ; lodge, lodging ; slave, slavish ; prude, prudish.*

An obligeing and humble disposition, is totally unconnected with a servile and cringeing humour.

By solaceing the sorrows of others, the heart is improved, at the same time that our duty is performed.

Labor and expense are lost upon a droneish spirit.

The inadvertancies of youth may be excused, but knaveish tricks should meet with severe reproof.

RULE XI.

Compounded words are generally spelled in the same manner, as the simple words of which they are formed : as, glasshouse, skylight, thereby, hereafter. *Many words ending with double* l, *are exceptions to this rule : as, already, welfare, wilful, fulfil : and also the words, wherever, Christmas, lammas,* &c.

The pasover was a celebrated feast among the Jews.

A virtuous woman looketh well to the ways of her houshold.

These people salute one another, by touching the top of their forheads.

That which is sometimes expedient, is not allways so.

We may be hurtfull to others, by our example, as well as by personal injuries.

In candid minds, truth finds an entrance, and a wellcome too.

Our passtimes should be innocent ; and they should not occur too frequently.

CONVERSATION III.

ETYMOLOGY AND SYNTAX.

OF NOUNS AND VERBS.

Tutor. Do you remember the explanations, which I have often given you, of the words, *analysis* and *synthesis ?*

George. I remember them well. *Analysis* is the separating of any thing into *parts*, to find the *elements* of which it is composed ; and *synthesis* is the joining of these parts together again, to make one whole.

Tutor. That is right; and you may now perceive that these terms may be applied to our present subject ; for you have learned that articulate *sounds* are the elements of language ; that letters are the representatives of these sounds, and compose syllables ; that syllables compose words ; that words compose sentences, and that sentences compose an *oration* or *discourse.* This process, you perceive, is *synthetic.* But when you take an *oration*, or any composition, and decompose it, or separate its different parts, and find the elements of which it is composed, you analyze it.

George. I suppose, then, when we begin upon Etymology and Syntax, our business will be to analyze sentences. And, as you told us, that after we had finished that part of Grammar, which is called *Orthography*, you would explain to us the two parts, which are called *Etymology* and *Syntax ;* I hope you will begin this morning.

Tutor. Yes, I am quite at leisure ; and I will now begin to explain to you, these useful parts of Grammar ; and I do it with more pleasure, because I perceive that you desire to understand your own language. It is pleasant to instruct you, when you express a wish to be informed ; but it is a very disagreeable task to teach children, if they have no curiosity, or love of learning ; if they discover no disposition to improve the minds which God has given them, and have no wish to become wiser and better.

Caroline. I am anxious that you should begin your explanations, for I think we shall understand them. There is a great pleasure in learning, when we comprehend what we are taught.

Tutor. *Etymology* treats of the different sorts of words, of their derivation, and various modifications on account of cases, moods, and tenses. *Syntax* treats of the arrangement of words in a sentence according to grammatical rules. But you cannot, at present, perfectly comprehend these definitions: I shall illustrate them more fully as we advance, and as I find you prepared to understand the subject.

Caroline. You say Etymology treats of the different sorts of words; I think there must be a great many sorts.

Tutor. Not so many, perhaps, as you imagine. Although there are nearly forty thousand words in the English language, yet there are only *ten* different sorts, viz. the NOUN, or SUBSTANTIVE, VERB, ARTICLE, ADJECTIVE, PARTICIPLE, ADVERB, PRONOUN, CONJUNCTION, PREPOSITION, and INTERJECTION. We call these different sorts of words, parts of speech.

A substantive, or Noun, is the name of any thing that exists, or of which we have any notion. The word Noun, means name. The name of any thing which we can see, taste, smell, hear, feel, or conceive of, is a noun. Book, apple, rose, song, pin, modesty, truth, bravery, are nouns. Nouns have four different properties, belonging to them, viz. *person, number, gender,* and *case.*

Nouns have two persons, the second and third. When we speak *of,* or *about* a thing, the word, which is the name of that thing, is a noun of the *third* person; when we speak *to* a person or thing, it is of the *second* person: as, when addressing a person, I say, The *book* is on the *table,* George;—the nouns book and table are of the *third* person, but George is of the *second* person, because, I speak *of* the book, and the table, but I speak *to* George. Girls, study your lesson. In this example, girls is a noun of the *second* person, and lesson of the *third* person.

Nouns have two numbers, the singular number, and the plural number. When a word is the name of one person or thing, it is of the singular number; when it denotes more than one, it is of the plural number. Thus, when I say, The man walks among the trees; *man* is a noun of the third person, singular number, but *trees* is a noun of the third person, plural number. But when I say, Trees, I wish you would grow faster, trees is a noun of the *second* person plural. Nouns have three Genders. GENDER is the distinction of nouns with regard to sex. When a noun denotes animals of the male kind, it is of the *Masculine Gender;* when it denotes animals of the female kind, it is of the *Feminine Gender;* and when it signifies objects that are neither males nor females, it is of the *Neuter Gender. Neuter* means neither one nor the other. A noun of neuter gender, then, means a noun, which is neither of the masculine gender, nor of the feminine gender. Thus, when I say ,The *boys* lent the *books* to the *girl;*—*boys* is a noun of the third person, plural number, of masculine gender; *girl* is a noun of the third person, singular number, of feminine gender; and *books* is a noun of the third person, plural number, of neuter gender.

Nouns have three cases; the Nominative case, the Possessive case, and the Objective case. Case is the condition, or situation of the noun in relation to other words in the sentence.

At present I will explain to you, only the Nominative case; the others will be explained hereafter. A noun which denotes an animal or thing that does an action is in the Nominative case.* Or, in other words, when a noun is the *actor* or *agent*, it is in the nominative case. And if a noun signifies an actor, there must be some word in the sentence expressing the action.

George. What are the words, which express actions, called?

---

*This definition is sufficient for the learner's *present* purpose. See Conv. XVIII, the definition in Italic, page 124.

3*

Tutor. VERBS. I shall *now* give you only such a definition of a Verb, as is sufficient for your present purpose; and, indeed, the only one which you can yet clearly comprehend; but, as we advance, I shall give you a more complete definition. And let me remark to you, once for all, that I shall present to you only such parts of the subject as I know you are prepared to understand; and give you such definitions as you can comprehend at the time they are given. Each Conversation will prepare you for the one that will follow.

George. That is the way in which you have instructed us in other subjects; and if you can do so in this, I am sure we shall be interested in it.

Tutor. I will proceed with the Verb. A verb is a word that expresses an action of some creature or thing. Thus, if I say, The boy runs—The ball rolls—The dog barks—The bird flies—The children play—The rain falls—you can be at no loss to know which words are the verbs. They are those that express the actions, viz. runs—rolls—barks—flies—play—falls. The nouns, boy, ball, dog, bird, children, rain, are *actors,* or persons and things that act or move, and, therefore, in the nominative case to the verbs that express their several actions.

You may perceive, then, how intimate the connexion is, between the nominative case and the verb : one denotes the actor, and the other the action. And you will readily see that, if only *one* animal or thing acts, there can be only *one action.* Or, in other words, when the word, denoting the *actor* signifies only *one thing,* the word denoting the *action* will signify only *one action.* Thus, when I say, The box rolls—*box* is in the singular number, because it denotes but one thing, and *rolls* denotes but one action, which the box does; therefore the verb *rolls* is of the singular number, just like the nominative *box.* If the nominative case, or the actor, is of the singular number, the verb must also be of the singular number. And the verb must also be of the same *person* that the nominative case is. If the nominative is of the *second person*, the verb must be the same—if the nominative is of the third person, then the verb must be of the third person. On this account I will give you a rule.

RULE I.

A verb must agree with its nominative case in number and person.

I shall now give you some sentences to *parse.* Parsing a noun is telling of what person, number, gender, and case it is : and also telling its grammatical relations in a sentence with respect to other words. Parsing any part of speech is telling all its properties and relations. These relations, then, must be perfectly understood before the scholar can parse. You cannot yet parse a verb completely, as you are not yet informed of all its distinctions and properties; but you can explain such as you have already learned.

When you parse verbs, you will only tell their persons and numbers, which are the same as those of their nominatives; and you will tell with what nominative the verb agrees, according to the rule which I have just given you. You will not give to the verb *gender* and *case.* I will parse for you one sentence, containing a nominative case and a verb ; the only sort of sentences which you are prepared to parse.

EXAMPLE.

When you know the person and number of the nominative, you know of what person and number the verb must be.

Smoke ascends. Smoke is a noun of the *third* person, singular number, of neuter gender, in the nominative case to the verb *ascends. Ascends* is a verb of the third person singular number, and agrees with its nominative case, *smoke. A verb must agree, &c.*

Now, parse this sentence several times, till the manner of parsing it is quite familiar to you, and then parse the following sentences :

EXERCISES IN PARSING.

Snow falls.	Fire burns.
Boys play.	Cats mew.
Men labour.	Ladies dance.
David studies.	Children study.
Emma writes.	Girls write.
Man talks.	Men talk.

Now try, in different parts of the conversation, to select these two parts of speech, from all the others, and parse the *nominative, and the verb*, correctly.—— I will now make some additional

REMARKS ON NUMBER.

Number is the consideration of an object, as one or more.

Some nouns, from the nature of the things which they express, are used only in the singular form : as, wheat, pitch, gold, sloth, pride, &c. ; others, only in the plural form : as, bellows, scissors, ashes, riches, &c.

Some words are the same in both numbers : as, deer, sheep, swine, &c.

The plural number of nouns is generally formed by adding *s* to the singular : as, dove, doves ; face, faces ; thought, thoughts. But when the substantive singular ends in *x, ch* soft, *sh, ss*, or *s*, we add *es* in the plural : as, box, boxes ; church, churches, lash, lashes : kiss, kisses ; rebus, rebuses. If the singular ends in *ch* hard ; the plural is formed by adding the *s :* as, monarch, monarchs ; distich, distiches.

Nouns, which end in *o*, have sometimes *es* added, to form the plural : as, cargo, echo, hero, negro, manifesto, potato, volcano, wo ; and sometimes only *s :* as, folio, nuncio, punctilio, seraglio. When the *o* is immediately preceded by a vowel, we add only *s*.

Nouns ending in *f*, or *fe*, are rendered plural by the change of those terminations into *ves :* as, loaf, loaves ; half, halves ; wife, wives : except grief, relief, reproof, and several others, which form the plural by the addition of *s*. Those which end in *ff*, have the regular plural : as ruff, ruffs ; except, staff, staves.

Nouns which have *y* in the singular, with no other vowel in the same syllable, change it into *ies* in the plural : as, beauty, beauties ; fly, flies. But the *y* is not changed, where there is another vowel in the syllable ; as, key, keys ; delay, delays ; attorney, attorneys.

Some nouns become plural by changing the *a* of the singular into *e :* as, man, men ; woman, women ; alderman, aldermen. The words, ox and child form oxen and children ; brother, makes either brothers or brethren. Sometimes the diphthong *oo* is changed into *ee* in the plural : as, feet ; goose, geese ; tooth, teeth. Louse and mouse make lice and mice. Penny, makes pence ; or pennies, when the coin is meant ; die, dice (for play) ; die, dies (for coining).

It is a general rule, that all names of things measured or weighed, have no plural ; for in them not number, but quantity is regarded : as, wool, wine, oil. When we speak, however, of different kinds, we use the plural: as, the coarser wools, the richer wines, the finer oils.

It is agreeable to analogy, and the practice of the generality of correct writers, to construe the following words as plural nouns : *pains, riches, alms ;* and also, *mathematics, metaphysics, polictics, ethics, optics, pneumatics,* with other similar names of sciences.

Dr. Johnson says, that the adjective *much* is sometimes a term of number, as well as of quantity. This may account for the instances we meet with of its associating with *pains* as a plural noun: as " much pains." The connexion, however, is not to be recommended.

The word *news* is now almost universally considered as belonging to the singular number.

The noun *means* is used both in the singular and the plural number.

As a general rule for the use of the word *means*, as either singular or plural, it would render the construction less vague, and the expression therefore less ambiguous, were we to employ it as singular when the mediation or instrumentality of one thing is implied ; and, as plural when two or more mediating causes are referred to. " He was careful to observe what means *were* employed by his adversaries, to counteract his schemes." Here *means* is properly joined with a plural verb, several methods of counteraction being signified.— " The king consented ; and, by *this* means, all hope of success was lost.". Here but one mediating circumstance is implied ; and the noun is, therefore, used as singular.

The following words, which have been adopted from the Hebrew, Greek, and Latin languages, are thus distinguished with respect to number.

Singular.	Plural.	Singular.	Plural.
Cherub.	Cherubim.	Phœnomenon.	Phœnomena.
Seraph.	Seraphim.	Appendix.	Appendices, or Appendixes.
Antithesis.	Antitheses.		
Automaton.	Automata.	Arcanum.	Arcana.
Basis.	Bases.	Axis.	Axes.
Crisis.	Crises.	Calx.	Calces.
Criterion.	Criteria.	Datum.	Data
Diæresis.	Diæreses.	Effluvium.	Effluvia.
Ellipsis.	Ellipses.	Encomium.	Encomia, or Encomiums.
Emphasis.	Emphases.		
Hypothesis.	Hypotheses.	Erratum.	Errata.

Metamor- phosis.	{ Metamor- phoses.	Genius.	Genii.*
Genus.	Genera.	Memoran- dum.	Memoranda, or Memorandums.
Lamina.	Laminæ.	Stratum.	Strata.
Index.	{ Indices, or Indexes.*	Radius.	Radii.
Medium.	Media.	Stamen.	Stamina.
Magus.	Magi.	Vortex.	Vortices.

Some words, derived from the learned languages, are confined to the plural number : as, antipodes, credenda, literati, minutiæ.

The following nouns being, in Latin, both singular and plural, are used in the same manner, when adopted into our tongue : hiatus, apparatus, series, species.

By studying this Conversation thoroughly, you will find the next quite easy to be understood : and will be able, at another time, to answer the following questions, which I shall ask you before I give you further instruction.

QUESTIONS.

What is a noun?
How many persons has it?
How do you distinguish the persons?
How many numbers have nouns?
What are they?
How do you distinguish them?
How many genders have nouns?
What are they?
How do you know them?
How many cases have nouns?
When is a noun in the nominative case?
What is a verb?
What belong to verbs?
Have they genders and cases?
How do you know the person and number of verbs?
Are verbs of the singular and plural number spelled alike?
What rule do you give when you parse a verb?
What is the use or necessity of this rule?
What nouns are used only in the singular form?
What are used only in the plural form?
What are the same in both numbers?
How is the plural number of nouns generally formed?
When the noun singular ends in _x_, _ch_ soft, _sh_, _ss_, or _s_, how is the plural formed?
But if the singular ends in _ch_ hard, how is the plural formed?

*Genii, when it signifies aerial spirits ; Geniuses, when signifying persons of genius.
*Indexes, when it signifies pointers, or tables of contents : indices, when referring to algebraic quantities.

How do nouns ending in *o*, form their plural ?

How those ending in *f*, or *fe* ? what exceptions ?

How those in *y* ? what exception ?

What is the general rule respecting the names of things weighed and measured ?

Is there any exception to this ?

What nouns change *a* into *e*, and *oo* into *ee*, to form the plural ?

What is the plural of *brother* ?

Of what number are *pains, riches, alms, ethics, optics,* &c. ?

Of what number is *news* ?

How is the noun *means* used ?

How are *hiatus, apparatus, series, species,* used ? Why ?

CONVERSATION IV.

OF NOUNS AND VERBS. CASES OF NOUNS.

Tutor. I find by the correctness with which you have answered the questions relating to our last conversation, that you will find no difficulty in understanding what I shall say in this. You were yesterday informed, that nouns have three cases, the Nominative, Possessive, and Objective ; but I explained only the *Nominative*, which denotes an actor. I shall now give you the *Possessive* and *Objective* cases.

When the noun is in the Possessive Case, it denotes the possessor of some thing, and is spelled differently from the nominative case : as, Boy's hat.—— The boy is the possessor of the hat, which is shown by an apostrophe and an s, after the word boy. When a noun of the plural number is in the possessive case, and ends in s, we only add an *aposthrophe* to it : as, Boys' hats.—If the plural number is formed otherwise than by adding *s* to the singular, the possessive case *plural* is formed by the apostrophe and the *s* also, just as we form the possessive case *singular* : as,—Man's house.—Men's house.—Woman's bonnet.—Women's bonnets. In these examples, *man's*, and *woman's* are in the possessive case, singular number, and the nouns *men's* and *women's*, are in the possessive case, *plural* number.

Caroline. I understand the Nominative and Possessive cases ; please to explain the Objective.

Tutor. The *Objective* case denotes the object of an action, and is spelled just as the nominative is. The following examples illustrate the three cases of nouns.

EXAMPLES.

Nom. Case.		Verb.		Poss. Case.	Obj. Case.
The	boy	beats	the	man's	horse.
The	horse	kicks	the	man's	boy.
The	man	struck	that	man's	man.
The	servant	lost	those	boys'	ball.

Take notice, that the last noun *boys'* is in the plural number, which is formed by adding *s* to the singular ; therefore, being in the possessive case, an apostrophe only is added, without another s.

You have now had nouns in their three cases ; and see that *case* means the different situation or relation of nouns in sentences. Every noun must be either in the Nominative, Possessive, or Objective Case.

When we put a noun in the three cases without making a sentence, but merely to show the *termination* of the noun in the different cases, we call it *declining* a noun. Termination means ending. The Possessive case you have seen has a termination, or ending, different from that of the Nominative, or Objective case.

The nouns, Man and Mother, are thus declined :

	Sing. num.			Sing. num.
Nom.	Man		*Nom.*	Mother
Poss.	Man's		*Poss.*	Mother's
Obj.	Man		*Obj.*	Mother.
	Plu. num.			Plu. num.
Nom.	Men		*Nom.*	Mothers
Poss.	Men's		*Poss.*	Mothers'
Obj.	Men		*Obj.*	Mothers.

When nouns in the singular number end in ss, we sometimes write the Possessive case with an apos-

trophe only, without another s; as *goodness' sake,
righteousness' sake;* because it would cause too
much of a hissing sound to say *goodness's sake,* &c.
But the apostrophic s, is not always omitted in words
ending in double s. We write the word *witness,*
when in the Possessive case, thus : *Witness's* testimony. When the word ends in *ence,* the *s* should
be omitted : as, for conscience' sake ; but, observe,
the apostrophe is used.

George. Yes, for conscience's sake, would not
only be disagreeable to the ear, but somewhat difficult to be pronounced 'with distinctness. But
although we have nouns in all their cases, we know
how to parse them only in the *Nominative.*

Tutor. I will give you two rules which will
inform you how to parse the Possessive and Objective cases.

RULE II.

*When two nouns come together, signifying different
things, the former implying possession must be in the
possessive case, and governed by the latter.*

Sometimes the latter noun which governs the
Possessive case is understood : as, this is John's hat,
but that is Peter's. The noun hat is understood
after Peter's, and it governs Peter's in the Possessive
case.

RULE III.

Transitive verbs govern the objective case.

Caroline. We do not know what a *transitive*
verb is.

Tutor. A *transitive* verb, is one that expresses
an action done to some *object,* and governs that
object in the objective case.

George. What does the word *transitive* mean ?

Tutor. It means *passing*—or having the power
of passing from one thing to another. When applied
to a verb, it means that the verb expresses an action
which the Nominative case does to some object: as,
men *build* houses—horses *eat* hay—fire *consumes*

4

wood. In these sentences, *build, eat, consumes*, are *transitive verbs*, and govern *houses, hay*, and *wood*, in the objective case, according to the rule, *Transitive verbs govern the objective case.*

Caroline. You say, that transitive verbs govern the objective case. I do not exactly understand the word *govern*, when used in grammar.

Tutor. You cannot now understand an explanation of grammatical government so well as you will be able to, after I shall have given you more instruction ; but since you have asked the question, I will give you such explanation as you can comprehend. *Government*, as it respects nouns, *is the influence that one word has over another, in causing it to be in any particular case*, rather than in *another*. When we say, *Peter's hat*, Peter is the possessor, and hat is the thing possessed by Peter. The relation between the *Possessor* and *thing* possessed, used to be expressed by *es* added to the former noun : as Pe*teres* hat ; but now, by leaving out the *e*, and writing the *s* with an apostrophe ' to show that the *e* is wanting. Now, then, when a thing or person is possessed by another thing or person, this relation may be expressed by this sign '*s*, or as I have before told you, when the noun ends in *ss*, it is sometimes expressed by this sign ' only, without the *s*. It is therefore plain that the latter noun or thing possessed, is what makes it necessary to add this sign '*s*, or this ' to the former noun *or possessor ;*—and this is what is meant by government. The *latter* noun, then, governs the *former* in the possessive case, when the latter noun denotes the *thing* possessed, and the former one, the *possessor*.

So a transitive verb governs the *Objective case*, of the noun, that denotes the object of an action ; it does *not* govern the *Possessive* or the *Nominative* case. When I mean to say, that *Peter* is the object which I strike, I cannot say, I strike Peter's, I must say, I strike Peter ; because the transitive verb does not govern the *Possessive*, but the *Objective* case.

Caroline. I suppose if a *transitive* verb expresses an action done to some object, an *intransitive* verb must express an action which is *not* done to any *object.*

Tutor. You are right. Intransitive verbs express action confined to the actor. Give me an example of an intransitive verb.

Caroline. George *runs.* Runs is an intransitive verb, because George's action is confined to himself, and does not affect any object.

Tutor. Very well explained. Now, George, give me an example of a *transitive* verb.

George. Caroline broke the glass. Broke is a *transitive* verb, because it expresses an action done by the Nominative case *Caroline*, to the object *glass.* *Broke* governs *glass* in the Objective case, according to Rule III, Transitive verbs govern, &c.

Caroline. Give us, if you please, a few such sentences as we are prepared to parse, that we may practise upon them.

Tutor. I will.

Horses draw men's carriages.

I will parse this sentence for you, and then you can parse the others which I shall give you yourselves. If you find it difficult, reflect upon what has been told you, and you will at length succeed. *Horses* is a noun of the third person, plural number, masculine gender, in the nominative case to the verb *draw.* *Draw* is a transitive verb of the third person, plural number, and agrees with its nominative case *Horses,* according to Rule I, which says, The verb must agree, &c. *Men's* is a noun of the third person, plural number, masculine gender, in the Possessive case, and is governed by the following noun *carriages,* agreeably to Rule II. Repeat the rule. *Carriages* is a noun of the third person, plural number, of neuter gender, in the Objective case, and is governed by the transitive verb *draw,* according to Rule III. Repeat the rule.

Parse the following sentences, in the same manner, only take care to call the verb *intransitive,* when there is no object acted upon.

EXERCISES IN PARSING.

Foxes kill people's geese. Women wash children's clothes. Women walk. Mothers make daughters' frocks.—Daughters increase mothers' pleasures—John whips Peter's dog—Peter's dog bites John's finger—George's wife's sister loves Emma's brother—In this last sentence *George's* is governed by *wife's*, and *wife's* by *sister*. ✓

David *plays*—Boys *play*—Take notice in these, as well as in the other sentences, that the singular verb ends in *s*, but in writing the plural verb the *s* is omitted. Now practise upon such sentences, in different parts of the Conversation.

I will now give you a few additional

REMARKS ON NOUNS.

Substantives or nouns, are either common or proper.

Proper names or substantives, are the names appropriated to individuals : as, George, London, Thames.

Common names or substantives, stand for kinds containing many sorts, or for sorts containing many individuals under them : as, animal, man, tree, &c.

When proper names have an article annexed to them, they are used as common names : as, " He is *the Cicero* of his age ; he is reading the lives of *the* Twelve *Cæsars.*"

Common names may also be used to signify individuals, by the addition of articles or pronouns : as, " *The* boy is studious ; *that* girl is discreet."*

To substantives belong gender, number, and case ; and they are all of the third person, when spoken *of*, and of the second, when spoken *to*, : as, " Blessings attend us on every side ; be grateful, children of men !" that is, *ye* children of men.

Some substantives, naturally neuter, are, by a figure of speech, converted into the masculine or feminine gender : as, when we say of the sun, *he* is setting ; and of a ship, *she* sails well.

Figuratively, in the English tongue, we commonly give the masculine gender to nouns which are conspicuous for the attributes of imparting or communicating, and which are by nature strong and efficacious. Those, again, are made femi-

---

* Nouns may also be divided into the following classes : *Collective* nouns, or nouns of multitude : as, the people, the parliament, the army : *Abstract* nouns, or the names of qualities abstracted from their substantives : as, knowledge, goodness, witness. *Verbal* or *participal* nouns : as, beginning, reading, writing.

nine, which are conspicuous for the attributes of containing, or bringing forth, or which are peculiarly beautiful or amiable. Upon these principles, the sun is said to be masculine; and the moon, being the receptacle of the sun's light, to be feminine. The earth is generally feminine. A ship, a country, a city, &c. are likewise made feminine, being receivers or containers. Time is always masculine, on account of its mighty efficacy. Virtue is feminine from its beauty, and its being the object of love. Fortune and the church, are generally put in the feminine gender.—There appears to be a rational foundation for these figurative distinctions, though they have not been adopted in all countries. Many of the substances, which, in one language, have masculine names, have, in others, names that are feminine.

Greek and Latin, and many of the modern tongues, have nouns, some masculine, some feminine, which denote substances in which sex never had existence. Nay, some languages are so particularly defective in this respect, as to class every object, inanimate as well as animate, under either the masculine or the feminine gender, as they have no neuter gender for those which are of neither sex. This is the case with the Hebrew, French, Italian, and Spanish. But the English, strictly following the order of nature, puts every noun which denotes a male animal, and no other, in the *masculine* gender; every name of a female animal, the *feminine*; and every animal whose sex is not obvious, or known, as well as every inanimate object whatever, in the *neuter* gender. And this gives our language a superior advantage to most others, in the poetical and rhetorical style: for when nouns naturally neuter are converted into masculine and feminine, the personification is more distinctly, and more forcibly marked.

The English language has three methods of distinguishing the sex, viz.

1. *By different words : as,*

Male.	Female.	Male.	Female.
Bachelor	Maid	Dog	Bitch
Boar	Sow	Drake	Duck
Boy	Girl	Earl	Countess
Brother	Sister	Father	Mother
Buck	Doe	Friar	Nun
Bull	Cow	Gander	Goose
Bullock or Steer	Heifer	Hart	Roe
		Horse	Mare
Cock	Hen	Husband	Wife
King	Queen	Singer	Songstress or Singer
Lad	Lass		
Lord	Lady	Sloven	Slut
Man	Woman	Son	Daughter
Master	Mistress	Stag	Hind

4*

Milter	Spawner	Uncle	Aunt
Nephew	Niece	Wizzard	Witch
Ram	Ewe		

2. *By a difference of termination : as,*

Male.	Female.	Male.	Female.
Abbot	Abbess	Jew	Jewess
Actor	Actress	Landgrave	Landgravine
Administrator	Administratrix	Lion	Lioness
Adulterer	Adultress	Marquis	Marchioness
Ambassador	Ambassadress	Mayor	Mayoress
Arbiter	Arbitress	Patron	Patroness
Baron	Baroness	Peer	Peeress
Bridegroom	Bride	Poet	Poetess
Benefactor	Benefactress	Priest	Priestess
Caterer	Cateress	Prince	Princess
Chanter	Chantress	Prior	Prioress
Conductor	Conductress	Prophet	Prophetess
Count	Countess	Protector	Protectress
Deacon	Deaconess	Shepherd	Shepherdess
Duke	Dutchess	Songster	Songstress
Elector	Electress	Sorcerer	Sorceress
Emperor	Empress		Sultaness
Enchanter	Enchantress	Sultan	Sultana
Executor	Executrix	Tiger	Tigress
Governor	Governess	Traitor	Traitress
Heir	Heiress	Tutor	Tutress
Hero	Heroine	Viscount	Viscountess
Hunter	Huntress	Votary	Votaress
Host	Hostess	Widower	Widow

3. *By a noun, pronoun, or adjective, being* prefixed *to the substantive : as*

A cock-sparrow	A hen-sparrow
A man-servant	A maid-servant
A he-goat	A she-goat
A he-bear	A she-bear
A male child	A female child
Male descendants	Female descendants

It sometimes happens, that the same noun is either masculine or feminine. The words *parent, child, cousin, friend, neighbor, servant,* and several others, are used indifferently for males or females. These words cannot properly be said to denote a distinct species of gender, as some writers on English grammar have asserted, and who denominate them the *common* gender. There is no such gender belonging to the language. The business of parsing can be effectually performed, without having recourse to a *common* gender.— us, we may say; *Parents* is a noun of the masculine *and* feminine gender ; *Parent*, if doubtful, is of the masculine *or* feminine gender ; *Parent*, if the gender is known by the construction, is of the gender so ascertained.

Nouns with variable terminations contribute to conciseness and perspicuity of expression. We have only a sufficient number of them to make us feel our want : for when we say of a woman, she is a philosopher, an astronomer, a builder, a weaver, we perceive an impropriety in the termination, which we cannot avoid ; but we can say, that she is a botanist, a student, a witness, a scholar, an orphan, a companion, because these terminations have not annexed to them the notion of sex.

If you have paid attention to what I have said, you will be able to answer the following questions before I give you any new information. I will write them for you, that you may find out the answers, which I shall expect you to give, when we meet again.

QUESTIONS.

What is a noun ?
How many persons have nouns ?
How many numbers ?
How many genders ?
How many cases ?
How do you distinguish the three cases ?
What rule do you give when you parse the possessive case ?
When you parse an objective case what rule ?
What is a verb ?
What distinction have I given respecting a verb ?
What is the difference between a *transitive* and an *intransitive* verb ?
Are verbs, in the singular number, written as they are in the plural ?
What is the distinction between a common and a proper noun ?
Of what person are all nouns ?
How are nouns, naturally neuter, made of masculine or feminine gender ?
Can proper nouns be converted into common nouns ? How ?

CONVERSATION V.

OF THE ARTICLES.

Tutor. In the two preceding Conversations, I endeavoured to explain to you the two principal parts of speech in the language, viz. the *Noun* and the *Verb*. Every thing that you see about you, called by some name. The substance on which I write, is called *paper* ; the thing with which I write, is called a *pen* ; the thing which you hold in your hand, is called a *book* ; and the thing which Caroline wears in her hair, is called a *comb* ; You perceive, then, that *things* are called by names, as well as persons ; and a word that is a name, you know, is a noun. The verb, you remember, is a word of a very different meaning from a noun ; the Verb signifies an *action* that some person or thing does. I will now introduce another part of speech, the *Article*.

An article is a word prefixed to nouns, to limit their signification.

In the English language, there are but two articles, *a* and *the* : *a* becomes *an*, when the following word begins with a vowel or a silent *h* ; as, *an acron, an hour*. Here you see that *acron* begins with a vowel ; and *h* in *hour* is silent ; therefore *an* is used ; for the first letter sounded in *hour* is the vowel *o*.

George. Must we always use *a* before a word beginning with *h* that is sounded.

Tutor. No : there is one exception. *An* must be used when the following word begins with an *h* that is *not* silent, if the accent is on the second syllable : as, *an heroic* action, *an historical* account. But when the *h* is sounded, and the accent is not on the second syllable, *a* is only to be used : as, *a hand, a husband, a heathen*.

Caroline. You said we must use *an*, and not *a*, before a word beginning with a vowel ; is there no exception to that ?

Tutor. Yes : there are two. *An* must not be used before the vowel *u*, when it is sounded long, but *a* : as, *a union, a university, a useful book*, &c. *A* must be used also before the word *one* ; as, *many a one*—because in pronouncing *one*, we sound it as if it were written with a *w*.

A or *an* is called the indefinite article; because it is used to point out one single thing of a kind in an indefinite manner : as, Give me *a* book—Bring me *an* apple ; not meaning any particular book, or any particular apple. *The* is called the definite article ; because it points out what particular thing or things are meant : as, Give me *the* book—Bring me *the* apples ; meaning some particular book, or apples—A noun used without an article to limit it is generally taken in the widest sense : as, *Man is mortal.* You readily see that this does not mean the same, as *a* man is mortal. The former phrase means, the creature, man, that is, all mankind ; the latter restricts the meaning to an individual. The rule we give, then, when we parse an article, is

RULE IV.

The article refers to a noun, expressed or understood, to limit its signification.

George. Do both the articles limit the nouns they refer to ?

Tutor. Yes ; but in different ways. *A* or *an* requires the following noun to be in the singular number, and therefore limits it as to its number.

Caroline. Does *a* or *an* always require the following noun to be singular ?

Tutor. Not always ; for when the words *few, great, many, dozen, hundred, thousand,* come between the article and noun, the noun is plural : as, *a few* men, *a great many* men, *a dozen* men, *a hundred* houses, *a thousand* houses.

George. I could not properly say, *a houses ;* but if I use *few,* or any of the words you mentioned, I perceive that the noun must be plural : as, a few houses, &c. But the definite article, I see, may be used with nouns of either number ; I can say, *the house,* or *the houses,* with equal propriety ; how then does the definite article limit its noun ?

Tutor. By referring to some particular thing or things, *known ;* while *a* or *an* refers to things unknown, and of course to no *particular* thing.

Caroline. When I say you saw a horse, which my father sold, does not *a* refer to a *particular* horse, which is known?

Tutor. You have put a very proper question, Caroline; and I am glad to observe you examine closely the principles I present to you; it is the only way to become a scholar. If you reflect on your question, however, you will find, that it is not the *article*, which ascertains the horse, spoken of to be a *particular* one, that is *known;* but it is that part of the sentence that follows the word horse. This will appear by stopping at the word horse: as, You saw a horse.—What horse is referred to?

George. None, in particular. I now perceive, that the indefinite article has not the power of pointing out a thing precisely; but that *other* words render the thing definite, which the *article* alone could not make so.

Caroline. I believe, that we now entirely comprehend the different uses of the articles.

Tutor. I think you do; and I shall now write several questions for you to answer, and then give you a parsing lesson.

QUESTIONS.

How many articles are there in the English language?
What are they called?
For what purpose are they used?
How does the indefinite article limit the noun?
How does the definite article limit it?
When must *a* become *an?*
In what instances must *a* be used before a vowel?
When must *an* be used before an *h* that is not silent?
When must *a* be followed by a plural noun?
What *rule* do you give when you parse the articles?

EXERCISES IN PARSING.

The men saw wood. A boy runs. A girl writes. The husband governs the family. An owl hoots. The owls hoot. An ostrich runs. A bird flies. The ladies teach the children. The merchant sells the goods. The farmers sell produce.

Practice, as before, in different parts of the Conversation.

To show you more particularly their use and importance, I give you the following

REMARKS ON THE ARTICLES.

The peculiar use and importance of the articles will be seen in the following examples: "The son of a king—the son of the king—a son of the king." Each of these three phrases has an entirely different meaning, through the different application of the articles *a* and *the*.

"Thou art *a* man;" is a very general and harmless position; but, "Thou art *the* man," (as Nathan said to David,) is an assertion capable of striking terror and remorse into the heart.

The article is omitted before nouns that imply the different virtues, vices, passions, qualities, sciences, arts, metals, herbs, &c.: as, "prudence is commendable; falsehood is odious; anger ought to be avoided;" &c. It is not prefixed to a proper name: as, "Alexander," (because that of itself denotes a determinate individual or particular thing, (except for the sake of distinguishing a particular family: as, "He is *a* Howard, or of the family of the Howards: or by way of eminence: as, "Every man is not *a* Newton; "He has the courage of an Archilles: or when some noun is understood: "He sailed down *the* (river) Thames, in *the* (ship) Britannia."

When an adjective is used with the noun to which the article relates, it is placed between the article and the noun: as, "a *good* man," an *agreeable* woman," "the *best* friend." On some occasions, however, the adjective precedes *a* or *an*: as, *such* a shame," as *great* a man as Alexander," "too *careless* an author."

The indefinite article is sometimes placed between the adjective *many*, and a singular noun: as,

> "Full *many a gem* of purest ray serene.
> "The dark unfathom'd caves of ocean bear;
> "Full *many a flow'r* is born to blush unseen,
> "And waste its sweetness on the desert air."

In these lines, the phrases, *many a gem* and *many a flow'r*, refer to *many gems*, and *many flowers*, separately, not collectively considered.

The definite article *the* is frequently applied to adverbs in the comparative and superlative degree; and its effect is, to mark the degree the more strongly, and to define it the more precisely: as, "*The* more I examine it, *the* better I like it. I like this *the* least of any.

"That which is nearly connected with us, or with which, from its vicinity, we have been long acquainted, becomes

speak of one person or thing, or more than one ;
therefore they have no number ; nor do they denote actors, possessors, or objects ; therefore they
have no case.

Tutor. You are right. In *our* language, Adjectives have no person, number, gender, or case ;
and the only variation which they admit, is that of
the degrees of comparison.

There are commonly reckoned three degrees of
comparison ; The POSITIVE, the COMPARATIVE,
and the SUPERLATIVE.

The Positive State expresses the quality of an
object, without increase or diminution : as, *good*
boys, *wise* boys, *great* boys.

The Comparative Degree increases or lessens
the Positive in signification : as, *wiser* boys—*greater* boys—*less wise* boys—or boys *less wise.* The
Adjective may be placed *after* the noun, as well as
before it, as in the last example.

The Superlative Degree increases or lessens the
Positive to the highest or lowest degree : as, *greatest, wisest, least wise* boys, or men, or people.

The simple word, or Positive, becomes the Comparative, by adding *r* or *er ;* and the Superlative,
by adding *st* or *est* to the end of it : as

Possessive.	Comparative.	Superlative.
wise,	wiser,	wisest.
great,	greater,	greatest.

The words *more* and *most, less* and *least,* have the
same effect : as,

Possessive.	Comparative.	Superlative.
wise,	more wise,	most wise.
wise,	less wise,	least wise.

You must perceive that the Adjective is a very
simple part of speech ; and when you parse it,
you will merely tell of what degree of comparison
it is ; and to what noun it belongs ; and then give
this rule ;

RULE V.

Every adjective belongs to some noun, expressed or understood.

Caroline. I suppose we are now prepared to parse sentences, composed of Nouns, Verbs, Articles, and Adjectives.

Tutor. Yes. I will first parse one for you, and then give you several more, which you must practise upon.

The little girls write a long letter.

The is the definite Article, and refers to the noun *girls.* Repeat Rule IV. *Little* is an Adjective of the Positive state, and belongs to the noun *girls.* Repeat Rule V. *Girls* is a noun of the third person, plural number, of the feminine gender, and nominative case to the verb *write.* *Write* is a transitive verb, of the third person, plural number, and agrees with its Nominative case, *girls.* Repeat Rule I. *A* is the indefinite Article, and refers to the noun *letter.* Repeat Rule IV. *Long* is an Adjective, of the Positive state, and belongs to the noun *letter.* Repeat Rule V. *Letter* is a noun of the third person, singular number, of neuter gender, and in the Objective case, governed by the transitive Verb *write.* Repeat Rule III.

Parse this sentence several times ; and when you can do it accurately, practise upon the following, in the same manner.

EXERCISES IN PARSING.

The great ships carry large burdens ; the smaller ships bear less burdens. Generous persons relieve the poor old men. Wealthy ladies help indigent females. The little children cry. The old birds fly. Wise mothers teach little girls. The man's discourse caused much excitement. The girl's friends abuse the children's parents. The parents' servants brush the boys' new clothes.

NOTE. *An adjective, used without a substantive, having the definite article before it, has the force and meaning of a substantive of the plural number, and must be parsed thus :* The *rich* help the *poor.*

Rich is an adjective used substantively, third person plural, in the nominative case to the verb *help.*

Poor is an adjective used substantively, of the third person, plural number, and in the objective case, governed by the transitive verb *help.* Repeat Rule III.

Private virtues adorn a man.

The grey horses prance.

NOTE.   *One, two, three, &c. are called numeral adjectives.*

The two armies conquered the enemies.

Thirty men killed twenty wolves.

NOTE.   *The words, first, second, third, &c. are called numeral adjectives of order.*

The third man killed the fourth wolf.

I shall now give you a number of questions, which you will be able to answer, if you recollect what I have said in this Conversation.

QUESTIONS.

What is an Adjective ?

Do adjectives vary, as nouns do, on account of number, gender or case ?

Do they ever vary ?

What variation have they ?

How many degrees of comparison have they ?

How is the Comparative formed ?

How the Superlative ?

Is the noun to which the adjective belongs, always expressed ?

What rule do you give, when you parse adjectives ?

Is an adjective ever used in the nature of a noun ?

Of what number is the adjective when used substantively ?

Now I will give you some

REMARKS ON THE ADJECTIVE.

Grammarians have generally enumerated three degrees of comparison ; but the first of them has been thought by some writers, to be improperly termed a degree of comparison ; as it seems to be nothing more than the simple form of the adjective, and not to imply either comparison or degree.— This opinion may be well founded, unless the adjective be supposed to imply comparison or degree, by containing a secret or general reference to other things: as, when we say, " he is a *tall* man," "this is a *fair* day," we make some reference to the ordinary size of men, and to the different weather.

The termination *ish*, may be accounted in some sort a degree of comparison, by which the signification is diminished below the positive: as, *black, blackish*, or tending to blackness; *salt, saltish*, or having a little taste of salt.

The word *rather* is very properly used to express a small degree or excess of a quality: as, "she is *rather* profuse in her expenses."

Monosyllables, for the most part, are compared by *er* and *est;* and dissyllables by *more* and *most* : as, mild, milder, mildest; frugal, more frugal, most frugal. Dissyllables ending in *y,* as, happy, lovely; and in *le* after a mute, as, able, ample; or accented on the last syllable, as, discreet, polite; easily admit of *er* and *est;* as, happier, happiest; abler, ablest; politer, politest. Words of more than two syllables hardly ever admit of those terminations.

In some words the superlative is formed by adding the adverb *most* to the end of them; as, nethermost, uttermost or utmost; undermost, uppermost, foremost.

In English, as in most languages, there are some words of very common use, (in which the caprice of custom is apt to get the better of analogy,) that are irregular in this respect: as, " good, better, best; bad, worse, worst; little, less least; much or many, more, most; near, nearer, nearest or next ..te, later, latest or last; old, older or eldest, oldest or eldest ;" and a few others.

An adjective put without a substantive, with the definite article before it, becomes a substantive in sense and meaning, and is written as a substantive: as, " Providence rewards *the good*, and punishes *the bad*.

Various nouns placed before other nouns assume the nature of adjectives; as, sea fish, wine vessel, corn field, meadow ground, &c.

Numeral adjectives are either cardinal, or ordinal: cardinal, as one, two, three, &c. : ordinal, as first, second, third, &c.

REMARKS ON THE SUBJECT OF COMPARISON.

If we consider the subject of comparison attentively, we shall perceive that the degrees of it are infinite in number, or at least indefinite. The following instances will illustrate this position.—A mountain is larger than a mite; by how many degrees ? How much bigger is the earth than a grain of sand ? By how many degrees was Socrates wiser than Alcibiades : or by how many is snow whiter than this paper? It is plain, that to these, and many other questions of a similar nature, no *definite* answers can be returned.

In quantities, however, that may be *exactly* measured, the degrees of excess may be exactly ascertained. A foot is just twelve times as long as an inch; and an hour is sixty times the length of a minute. But in regard to *qualities*, and to those quantities which cannot be measured exactly, it is impossible to say how many degrees may be comprehended in the comparative excess.

But, though these degrees are infinite or indefinite in fact, they cannot be so in language: it is not possible to accommodate our speech to such numberless gradations; nor would it be convenient, if language were to express many of them. In regard to unmeasured quantities and qualities, the degrees of more and less, (besides those marked above,) may be expressed intelligibly, at least, if not accurately, by certain adverbs, or words of like import: as, "Virtue is *greatly* preferable to riches; "Socrates was *much* wiser than Alcibiades; "Snow is *a great deal* whiter than this paper;" "The tide is *considerably* higher to-day than it was yesterday;" "Epaminondas was *by far* the most accomplished of the Thebans;" "The evening star is a *very* splendid object, but the sun is *incomparably* more splendid; "The Deity is *infinitely* greater than the greatest of his creatures." The inaccuracy of these, and the like expressions, is not a material inconvenience; and, if it were, it is unavoidable: for human speech can only express human thought; and where thought is necessarily inaccurate, language must be so too.

When the word *very, exceedingly,* or any other of similar import, is put before the positive, it is called by some writers the superlative of eminence, to distinguish it from the other superlative, which has been already mentioned, and *is* called the superlative of comparison. Thus *very eloquent,* is termed the superlative of eminence; *most eloquent,* the superlative of comparison. In the superlative of eminence, something of comparison, is however, remotely or indirectly intimated; for we cannot reasonably call a man very eloquent, without comparing his eloquence with the eloquence of other men.

The comparative may be so employed, as to express the same pre-eminence or inferiority as the superlative. Thus, the sentence, "Of all acquirements, virtue is the *most valuable,*" conveys the same sentiment as the following: "Virtue is *more valuable* than every other acquirement."

When we properly use the comparative degree, the objects compared are set in *direct opposition,* and the one is not considered as a part of the other, or as comprehended under it. If I say, "Cicero was more eloquent than the Romans," I speak absurdly; because it is well known, that of the class of men expressed by the word *Romans,* Cicero was one. But when I assert that "Cicero was more eloquent than all the *other* Romans, or any other *Roman;*" I do not speak absurdly ; for, though the persons spoken of were all of the same class or city, Cicero is here set in contradistinction to the rest of his countrymen, and is not considered as one of the persons with whom he is compared. Moreover, if the Psalmist had said, "I am the wisest of my teachers," the phrase would have been improper, because it would imply that he was one of his teachers. But when he says, "I am wiser than my teachers," he does not consider himself as one of them, but places himself in contradistinction to them. So also, in the expression, "Eve was the fairest of her daughters," the same species of impropriety is manifest ; since the phrase supposes, that Eve was one of her own daughters.—Again, in the sentence, "Solomon was the wisest of men." Solomon is compared with a kind of beings, of whom he himself was one, and therefore the superlative is used. But the expression, "Solomon was of all men the wiser," is not sense : because the use of the comparative would imply, that Solomon was set in opposition to mankind ; which is so far from being the case, that he is expressly considered as one of the species.

As there are some qualities which admit of comparison, so there are others which admit of none. Such, for example, are those which denote that quality of bodies arising from their figure : as when we say, "A *circular* table ; a *quadrangular* court ; a *conical* piece of metal," &c. The reason is, that a million of things participating the same figure, participate it equally, if they do at all. To say, therefore, that while A and B are both quadrangular, A is more or less quadrangular than B, is absurd. The same holds true in all attributives denoting *definite qualities*, of whatever nature. Thus the *two-foot* rule C cannot be *more a two-foot* rule, than any other of the same length. For there can be no comparison without *intension* or *remission*, and as there can be no intension or remission in *things always definite*, these attributes can admit of no comparison. By the same method of reasoning, we discover the cause why no substantive is susceptible of these degrees of comparison. A mountain cannot be said more to be, or to exist, than a molehill ; but the more or less must be sought for in their qualities.

You can now answer the following

QUESTIONS.

How are adjectives of one syllable compared ?

How do you compare those of two syllables ?

How do you compare dissyllables, ending in *y*, in *le* after a mute, and those accented on the last syllable ?

Do adjectives of *more* than two syllables admit of the terminations, *er* and *est* ?

What adjectives are compared irregularly ?

What words form the superlative by adding *most* to the end of them?

What is the effect of the termination *ish* ?

Do adjectives ever become nouns?

Do nouns ever become adjectives?

How are *numeral* adjectives divided?

Which are ordinal?

Which are cardinal?

What sort of adjectives cannot be compared?

CONVERSATION VII.

OF THE PARTICIPLES.

George. We now understand the Nouns, Verbs, Articles, and Adjectives very well, and we can parse them without difficulty.

Caroline. We have found great advantage in studying the questions, which you have written after each Conversation; for in order to answer all these questions, we are obliged to recollect all your explanations; and then we find it easy to parse the examples.

Tutor. I shall now explain to you the part of speech, called *Participle*; and then introduce it into your exercises in parsing. A participle is a word which is derived from a verb, and participates of the nature of a *verb*, and also of an *adjective*. It participates of the nature of a verb, because it expresses *action* as a verb does; and it partakes of the nature of an *adjective*, because it frequently belongs to some noun, and is used as an adjective. There are three kinds of participles: *present, perfect,* and *compound perfect participles.*

A present participle, which is the only one I shall now explain to you, denotes an action, continuing, or still going on, and ends in *ing :* as, I see a boy *beating* a dog—I see the dog *running, walking, fighting, eating, drinking, &c.* These are present participles, derived from the verbs *beat, run, walk, fight, eat, drink, &c.* The rule you will give when you parse this participle is,

RULE VI.

The participle ending in ing, when not connected with the auxiliary verb, to be, refers to some noun or pronoun denoting the subject or actor.

George. I suppose, then, according to the rule, that the first participle, which you mentioned, *beating*, refers to the noun boy—and *running, walking, eating, drinking, fighting*, all refer to the noun *dog*.

Tutor. You are right.

Caroline. You say that a participle refers to the noun denoting the *actor ;* but you said that the *verb* agrees with its *nominative*, which is the word denoting the *actor ;* and why cannot a participle agree in the same manner?

Tutor. I shall be able to explain this to you better, a few days hence, than I can now. But I will try to make you comprehend the reason.—When I say, the boy *beats* the dog, you perceive that the verb ends in *s*, and is of the third person singular, to agree with its nominative *boy*. If I make the nominative of the plural number, and say, the *boys*, I must write the verb without the *s :* thus, the boys *beat*, &c. because *beat* is the plural verb, and *beats* is singular; and the verb, you know, must agree with its *nominative* in number and person.

The participle never varies its termination ; it is spelled in the same manner whether the word denoting the actor, be singular or plural, as you may see by the following examples : I see the *boys* running, or the *boy* running.

Caroline. I understand that the participle does not agree with a noun, but simply *refers* to it; and I know it must of necessity, refer to some word that denotes the *actor*, because the participle expresses an action as the verb does, and there can be no *action* without an *actor ;* and, as the real action is always connected with the person or thing that does it; so the words denoting the *actor* and *action*, must have some sort of relation to each other.

Tutor. You begin to understand, I perceive, the relation that words have to one another.

George. You said that the participle partakes of the nature of an *adjective,* and sometimes belongs to a noun like an adjective; will you give us some examples?

Tutor. Yes: I see a *running* stream, and *flying* clouds. Here you see that the participles, *running* and *flying*, are used as adjectives. And when participles are so used, you may call them adjectives.—Some grammarians call them participial adjectives. But I have another relation to explain, respecting the participle. When I say, *The master sees the great boy teaching the little child*—what *case* do you think the noun child, is in?

George. Child is the *object* of the action, expressed by the *participle teaching*, therefore I should take it to be in the objective case, but we have no rule yet, which tells us that an objective case is governed by a participle.

Tutor. You are right; and, as you understand the principle and the relation of the words, you might make a rule yourself. I will however, give you one.

RULE VII.

Participles of TRANSITIVE *verbs govern the objective case.*

Now parse all the words in the sentence I gave you a few minutes since—*The master, &c.*—and then parse the following examples, containing the five parts of speech with which you are acquainted : viz. Nouns, Verbs, Articles, Adjectives, and Participles.

EXERCISES IN PARSING.

The hunters shoot the deer running.
The flying clouds obscure the sun.
The rattling hail pelts the windows.
The laboring men cultivate the earth.

The child sees the hawk killing the chickens.
The servant watches the horse eating oats.

Caroline. We can parse these sentences very easily, because we before knew how to parse all the words except the participle.

Tutor. When we meet again, you must answer the following

QUESTIONS.

What is a Participle?
Why is it called *Participle?*
How does it differ from the verb?
How many participles are there?
What are they called?
Which have I explained?
What rule do you give when you pass the participle?
What rule when you pass the objective case which is governed by it?
I will now give you a few more particular

REMARKS ON THE PARTICLE*.

The participle derives its name from its participating, not only of the properties of a verb, but also of those of an adjective: as, "I am desirous of *knowing him;*" "*admired* and *applauded* he became vain;" "*Having finished* his work he submitted it," &c.

In the phrase, "An admired performance," the word *admired* has the form of the imperfect tense, and of the participle passive of the verb *to admire;* and, at the same time, it denotes a quality of the substantive *performance,* which shows it to be an adjective.

There are three participles, the Present or Active, the Perfect or Passive, and the Compound Perfect: as, "loving, loved, having loved."

Agreeably to the general practice of grammarians, I have represented the present participle as active; and the past as passive: but they are not uniformly so; the present is sometimes passive; and the past is frequently active. Thus, "The youth *was consuming* by a slow malady;" "The Indian *was burning* by the cruelty of his enemies;" "The number is *augmenting* daily?" "Plutarch's Lives are *reprinting;*" appear to be instances of the present participle's being used passively. "He *has instructed* me;" "I have gratefully *repaid* his kindness;" are examples of the past participle's being applied in an active sense. It may also be

* These remarks the learner may omit, till the moods and tenses of the verb shall have been explained.

observed, that the present participle is sometimes associated with the past and future tenses of the verb ; and the past participle connected with the present and future tenses.—The most unexceptionable distinction which grammarians make between the participles, is, that the one points to the continuation of the action, passion, or state, denoted by the verb; and the other to the completion of it. Thus, the present participle signifies *imperfect* action, or action begun and not ended : as, "I am *writing* a letter." The past participle signifies action *perfected*, or finished : as, "I have *written* a letter ;" "The letter is *written*."*

The participle is distinguished from the adjective. by the former's expressing the idea of time, and the latter's denoting only a quality. The phrases "*loving* to give as well as to receive," "*moving* in haste," "*heated* with liquor," contain participles giving the idea of time ; but the epithets contained in the expressions, "a *loving* child. "a *moving* spectacle," "a *heated* imagination," mark simply the qualities referred to, without any regard to time ; and may properly be called participial adjectives.

Participles not only convey the notion of time ; but they also signify actions, and govern the cases of nouns and pronouns, in the same manner as verbs do.

Participles sometimes perform the office of substantives, and are used as such ; as in the following instances ; "The *beginning* ;" "a good *understanding* ;" "excellent *writing* ;" "The chancellor's *being attached* to the king secured his crown ;" "The general's *having failed* in this enterprise occasioned his disgrace ;" "John's *having been writing* a long time had wearied him."

That the words in italics of the three latter examples, perform the office of substantives, and may be considered as such, will be evident, if we reflect. that the first of them has exactly the same meaning and construction as, "The chancellor's attachment to the king secured his crown ;" and that the other examples will bear a similar construction. The words, *being attached*, govern the word *chancellor's* in the possessive case, in the one instance, as clearly as *attachment* governs it in that case, in the other ; and it is only substantives, or words and phrases which operate as substantives, that govern the genitive or possessive case.

. The following sentence is not precisely the same as the above, either in sense or construction, though, except the possessive case, the words are the same: "The chancellor being attached to the king, secured his crown." In the former, the words, *being attached*, form the nominative case to

---

*When this participle is joined to the verb *to have*, it is called *perfect* ; when it is joined to the verb *to be*, or understood with it, it is denominated *passive*.

the verb, and are stated as the cause of the effect; in the latter, they are not the nominative case, and make only a circumstance to *chancellor*, which is the proper nominative. It may not be improper to add another form of this sentence, by which the learner may better understand the peculiar nature and form of each of these modes of expression: "The chancellor being attached to the king, his crown was secured." This constitutes what is properly called, the CASE ABSOLUTE; or, the NOMINATIVE ABSOLUTE.

You can now answer the following

QUESTIONS.

In what respect is a participle like a verb?

How does it differ from a verb?

How is it like an adjective?

How does it differ from it?

Is the participle ending in *ing* always used in an active sense?

Is the *perfect* or *passive* participle always used in a passive sense?

When is *this* participle properly called *passive*, and when *perfect*?

Is a participle ever used as a noun?

Can you give examples with the *present, passive*, and *compound perfect* participle so used?

CONVERSATION VIII.

OF ADVERBS.

Caroline. The Adverb, I believe, is the next part of speech in order; so I suppose we are to have that in this Conversation.

Tutor. Yes; an Adverb is a word which has its grammatical connexions always with a *Verb, Participle, Adjective*, or another *Adverb*; so that you are now prepared to receive the explanations concerning this part of speech, and understand its relations in a sentence. It has no connexion with a noun or any other part of speech except the four, which I have just mentioned. It is called *adverb*, because it is more frequently added to the verb than to any other part of speech;

6

and when added to a *verb*, or a *participle*, it usually expresses the *time*, the *manner*, or the *place*, in which an action is done : as, the boy walks *slowly, leisurely, quickly, hastily,* or *badly,&c.* : or with a participle : as, I see the boy *walking slowly, leisurely, quickly, &c.* these adverbs qualify the participle ; and you see that all these express the *manner* in which the *actions* are done, that are denoted by the verb or participle.

There are many sorts of adverbs.

Adverbs of *time present* are such as these : Now, to-day, &c.

Of time past : Already, heretofore, before, lately, yesterday, hitherto, long since, long ago, &c.

Of time to come : To-morrow, not yet, hereafter, henceforth, by and by, &c.

Of time indefinite : Oft, often, oft-times, then, when, ever, never, again, &c.

Of place : There, where, elsewhere, anywhere, nowhere, hither, whither, thither, whence, hence, thence, upwards, downwards, forwards, backwards, whithersoever, &c.

When an adverb is joined to an adjective or adverb, it generally expresses the degree of the adjective or adverb ; for some adverbs have degrees of comparison like adjectives : as, the adverbs, soon, often, much, well ; and these are compared thus :

Positive.	Comparative.	Superlative.
soon,	sooner,	soonest.
often,	oftener,	oftenest.
much,	more,	most.
well,	better,	best.

Adverbs ending in *ly*, are compared by *more* and *most* :

Positive.	Comparative.	Superlative.
wisely,	more wisely,	most wisely.
ably,	more ably,	most ably.

And adverbs express the degrees of Adjectives : as

Positive.	Comparative.	Superlative.
wise,	more wise,	most wise.
wise,	less wise,	least wise.
prudent,	more prudent,	most prudent.

When such phrases as the following ; *none at all,* *a great deal, many times, a few days ago ;* are used to express the *manner,* or time, and are joined to verbs or participles, you will call them *adverbial phrases.*

George. I suppose we can now parse sentences containing six parts of speech : Nouns, Verbs, Articles, Adjectives, Participles, and Adverbs.

Tutor. Yes: and you must be careful to remember how each is parsed.

In parsing a *Noun,* tell its person, number, gender, and case.

In parsing the *Verb,* tell whether it is transitive or intransitive ; also tell its person, number, and with what nominative it agrees, and give Rule I.

In parsing the *Article,* tell what kind, and what it refers to, and give Rule IV.

In parsing the *Adjective,* tell the degree of comparison, and what noun it belongs to, and give Rule V.

In parsing the *Participle,* tell what it refers to, and give Rule VI.

In parsing the *Adverb,* tell of what kind it is, whether of time, place, or quality, &c. and what particular word it qualifies, and give

RULE VIII.

Adverbs qualify verbs, participles, adjectives, and other adverbs.

By observing these directions, you can parse these sentences, which I have written for you to practise upon.

EXERCISES IN PARSING.

Good boys study well. *Very* industrious children study a great deal. *Very* idle girls learn none at all.

NOTE. You perceive in these sentences, that the word *very* does not belong to the nouns *children* and *boys ;* for the sense is not *very children—very boys,* but it belongs to the adjectives *industrious* and *idle,* and is therefore an adverb, and qualifies an adjective. A word is always an adverb when it qualifies a *verb*, an *adjective*, a *participle*, or another *adverb*, as I have before explained to you.

Now parse the following examples :

Old houses soon fall—The new ship sails fast—Good people love young children learning well—Large cities contain many poor inhabitants—Persons seeing little girls, learning grammar thoroughly, feel much pleasure—Behaving carelessly, boys do mischief—Running swiftly, horses break carriages—Servants driving horses very carelessly, often break people's limbs.

The definite article is frequently prefixed to adverbs of the comparative and superlative degrees, to mark the degree more strongly : as,

The *more* the wind blows, the *faster* the ship sails—The *more* the boy studies the lesson, the *better* the boy understands the lesson.

You must now try to remember the following

REMARKS ON ADVERBS.

Adverbs seem originally to have been contrived to express compendiously in one word, what must otherwise have required two or more : as, "He acted wisely," for he acted with wisdom ; " prudently," for with prudence ; " He did it here," for, he did it in this place ; "exceedingly," for, to a great degree ; "often and seldom," for many, and for a few times ; " very," for in an eminent degree, &c.—Phrases which do the office of adverbs, may properly be termed adverbial phrases : " He acted in the best manner possible." Here, the words, *in the best manner possible*, as they qualify the verb *acted*, may be called an adverbial phrase.

There are many words in the English language, that are sometimes used as adjectives, and sometimes as adverbs : as, " More men than women were there ;" or, " I am more diligent than he." In the former sentence, *more* is evidently an adjective, and in the latter an adverb. There are others that are sometimes used as substantives, and sometimes as adverbs : as, " To-day's lesson is longer than yesterday's :" here *to-day* and *yesterday* are substantives, because they are words that make sense of themselves, and admit besides of a possessive case : but in the phrase, " He came home yesterday, and sets out again to-day," they are adverbs of time ; because they answer to the question *when*. The adverb *much* is used as all three : as, " Where much is given, much is required ;" " Much money has been expended :" " It is much better to go than to stay." In the first of these sentences, *much* is a substantive ; in the second, it is an adjective ; and in the third, an adverb. In short, nothing but the sense can determine what they are.

Adverbs, though very numerous, may be reduced to certain classes, the chief of which are those of Number, Order, Place, Time, Quantity, Manner or Quality, Doubt, Affirmation, Negation, Interrogation, and Comparison.

1. Of *number* : as, " Once, twice, thrice," &c.

2. Of *order* : as, " First, secondly, thirdly, fourthly, fifthly, lastly, finally," &c.

3. Of *place* : as, " Here, there, where, elsewhere, anywhere, somewhere, nowhere, herein, whither, hither, thither, upwards, downwards, forwards, backwards, whence, hence, thence, whithersoever, &c.

4. Of *time.*

Of *time present* : as, " Now, to-day," &c.

Of *time past* : as, " Already, before, lately, yesterday, heretofore, hitherto, long since, long ago," &c.

Of *time to come* : as, " To-morrow, not yet, hereafter, henceforth, henceforward, by and by, instantly, presently, immediately, straightways," &c.

Of *time indefinite* : as, " Oft, often, oft-times, oftentimes, sometimes, soon, seldom, daily, weekly, monthly, yearly, always, when, then, ever, never, again," &c.

5. Of *quantity* : as, Much, little, sufficiently, how much, how great, enough, abundantly," &c.

6. Of *manner* or *quality* : as, " Wisely, foolishly, justly, unjustly, quickly, slowly," &c. Adverbs of quality are the most numerous kind ; and they are generally formed by adding the termination *ly* to an adjective or participle, or changing *le* into *ly* : as, " Bad, badly ; cheerful, cheerfully ; able, ably ; admirable, admirably."

7. Of *doubt* : as, "Perhaps, peradventure, possibly, perchance."

8. Of *affirmation* : as, " Verily, truly, undoubtedly, doubtless, certainly, yea, yes, surely, indeed, really," &c.

9. Of *negation* : as, " Nay, no, not, by no means, not at all, in no wise," &c.

10. Of *interrogation* : as, " How, why, wherefore, whither," &c.

11. Of *comparison* : as, " More, most, better, best, worse, worst, less, least, very, almost, little, alike, &c.

Besides the adverbs already mentioned, there are many which are formed by a combination of several of the prepositions with the adverbs, of place, *here, there,* and *where* : as, " Hereof, thereof, whereof ; hereto, thereto, whereto ; hereby, thereby, whereby ; herewith, therewith, wherewith ; herein, therein, wherein ; therefore, (i. e. there-for,) wherefore, (i. e.

where-for,) hereupon, or hereon, thereupon, or thereon, whereupon, or whereon, &c. Except *therefore*, these are seldom used.

In some instances, the preposition suffers no change, but becomes an adverb merely by its application : as, when we say, " he rides *about* ;" " he was *near* falling ;" " but do not *after* lay the blame on me."

There are also some adverbs, which are composed of nouns, and the letter *a* used instead of *at, on*, &c. : us, "Aside, athirst, afoot, asleep, aboard, ashore, abed, aground, afloat," &c.

The words, *when* and *where*, and all others of the same nature, such as, *whence, whither, whenever, wherever*, &c. may be properly called *adverbial conjunctions*, because they participate the nature both of adverbs and conjunctions : of conjunctions, as they conjoin sentences ; of adverbs, as they denote the attributes either of *time*, or of *place*.

It may be particularly observed, with respect to the word *therefore*, that it is an adverb, when, without joining sentences, it only gives the sense of, *for that reason*. When it gives that sense, and also connects, it is a conjunction : " He is good, *therefore* he is happy." The same observation may be extended to the words *consequently, accordingly*, and the like. When these are subjoined to *and*, or joined to *if, since*, &c. they are adverbs, the connexion being made without their help : when they appear single, and unsupported by any other connective, they may be called conjunctions.

The inquisitive scholar may naturally ask, what necessity there is for *adverbs of time*, when verbs are provided with *tenses*, to show that circumstance. The answer is, though tenses may be sufficient to denote the greater distinctions of time, yet, to denote them all by the tenses would be a perplexity without end. What a variety of forms must be given to the verb, to denote *yesterday, to-day, to-morrow, formerly, lately, just now, now, immediately, presently, soon, hereafter*, &c. It was this consideration that made the adverbs of time necessary, over and above the tenses.

QUESTIONS.

What is an adverb ?

To what does the adverb belong ?

To what does the *adjective* belong ?

When a word qualifies a verb, participle, adjective, or other adverb, what part of speech is it ?

Are adverbs compared ?

How are adverbs ending in *ly* compared ?

What is the rule when you parse an adverb ?

Does an article ever refer to an adverb ?

For what purpose does the article refer to it ?

For what purpose do adverbs seem to have been originally contrived ?

What is an adverbial phrase?

What words are used sometimes as adverbs, sometimes as adjectives, and sometimes as nouns? Can you give examples?

When are the words, *to-day, yesterday,* and *to-morrow* nouns, and when adverbs?

How many classes of adverbs are there?

What are they?

What are the adverbs of *number*?

What are the adverbs of *order*?

What are the adverbs of *place*?

What are the adverbs of *time present*?

What are the adverbs of *time past*?

What are the adverbs of *time to come*?

What are the adverbs of *time indefinite*?

What are the adverbs of *quantity*?

What are the adverbs of *quality* or *manner*?

What are the adverbs of *doubt*?

What are the adverbs of *affirmation*?

What are the adverbs of *negation*?

What are the adverbs of *interrogation*?

What are the adverbs of *comparison*?

What adverbs are composed of nouns, and the letter *a*?

What words are called *adverbial conjunctions*?

Why may they be so called?

When are the words, *therefore, consequently,* and *accordingly,* adverbial conjunctions, and when adverbs?

CONVERSATION IX.

OF PRONOUNS.

OF THE PERSONAL AND ADJECTIVE PRONOUNS.

Tutor. I shall this morning make you acquainted with the *Pronoun.*

George. What is meant by *pro*?—A noun we know is a *name.*

Tutor. *Pro* means *for,* or *instead of.*

Caroline. Now, I think I understand what a pronoun is. It means *instead of* a noun, or it is a word used instead of a noun.

Tutor. It is a word used instead of a noun to prevent the too frequent repetition of the same word.

Thus if we had no pronouns in the language, I should say, 'Caroline is a good girl, because *Caroline* studies *Caroline's* lessons well, and *Caroline* will soon understand *Caroline's* grammar.' But we have pronouns which are used to prevent this disagreeable repetition.

George. And therefore, instead of repeating the word *Caroline*, so many times as you did just now, I should say, 'Caroline is a good girl, because *she* studies *her* lessons well, and *she* will soon understand *her* grammar.'—It is plainly to be seen, that *she* and *her* are *pronouns*, used instead of the noun *Caroline*.

Caroline. And if the same could be said of George, I should say, "*He* studies *his* lessons well,' &c.

Tutor. Yes: and you must readily perceive that *gender* belongs to pronouns; for when you speak of *George*, you say *he* and *his*; but when you speak of *Caroline*, you say *she* and *her*; but when you speak of a thing that is neither masculine nor feminine, *it* is used: as, "I hold a book; *it* belongs to you, and you must use *it* carefully." Now you see that pronouns must be of the same gender, as the nouns are for which they stand.

George. I should think, that they must agree in number too, for when I speak of *two* or more books, I do not say *it*—but I say *they* or *them*.

Tutor. I will give you a rule concerning pronouns.

RULE IX.

Pronouns must agree with the nouns for which they stand in number and gender.

Caroline. Do not pronouns agree with their nouns in person too?

Tutor. They may agree in person, or they may not. Pronouns are frequently used in such a manner, that they cannot agree in person with the nouns for which they stand. When I say, "Go and say to those children, *you* must come in," you perceive that the noun *children* is of the *third* person, but the pronoun *you* is of the *second;* yet *you* stands for *children.*

Caroline. I understand it. The pronouns may agree in person with their noun, but they do not *always;* but they must *always* agree in number and gender, therefore we may put that fact into the form of a rule.

Tutor. You are right, Caroline.—There are four kinds of pronouns, viz: the PERSONAL, the ADJECTIVE, the RELATIVE, and the INTERROGATIVE PRONOUNS.

At this time I shall only notice those called *Personal,* and those called *Adjective* pronouns. There are five *Personal* pronouns, viz: I, thou, he, she, it, and their plurals.

I. is the first person	
Thou, is the second person	} Singular.
He, she, or *it,* is the third person	
We, is the first person	
Ye, or *you,* is the second person	} Plural.
They, is the third person	

The *noun,* you know, has but two persons, viz : the *second,* when it denotes the person or thing *spoken to;* and the *third,* when it denotes the person or thing *spoken of.* But you must perceive that the pronoun is also used to denote the person *speaking;* for when *I* or *we* is used, it denotes the person or persons speaking. Pronouns, therefore, have *three* persons, viz : the *first, second,* and *third.*

George. What is meant by person?

Tutor. Suppose that Caroline should go out of the room, and leave you and me together, and I should talk to you about Caroline: you perceive that *I* should be the person *speaking, you* would be the person *spoken to,* and *she* would be the person *spoken of.* When people are talking together, all this is very plain ; for they can easily perceive who it is that speaks, who it is that is spoken to, and who it is that is spoken of ; but when we wish to represent this on paper, we must have particular words or signs to represent each person, and they must be such signs as will distinguish the person who speaks, from the one that is spoken *to,* and distinguish the one that is spoken to, from the one that is spoken to, and the one that is spoken *of,* from both the others. In all conversations, or composition, there may be these three persons; and as we frequently speak *to things* as well as *to persons,* and *of things* as well as *of persons,* we are obliged to consider *things* in grammar, as we do *persons,* and we use such words as will denote when the thing is spoken *to,* and when it is spoken *of.* *Person,* then, in grammar, is the property of a noun or a pronoun, which shows us whether the noun or *pronoun* denotes the person speaking, the person spoken to, or the one that is spoken *of.* This property of the noun or pronoun also causes the verb *to vary* in the *second* and *third* persons singular: as,

First person singular,	I walk.
Second person singular,	Thou walk*est.*
Third person singular,	He walk*s,* or walk*eth.*

In these examples you see, that *walk* is first person to agree with its nominative *I,* but when the verb is joined with *thou* for its nominative, it ends in *est,* and when it agrees with *he,* it ends in *s,* or *eth;* and so in other verbs: as,

I go	I speak,	I eat,
Thou go*est,*	Thou speak*est,*	Thou eat*est,*
He goes, or goeth,	He speaks, or speak*eth,*	He eats, or eat*eth.*

Whenever you see a verb end in *est,* you know it to be of the *second person singular,* and it must agree with a nominative of the second person singular; and when you see a verb ending in *s,* or *eth,* you know it to be of the *third* person singular: and it must agree with a nominative of the third person singular. So, then, if the nominative of the second or third person should not be *written,* as it frequently happens, you will know of what person the verb is, by its spelling: Thus, *walkest, goest, buildest, &c.* are all of the second person singular; and *walks* or *walketh*, *eats* or *eateth*, *drinks* or *drinketh*, *builds* or *buildeth*, &c. are all of the third person singular; and they must agree with their nominatives according to Rule I, viz: *A verb must agree with its nominative case in number and person.*

Caroline. I now see more clearly the use of this rule; for it would not be grammatical to say, *I reads* or *readeth, I goes* or *I goeth :* because the verbs *reads, readeth, goes, goeth,* are of the *third* person singular, and *I* is a nominative of the *first* person. Nor would it be correct to say, *thou go,* or *thou goes ;* because neither of these verbs is of the second person, as it should be to agree with the nominative *thou ;* therefore the verb should be *goest ;* then the verb would agree with its nominative agreeably to the rule.

Tutor. You are right, Caroline. Now, George can you give me an example of bad English, which this rule enables you to correct?

George. I think I can "*The boys whispers.*"— "*The children plays*"—"*The people saith,*" are ungrammatical, because the verbs *whispers, plays, saith,* are all of the third person *singular,* and their nominatives are third person *plural ;* so they do not agree with their nominatives. They should be *whisper, play, say.*

Tutor. Very well. I shall now give the personal pronouns in their different cases. The personal pronouns are declined in the following manner :

SINGULAR NUMBER.

Person First.	2d.	3d. Mas.	3d. Fem.	3d. Neu.
Nom. I.	Thou.	He.	She.	It.
Poss. Mine.	Thine.	His.	Hers.	Its.
Obj. Me.	Thee.	Him.	Her.	It.

PLURAL NUMBER.

Nom. We.	Ye or you.	They.	They.	They.
Poss. Ours.	Yours.	Theirs.	Theirs.	Theirs.
Obj. Us.	You.	Them.	Them.	Them.

ADJECTIVE PRONOUNS are a kind of pronouns that belong to nouns like adjectives ; and are, on that account, called pronouns *adjective*, or adjective pronouns. They are therefore of a mixed nature, participating of the properties both of pronouns and adjectives. They may be divided into four sorts. Those which imply possession are called *possessive adjective pronouns*, viz.

My, thy, his, her, our, your, their.

Those that denote the persons or things that make up a number, each taken separately and singly, are called *distributive adjective pronouns*, viz.

Each, every, either.

These you will perceive must be used with nouns of the *singular* number only.

George. I see clearly it would be improper to say, *every boxes—each houses—either persons*, &c. I should say, *every box—each house—either person.* But what are the other two kinds of adjective pronouns ?

Tutor. The *demonstrative* and *indefinite.* The *demonstrative* are those which precisely point out the subject to which they relate : they are,

This and *that*, and their plurals, *these* and *those*, and the words *former* and *latter.* The last two are declinable.

The *indefinite* are those which express their subjects in an indefinite or general manner. Of this kind are the following :

Some, one, any, other, all, such, &c.

George, let me hear you repeat the adjective pronouns.

George. The adjective pronouns are,

Possessive. My, thy, his, her, our, your, their.

Distributive. Each, every, either.

Demonstrative. This and that, these and those, former and latter.

Indefinite. Some, one, any, other, all, such, &c.

Tutor. You have repeated them very accurately. Several of these words are sometimes used apart from any nouns ; or in other words, they do not *always* belong to a noun like an *adjective*.

Caroline. When they are not used with a noun like an adjective, either expressed or understood, then I suppose they are not to be called *adjective* pronouns, but *pronouns* only.

Tutor. You are right ; for the meaning of the word *adjective* is *added*—therefore, when a word is not *added* to a noun it is not an *adjective*. For example, when *his* and *her* are not added to a noun, they are personal pronouns, and by declining *he* and *she* you will find what case they are in. So, *each, every,* and *either,* when used without a noun, are *distributive pronouns.* So also, with the *demonstratives.* You will call them *demonstrative pronouns,* when they are not prefixed to any nouns necessarily expressed or understood. And *some, one, any, other, all,* and *such,* you will call *indefinite* pronouns, when they are not prefixed to nouns expressed or understood.

George. Will you give us some examples of these words, when used as *pronouns merely,* and some examples in which they are used as *adjective pronouns ?*

Tutor. I shall in a few minutes, give you some parsing lessons to practise upon ; and in them, I will give you such examples as will illustrate the use of these words as pronouns *merely,* and also as adjective pronouns. But I have to remark to you, that none of these pronouns are declinable except *his* and *her,* which you know are the possessive and objective cases of *he* and *she ;* and the words *one* and *other,* and *former* and *latter.*

One is declined in the following manner :

Singular.		Plural.
Nom.	One.	Ones.
Poss.	One's.	Ones'.
Obj.	One.	Ones.

And *other* is declined thus :

7

	Singular.	Plural.
Nom.	Other.	Others.
Poss.	Other's.	Others'.
Obj.	Other.	Others.

One and *other* when declinable, or used apart from any noun, you will call *indefinite pronouns*, as well as the others mentioned with them. The word *another* is composed of the indefinite article and the word *other ;* and it may be declined and used as a pronoun merely, like *other*, or as an *adjective pronoun.* The word *none* is composed of *not* and *one ;* and it seems originally to have signified only a single person or thing ; but there is good authority for using it in both numbers. *None*, then, is an *indefinite pronoun,* either of the singular or plural number, as the sense may require.

When *none* is used as an *adjective pronoun*, it follows the noun to which it belongs : as, " *Terms* of peace were *none* vouchsafed." *Self* is added to possessive adjective pronouns : as, myself, *yourselves ;* and sometimes to personal pronouns : as, himself, themselves, &c. and these, you will call compound personal pronouns ; and myself and *yourself*, &c., the same in the singular number. *Himself* and *themselves* are now used in the nominative case, instead of *hisself* and *theirselves*. I will now give you a number of questions, and when you can answer them all you will be prepared to parse the sentences, which I shall give you to practise upon.

QUESTIONS.

What is a pronoun ?
How many personal pronouns are there ?
How many persons have pronouns ?
How many cases have they ?
What is the first person ?
How do you decline it ?
What is the personal pronoun of the second person ?
How is it declined ?
How do you decline the personal pronoun of the third person, masculine gender ?
How the third person of feminine gender ?

How the third person of neuter gender ?

When you decline the pronoun of the second person, you find that *you* is used in the nominative case, as well as in the objective. When you see the word *you,* written in a sentence, then, how will you know whether it is a nominative or an objective ease ?

How will you know when the pronoun *it,* is a nominative or an objective case ?

When you say a word is of the first, second, or third person, what do you understand by the word *person ?*

What are *adjective pronouns ?*

How many kinds are there ?

What are the *possessive ?*

What are the *distributive ?*

What are the *demonstrative ?*

What are the indefinite ?

Which of the *possessive* are declinable ?

Are these two called *adjective* pronouns when they are declinable and have cases ?

What are they called ?

Which of the indefinite are *declinable ?*

Decline *one.*

Decline *other.*

Are any of the *distributive* or *demonstrative* declinable ?

Decline *former* and *latter.*

When are all these considered as *adjective* pronouns, and when as pronouns merely ?

What do you understand by the word *adjective ?*

What rule have you for pronouns ?

What is the personal termination of the verb of the second person singular ? or in other words, how does the verb of the second person singular end ?

What is the personal termination of the verb of the third person singular ? ,

Now parse the following sentences, in which you will find the *personal* and *adjective pronouns,* combined with those parts of speech which you had before; and when parsing the adjective pronoun, you will give

RULE X.

Every adjective *pronoun belongs to some noun, or pronoun, expressed or understood.*

EXERCISES IN PARSING.

I see that man teaching his child. Your father loves his children very much. My friends visit me very often. People many times complain unreasonably. I run. Thou runnest. He runs. He runneth. We run. You run. They run. Thou teachest me. I teach thee. He teaches us. She loves him. He pities her. Her they instruct. Them we command. You they feed. Them you carry. Every man helps a little. Some persons labour, others labour not; the* former increase, the latter decrease.—Those horses draw the new coach very easily.—Each pupil daily recites his own† lesson twice. You have not any other books.

Note. *A pronoun in the possessive case, like a noun, is governed by the following noun expressed or understood.*

One loves one's self. Our neighbors invite their friends. Her boys play a great deal. Her son loves her. Thy daughter pleases her teacher. Your dogs hurt mine. My servant assists yours.

Note. *Adjectives, and adjective pronouns, belong to pronouns as well as to nouns.*

The old bird feeds the young ones.
Every one learns his task well.
Great boys teach the small ones.

I will now close this Conversation with a few additional

REMARKS.

Mine and *thine*, instead of *my* and *thy*, were formerly used before a substantive, or adjective, beginning with a vowel, or a silent *h*; as, "Blot out all *mine* iniquities."

The following sentences exemplify the possessive adjective pronouns.—"*My* lesson is finished; *Thy* books are defaced; "He loves *his* studies; She performs *her* duty; We own *our* faults; *Your* situation is distressing; I admire *their* virtues."

The following are examples of the possessive cases of the personal pronouns. "This desk is *mine*; the other is *thine*;

*The article refers to a pronoun as well as to a noun.
†The word *own* may be parsed as a possessive adjective pronoun.

These trinkets are *his*; those are *hers*; This house is *ours*, and that is *yours*; *Theirs* is very commodious."

Each relates to two or more persons or things, and signifies either of the two, or every one of any number taken separately.

Every relates to several persons or things, and signifies each one of them all, taken separately. This pronoun was formerly used apart from its noun; but it is now constantly annexed to it, except in legal proceedings: as, in the phrase, " all and *every* of them."

Either relates to two persons or things taken separately, and signifies, the one or the other. To say, " either of the three," is therefore improper. It should be, "any of the three."

Neither imports " *not either;*" that is, not one nor the other: as," Neither of my friends was there." If more than two are alluded to, it should be, " None of my friends was there."

This refers to the nearest person or thing, and *that* to the most distant: as, " *This* man is more intelligent than *that*." *This* indicates the latter, or last mentioned: *that* the former, or first mentioned: as, " Both wealth and poverty are temptations; *that*, tends to excite pride, *this*, discontent."

One has a possessive case, which it forms in the same manner as substantives: as, *one*, *one's*. This word has a general signification, meaning people at large; and sometimes also a peculiar reference to the person who is speaking: as, " *One* ought to pity the distresses of mankind." " *One* is apt to love *one's* self." This word is often used, by good writers, in the plural number: as, " The great *ones* of the world;" " The boy wounded the old bird, and stole the young *ones;*" " My wife and the little *ones* are in good health."

Others is only used when apart from the noun to which it refers, whether expressed or understood: as, " When you have perused these papers, I will send you the *others*."— When this pronoun is joined to nouns, either singular or plural, it has no variation: as, " the other man," " the other men."

The following phrases may serve to exemplify the indefinite pronouns. " *Some* of you are wise and good;" "A few of them were idle, the *others* industrious;" " Neither is there *any* that is unexceptionable;" " *one* ought to know *one's* own mind;" " They were *all* present;" " *Such* is the state of man, that he is never at rest;" " *Some* are happy, *others* are miserable."

The word *another* is composed of the indefinite article prefixed to the word *other*.

None is used in both numbers: as, " *None* is so deaf as he that will not hear;" " *None* of those are equal to these." It

7*

seems originally to have signified, according to its derivation, *not one*, and therefore to have had no plural; but there is good authority for the use of it in the plural number: as, "*None* that *go* unto her *return* again." *Prov.* ii. 19.—— "Terms of peace *were none* vouchsaf'd." Milton. "*None* of them *are* varied to express the gender." "*None* of them *have* different endings for the numbers." Lowth's *Introduction*. "*None* of their productions *are* extant." Blair.

CONVERSATION X.

OF RELATIVE & INTERROGATIVE PRONOUNS.

In our last Conversation, I told you, that there were four kinds of pronouns, viz. personal, adjective, relative, and interrogative pronouns. The first two I have explained to you; the last two I will endeavor to make you acquainted with this morning.

Relative pronouns are such as, in general, relate to some preceding noun or pronoun. The preceding, noun or pronoun, is called the *antecedent*. Antecedent means going before. The noun or pronoun, therefore, that goes before the relative, which the relative stands for or relates to, is its *antecedent;* and the relative must be made to agree with its antecedent in person, number, and gender; because the relative is a pronoun used to save the repetition of its antecedent. The relative pronouns are, *who*, *which*, and *that*. Thus, instead of saying, "The boy learns well, the boy studies;" we say, "The boy learns well, *who* studies." *Who*, in this sentence, is a relative pronoun, third person, singular number, masculine gender, agreeing with its antecedent noun *boy*, and in the nominative case to *studies*.

And when you parse a relative, always give this rule:

RULE XI.

Relative pronouns agree with their antecedent in person, number, and gender.

I have said that *who, which,* and *that* are relatives. That is a relative, only when it has the sense of *who* or *which;* that is, when you can use *who* or *which* in its place. Thus when I say, " Here is a box *that* I bought," it is the same sense, as if I were to say, " Here is a box *which* I bought." " The man *that* came," &c. is the same sense, as the " man *who* came."

George. But I remember the word *that,* was among the *demonstrative adjective pronouns.* How shall I know when it is a *demonstrative,* and when it is a *relative* pronoun ?

Tutor. When *that* is a *demonstrative,* it points out something precisely, and it cannot be changed into *who* or *which,* as it can when it is a relative. For example, " Give me *that* box"—" See *that* box." In these phrases *that* is a demonstrative, and you preceive that you cannot supply its place by *who* or *which,* as you can in these. " The boy *that* studies will improve,"—" The wood *that* I bought is good."

Caroline. Are the relatives declined as the personal pronouns are ?

Tutor. The relative *who* is thus declined : *Singular,* Nominative *Who,* Possessive *Whose,* Objective *Whom.* The *plural* is the same. This relative does not vary on account of its person, number, or gender.

George. How then shall we know its person, number and gender ?

Tutor. By its antecedent.

Caroline. I could have answered that question, for I remember the tenth rule, " Relative pronouns agree with their antecedents in *person, number,* and *gender.*" But is it proper to say, The master *which* teaches me, teaches George ?

Tutor. No : when the antecedent denotes persons, or intelligent beings, you must use *who, whose,* and *whom ;* therefore you should say, the master, *who* teaches, &c. But when the antecedent denotes *animals* or *things,* you must use *which* or *that.*

George. Are *which* and *that* declinable ?

Tutor. No : these relatives are indeclinable.— They are used in the nominative, and objective cases, and are spelled in the same manner in both ; but they have no possessive case.

Caroline. Is *that* never used as a relative, when the antecedent denotes persons, or intelligent beings ?

Tutor. Yes, in several instances : as first, when *who* has been used in the same member of the sentence, to prevent the too frequent recurrence of the same word, we use *that.* Secondly, when persons make but part of the antecedent : as, " The *man* and the *horses that* were drowned, have been found." In this sentence, neither *who* nor *which* would be proper. Thirdly, when we ask a question with *who* : as, " Who *that* is honest would behave thus ?" Fourthly, *that* is more elegantly used as a relative than *who* or *which* after adjectives of the superlative degree : as, " Moses was the *meekest* man *that* ever lived." "Solomon was the *wisest* man *that* we read of." " This is the *best* pen *that* I ever had." Fifthly, *that* is used after the adjective *same* in preference to *who* or *which* : as, " He is the *same* man *that* you saw." The word *as,* when it follows *such,* is used as a relative, in preference to *who, which* or *that* : as, " I like such people *as* are agreeable." "I am pleased with such pupils *as* improve," &c.

George. What are the interrogative pronouns ?

Tutor. *Who, which,* and *what,* when used in asking questions, are *interrogative* pronouns. *Who* and *which,* when they relate to antecedents, are *relatives ;* when used in asking questions, *interrogatives.* *Who* is declined in the same manner when an *interrogative*, as it is when a *relative*. *What* is indeclinable. This word should not be used as a *relative*. "The book *what* you gave me, &c. is bad English. It should be, "The book *which*, or *that*, you gave me, "&c.

Which and *what* are sometimes joined to nouns like adjectives, and then they become interrogative *adjective* pronouns: as, "*What* man is *that* ?" "*Which* pen will you have ?"

Caroline. We know now, that *who, which,* and *that*, are called *relative pronouns*, because they relate to some antecedent, and that *adjective pronouns* are so called, because they belong to some noun, like an adjective ; and that *interrogative pronouns* are so called, because they are used in asking questions ; for a question means an *interrogation ;* but we do not know why *personal pronouns* are so called.

Tutor. They are so called, because they denote what person they are of, by their spelling. They do no not depend on any other word for their *person.* Thus, if I write the word *I,* or *thou,* or *he,* or *she,* or *it,* without any connexion with another word, you know what person each of them is : but if I write the word *who,* or *which,* or *that,* you cannot tell what person it is. But if I write *he* as an antecedent before the relative, then we know the *person* of the relative, as well as its number and gender ; because the *relative* depends on the antecedent for its *person, number* and *gender,* and agrees with it according to the tenth rule. Thus, when I say, "I who—Thou who—He who—We who—You who—They who"—in all these instances, you perceive that *who* does not vary, and you can know its person, &c. only by its antecedents, I, thou, he, &c. But it is not so with respect to its antecedents, I, thou, he, &c. which are *personal* pronouns. *They* have person of themselves, and denote their person by their spelling.

Caroline. I think we now understand why the different kinds of pronouns are distinguished by particular names or terms. These distinctions of the pronouns show us, in some degree, their different natures and connexions.

Tutor. I shall now ask you a number of questions, which I presume you can answer.

QUESTIONS.

What are Relative Pronouns ?

How do you decline *who* ?

Are *which* and *that* declinable ?

When must *who* be used ?

In what instances is *that* more elegantly applied to *persons* than *who* ?

In what instances must *that* be used as a relative, where neither *who* nor *which* would be proper ?

When must *as* be used as a relative ?

How do you know the person, number, and gender of a relative pronoun ?

How do you know when *that* is a relative, and when a demonstrative ?

Which and *that* being indeclinable, how will you know their case ?   See the Rule below.

What are the interrogative pronouns ?

When which and what are added to nouns, what are they ?

I will now give you some exercises which you are prepared to parse.

EXERCISES IN PARSING.

Who does that work ?—Who recites this lesson ? —Whom see I ?—Whom seest thou now—Whom sees he ?—Whom see ye sometimes ?—Whom lovest thou most ?—What dost thou to-day ?—What person seest thou teaching that boy ?—Which girl instruct they ?—I have an excellent house.—Thou hast a handsome little sister.—He has an honest friend. —He hath two new knives.—We have most worthy friends.—You have a most agreeable temper.— They have an easy task —What has he ?—What book has he ?—Which road takest thou ?—What child teaches he ?—Us they teach.—Them we teach. —Her I instruct.—Thee he often praises.

RULE XII.

When no nominative comes between the relative and the verb, the relative is the nominative to the verb; but when a nominative DOES come between the relative and the verb, the relative must be in the possessive case, and governed by the following noun, or in the objective, and governed by the following verb, participle, or preposition, in its own member of the sentence.

EXERCISES IN PARSING.

The man who teaches you, pleases your father. —The person whom I teach, loves his friends.—— The woman whose house they hire, owns many houses.—Thee, whom thy friends admire, we also love.——Them, whom thou pleasest, some others displease.——Whom ye ignorantly worship, him declare I.—Him, whom you see, I love still.——The house which he occupies, our neighbour owns.——The elegant books, which the little boys read, the old man sells.——I, whom you call, hear your voice.——Thou, who makest my shoes, sellest many more.——I have good books, you have better, he has the best.

CONVERSATION XI.

OF PREPOSITIONS.

Tutor. We commence this morning with the Preposition, which is a part of speech very easily understood. Prepositions serve to connect words with one another, and to show the relations between them. Prepositions, being words used to express connexions, have no person, number, gender, or case. They agree with nothing; but they govern nouns and pronouns that follow them in the objective case.

The principal prepositions are the following :

of	in	betwixt	near	over against
out of	into	beneath	up	across
to	over	from	down	except
for	under	beyond	before	athwart
by	through	at	behind	towards
with	about	instead of	off	beside
within	amidst	notwithstanding	on	according to
without	below	concerning	upon	throughout
around	between	touching	amongst	

There are others which need not be mentioned, because by examining and parsing these, you will easily understand the nature and character of this part of speech, and be able to distinguish it from others whenever you see it.

George. You say that prepositions govern the objective case. They do not express any action done to an object, as a verb or participle does.

Tutor. That is true. The objective case that is governed by a preposition, is not the object of an *action*, but the object merely of a *relation*. They require the noun or pronoun following, to be in the *objective* case, and not the nominative or possesive case. This you will perceive by putting pronouns after the prepositions which I have written. You will see that the pronouns must be *me, thee, him, her, us, them,* and not *I, thou, he, she, they.* To say, Of *I,* to *thou,* with *they,* &c. you immediately perceive to be contrary to usage, and that it is nonsense.

When *nouns* are placed after prepositions, then, they must be in the same case that a pronoun would, if placed where the noun is, for nouns and pronouns have the same construction.

When you parse an objective case, governed by a preposition, you will give this rule :

RULE XIII.

*Prepositions govern the objective case.**

*The adverb *like,* and the adjectives *worth* and *like,* when they belong to preceding nouns or pronouns, also govern the objective case : as, She dances *like him ;* she is *like him ;* she is *worth him* and *all his family.*

Caroline. I do not perceive very clearly how prepositions connect words together ; nor do I well understand how they show the relation between them.

Tutor. I will illustrate the nature and office of a preposition by a few examples.

The boy writes———a pen. The man walks——— the river. My horse is———the stable. You live ———St. Paul's. The man fell———the water. The Theatre is situated———the Park.

In each of these expressions, you perceive either a total want of connexion, or such a connexion as produces either falsehood or nonsense. Fill up each vacancy in its order, by the following prepositions, *with, towards, in, opposite to,* or *over against, into, opposite to,* and you will see that the *connexion* will be perfect, and the sense complete.

George. I now see the necessity and use of prepositions as connectives, but I should like to hear one word, if you please, on the subject of *relation.*

Tutor. When I say this box lies *on* the table, you may perceive that *on* shows the existing relation between the box and the table, or the relative position each has in respect to the other. And so when I say, I throw the box *under* the table—*up* the chimney—*through* the window—*down* stairs— *into* the fire, &c. the several prepositions show the different relations between the box and the other things mentioned. Prepositions, then, being words that show the relation between persons, places, and things, necessarily show the relation also, between the *words,* that denote the persons, places, and things.

Caroline. I think the office of the preposition, is quite distinct from that of any other part of speech, we have been made acquainted with ; and that we now clearly comprehend its use, and know how to parse it.

8

Tutor. I think you do ; but I shall here make a few remarks concerning the verbs, which you were not before prepared to comprehend. There are three sorts of verbs, viz. the active, the passive, and the neuter verbs. The passive and neuter verbs, I shall reserve for some future Conversation. The one which I have explained to you, and which you have been parsing, is called the *active* verb, because it expresses an action, that is performed by its *nominative ;* and the nominative case to such a verb, may therefore be defined to be the *actor*, as it is the word that denotes the person or thing that acts. This active verb then, is either *transitive*, or *intransitive.* In a former Conversation, I explained the distinction between transitive and intransitive verbs. But I can now, perhaps, make you see the distinction more clearly. The *transitive* verb does not always in reality, express an action done to the object, expressed by the objective case which it governs. This, you will perceive in the use of the verbs, *resemble, understand, believe*, and many others : as, " James *resembles him*"—" You *understand her*"—" We *believe you.*"—The transitive verb, however, has a *direct* reference to the object, and does not permit a preposition to be placed between it and its object. But the object which follows an *intransitive* verb, must be governed by a preposition, either expressed or understood, and the idiom of our language generally requires the preposition to be expressed ; as you may remember from the examples I gave, to show you that prepositions connect words. Thus when I say, " *I walk the window,*" you perceive that some preposition must be placed before the word window : as, " I walk *to*, or *by*, or *towards*, the window." But the *transitive* verb requires no preposition to follow : as, " I *strike* the window"—" I *break* the window," &c. I will now give you a few more examples ; first of *transitive* verbs, and next of *intransitive* verbs.

Men build ships.

He instructs me.

She teaches him.

We love thee.

They carry her.

Men build houses.

Intransitive Verbs.

He looks me.

She dances him.

The man goes Boston.

They play her.

Men labour houses.

We complain thee.

Supply such prepositions, in these sentences, as will make sense. Reflect upon these examples, until you have a clear notion of the *transitive* and *intransitive* verbs.

Verbs are frequently compounded of verbs and prepositions : as, to *uphold*—to *invest*—to *overlook* : and this composition gives a new sense to the verb : as, to *understand*—to *withdraw*—to *forgive*. But the preposition is more frequently placed after the verb, and separately from it, like an adverb : in this situation it does not less affect the sense of the verb, and give it a new meaning, and may be considered a part of the verb, as it is, when placed before it. When you parse such verbs, you may call them *compound verbs*. And remember if the preposition gives a new meaning to your verb, which it would not have without it, it becomes a part of the verb, whether placed before, or after it. Thus, *to cast*, means *to throw* ; but in the phrase *to cast up* an account—*to cast up*, means to compute. So, to *fall on*, to *bear out*, to *give over*, &c. have very different meanings, from what they would, if the prepositions or adverbs after them, were not used. You now know that three parts of speech govern the objective case, viz. transitive verbs, praticiples, and prepositions. An objective case is always governed by one of these three. I will now see if you remember what I have said, by asking you a few questions.

QUESTIONS.

What is a preposition ?
What case does it govern ?
Is it ever compounded with a verb ?
What kind of verbs are these called ?
Explain the difference between a transitive and intransitive verb.
What parts of speech govern the objective case ?

I shall now give you a parsing lesson to practise upon.

EXERCISES IN PARSING.

An honest advocate pleads the cause of his client with much zeal. Good children tell no lies : they speak the truth ; they love their parents ; they respect their superiors. Envy nourishes many bad passions. Behave ye kindly to your friends ; treat them with candour. Love not idleness, it destroys many. Persons who have ingenuous minds, suspect not others of disengenuousness. The man whom my friend supports, treats him ill. The army which encamps on the banks of the river, marches thence to-day. The pen, with which I write, makes too large a mark. My neighbour's little girls, going to school, the other day, lost their books. My workmen ploughing the ground, broke the plough. She is like him. She writes like him She is worth him and all his connexions.

I will close this Conversation with some further

REMARKS ON PREPOSITIONS.

Prepositions, in their original and literal acceptation, seem to have denoted relations of place ; but they are now used *figuratively* to express other relations. For example, as they who are *above* have, in several respects, the advantage of such as are *below*, prepositions expressing high and low places, are used for superiority and inferiority in general : as, "He is *above* disguise ;" " we serve *under* a good master ;" " he rules *over* a willing people ;" " we should do nothing *beneath* our character."

The importance of the prepositions will be further perceived by the explanation of a few of them.

Of denotes possession or belonging, an effect or consequence and other relations connected with these : as, " The
house *of* my friend ;" that is " the house belonging to my
friend ;" " He died *of* a fever ;" that is, " in consequence
of a fever."

To or *unto*, is opposed to *from* : as, " He rode from Salis-
bury *to* Winchester."

For indicates the cause or motive of any action or circumstance, &c. : as, " He loves her *for* (that is, on account of) her
amiable qualities."

By is generally used with reference to the cause, agent,
means, &c. : as, " He was killed *by* a fall ;" that is, " a fall
was the cause of his being killed ;" " This house was built *by*
him ;" that is, " he was the builder of it."

With denotes the act of accompanying, uniting, &c. : as,
" We will go *with* you ;" " They are on good terms *with*
each other."—*With* also alludes to the instrument or means :
as, " He was cut *with* a knife."

In relates to time, place, the state or manner of being or
acting, &c. : as, " He was born *in* (that is, during) the year
1720 ;" " He dwells *in* the city :" " She lives *in* affluence."

Into is used after verbs that imply motion of any kind : as,
" He retired *into* the country ;" " Copper is converted *into*
brass."

Within, relates to something comprehended in any place or
time : as, " They are *within* the house :" He began and finished his work *within* the limited time."

The signification of *without* is opposite to that of *within* :
as, " She stands *without* the gate :" But it is more frequently opposite to *with* ; as, " You may go *without* me."

The import and force of the remaining prepositions will be
readily understood, without a particular detail of them. I
shall therefore conclude this head with observing, that there
is a peculiar propriety in distinguishing the use of the prepositions *by* and *with* ; which is observable in sentences like the
following :. " He walks *with* a staff *by* moonlight ;" " He was
taken *by* stratagem, and killed *with* a sword." Put the one
preposition for the other, and say, " he walks *by* a staff *with*
moonlight ;" " he was taken *with* stratagem, and killed *by* a
sword ;" and it will appear, that they differ in signification
more than one, at first view, would be apt to imagine.

Some of the prepositions have the appearance and effect
of conjunctions : as, " *After* their prisons were thrown open,"
&c. " *Before* I die ;" " They made haste to be prepared
against their friends arrived :" but if the noun *time*, which is
understood, be added, they will lose their conjunctive form :
as, " After [the time when] their prisons," &c.

The prepositions *after, before, above, beneath,* and several
others, sometimes appear to be adverbs, and may be so considered : as. " They had their reward soon *after* ;" " He

8*

died not long *before ;*" " He dwells *above ;*" but if the nouns *time* and *place* be added, they will lose their adverbial form : as, " He died not long *before that time,*" &c.

Prepositions as well as some other species of words, have a variety of significations. It will both gratify and instruct you to examine some of the various meanings which are attached to the preposition FOR. You will find, that each of the phrases denoting these meanings, may, with propriety, be substituted for the preposition.

1.   It signifies, *because of :* as, " Let me sing praises *for* his mercies and blessings."

2.   *With regard to, with respect to :* as, " *For* me, no other happiness I own."

3.   *In the character of :* as, " Let her go *for* an ungrateful woman."

4.   *By means of ; by interposition of :* as, " If it were not *for* Divine Providence, the world would be a scene of confusion."

5.   *For the sake of :* as " He died *for* those who knew him not."

6.   *Conducive to :* as, " It is *for* the general good."

7.   *With intention of going to a certain place :* as " We sailed from Peru *for* China."

8.   *In expectation of :* as, " He waited long *for* the return of his friend."

9.   *Instead of :* as, " We take a falling meteor *for* a star."

10.   *In search of :* as, " He went far back *for* arguments."

11.   *In favour of :* as, " One party was *for* the king, the other *for* the people."

12.   *Becoming :* as, " It were more *for* his honour to submit on this occasion."

13.   *Notwithstanding :* as, " *For* any thing we knew to the contrary, the design may be accomplished."

14.   *To preserve :* as, " I cannot *for* my life comply with the proposal."

15.   *In proportion to :* as, " He is not very tall, yet *for* his years he is tall."

16.   *For the purpose of :* as, " It was constructed *for* sailing in rough weather."

17.   *To be :* as, " No one ever took him *for* a very prudent man."

18.   *In illustration of :* as, " Thus much, *for* the first point under consideration."

19.   *In exchange for :* as, " They received gold *for* their glass beads."

20   *During :* as, " He was elected to the office *for* his life."

21.   *In recompense of :* as, " *For* his great and numerous services, they voted him a statue."

22.   After O, it denotes *an expression of desire :* as, " O *for* better times : " O *for* a place of rest and peace."

Before the conclusion of this Conversation, I shall present you with a list of Prepositions, which are derived from the Latin and Greek languages, and which enter into the composition of a great number of our words. If their signification should be carefully studied, you will be the better qualified to understand, with accuracy, the meaning of a numerous class of words, in which they form a material part.

The Latin prepositions used in the composition of English, words, are the following : *a, abs, ad, ante*, &c.

A, AB, ABS—signify *from* or *away*: as, to *avert*, to turn from; to *abstract*, to draw away.

AD—signifies *to* or *at*: as, to *adhere*, to stick to; to *admire*, to wonder at.

ANTE—means *before*; as, *antecedent*, going before; to *ante-date*, to date before.

CIRCUM—means *round about*: as, to *circumnavigate*, to sail round.

CON, COM, CO, COL—signify *together*: as, to *conjoin*, to join together; to *compress*, to press together; to *co-operate*, to work together; to *collapse*, to fall together.

CONTRA—*against*: as, to *contradict*, to speak against.

DE—signifies *from, down*; as, to *depart*, to retire from; to *deject*, to cast down.

DI—*asunder*: as, *dilacerate*, to tear asunder.

DIS—reverses the meaning of the word to which it is prefixed: as, to disagree, to dispossess.

E, EX—*out*: as, to *eject*, to throw out; to *exclude*, to shut out.

EXTRA—*beyond*: as, *extraordinary*, beyond the ordinary course.

IN—before an adjective, like *un*, signifies privation: as, *indecent*, not decent; *before* a verb it has its simple meaning: as, to *infuse*, to pour in; to *infix*, to fix in.

INTER—*between*: as, to *intervene*, to come between; to *interpose*, to put between.

INTRO—*into, inwards*: as, to *introduce*, to lead into; to *introvert*, to turn inwards.

OB—denotes opposition: as, to *object*, to oppose; to *obstruct*, to block up; *obstacle*, something standing in opposition.

PER—*through*: as, to *perambulate*, to walk through; to *perforate*, to bore through.

POST—*after*: as, *post meridian*, afternoon; *Postscript*, written after, that is, after the letter.

PRÆ—*before*: as, to *pre-exist*, to exist before; to *prefix*, to fix before.

PRO—*forth* or *forwards*: as, to protend, to stretch forth; to *project*, to shoot forwards.

PRÆTER—*past* or *beyond*: as, *preterperfect*, past perfect; *preternatural*, beyond the course of nature.

RE—*again* or *back*: as, *reprint*, to print again; to *retrace*, to trace back.

RETRO—*backwards: retrospective*, looking backwards; *retrograde*, going backwards.

SE—*aside, apart:* as, to *seduce*, to draw aside; to *secrete*, to put aside.

SUB—*under:* as, *subterranean*, lying under the earth; to *subscribe*, to *subsign*, to write under.

SUBTER—*under:* as, *subterfluous*, flowing under.

SUPER—*above*, or *over:* as, *superscribe*, to write above; to *supervise*, to overlook.

TRANS—*over, beyond, from one place to another:* as, to *transport*, to carry over; to *transgress*, to pass beyond; to *transplant*, to remove from one soil to another.

The Greek prepositions and particles used in the composition of English words, are the following; *a, amphi, anti, hyper*, &c.

A—signifies privation: as, *anonymous*, without name.

AMPHI—*both*, or *the two:* as, *amphibious*, partaking of both, or of two natures.

ANTI—*against:* as, *antimonarchical*, against government by a single person; *antiministerial*, against the ministry.

HYPER—*over and above:* as, *hypercritical*, over, or too critical.

HYPO—*under*, implying concealment, or disguise: as, *hypocrite*, one dissembling his real character.

META—denotes change or transmutation: as, to *metamorphose*, to change the shape.

PERI—*round about:* as, *periphrasis*, circumlocution.

SYN, SYM—*together:* as, *synod*, a meeting, or coming together; *sympathy*, fellow-feeling, feeling together.

CONVERSATION XII.

OF CONJUNCTIONS AND INTERJECTIONS.

Tutor. I will now give you the last two parts of speech, viz. the Conjunction and Interjection.

A CONJUNCTION is a part of speech chiefly used to connect sentences; so as, out of two or more sentences, to make but one. It sometimes connects only words. Conjunctions are divided into two sorts, the COPULATIVE and the DISJUNCTIVE.

The conjunction copulative serves to connect, or continue a sentence, by expressing a condition, a supposition, a cause, &c.: as, "He *and* his sister study." "I will go, *if* he will permit me." "The man is happy, *because* he is good."

The conjunction disjunctive serves not only to connect and continue the sentence, but also to express opposition of meaning in different degrees: as, "He *or* his sister studies." "I would go, *but* he will not permit me." "*Though* she is rich, *yet* she is not amiable."

George. I see clearly a difference between the copulative and the disjunctive conjunction; for when I say, Peter and John study, the expression implies, that *they both* study. But, when I say, Peter *or* John studies, the expression shows, that only *one* studies—and therefore I use the verb *studies*, in the third person singular, not *study*, in the plural.

Tutor. Very well. I will now mention the principal conjunctions, and you must make them familiar to you; but you must study the character of the two sorts of conjunctions, so that you may know to which class any one belongs, wherever you may see it. The *nature* and *office* of each part of speech must be carefully studied—not *particular words*; for the same word may, in different senses, be used as several parts of speech. Of this I shall, by-and-by, give you examples.

The principal conjunctions are the following:

The *Copulative.* And, if, that, then, both, since, for, because, therefore, wherefore, besides, further.

The *Disjunctive.* But, or, nor, either, neither, as, than, lest, unless, yet, notwithstanding, though, whether, except, as well as.

Caroline. The conjuctions are so different from the other parts of speech, that I think we should have known them, even if you had not written them.

Tutor. I shall now say something to you about simple and compound sentences, that you may more clearly perceive the use and importance of conjunctions.

A *simple sentence* contains only one nominative, and one verb that agrees with that nominative. There may be other words in it; indeed a simple sentence may contain several parts of speech, and be longer than many compound sentences; yet, if it contains but one nominative, and one verb, which agrees with that nominative, it is but a *simple* sentence. Thus, " *Grass grows,*" is a simple sentence; and, " *Excellent grass grows in great abundance, in all the northern regions of our country, particularly in the New-England States,*" is but a simple sentence, for it contains but one nominative, *grass*, and one verb, *grows.*

A compound of any thing, you know, is made up of simples; so a compound sentence is compounded of two or more simple ones, connected together by conjunctions, expressed or understood. Thus, " *Grass grows,* and *water runs,*" is a compound sentence. I will now give you several simple members, which you will perceive have no relation to each other, till conjunctions are used to connect them.

He is older — I am. She can improve — she pleases. He has talents — opportunities to cultivate them, — friends desirous — he should make a figure.

Here you see the want of conjunctions. Fill up the blanks by the following conjunctions in their order, *than, if, and, and, that,* and you will better understand the importance of this part of speech.

George. This illustrates the use of the conjunction very clearly. When these conjunctions can be placed between the simple members, they connect them, and make one compound sentence.

Tutor. Some conjunctions can be used to connect *sentences only.* That is, after one complete sentence is finished, the next may be commenced with one of these conjunctions, to show that it has some connexion with the former : or to express something in addition to what has been said. The conjunctions, *besides, further, again, &c.* are of this sort. These are never used to join the simple members of a compound sentence.

If, then, lest, though, unless, yet, notwithstanding, because, and the compound conjunctions, *so, that,* and *as well as,* are used only to connect simple members of a compound sentence. And some may be used either to connect sentences, or simple members of compound sentences ; such are, *and, but, for, therefore, &c.* Some may be used also to connect *words.* These are, *and, or, nor, as, &c.* And when conjunctions connect nouns and pronouns, the following rule must be observed.

RULE XIV.

The nouns, and pronouns, connected by conjunctions, must be in the same case.

George. Are the words which are used as conjuctions, ever used as other parts of speech ?

Tutor. Yes, it frequently happens that the same word is used as two or three different parts of speech in one sentence. Thus, " He laboured *for* a dollar a day, *for* he could get no more." In this sentence you perceive that the first *for* is a *preposition,* and governs *dollar* in the objective case, and that the second is a *conjunction,* connecting the two members of the compound sentence.

For is a conjunction, whenever it has the meaning of *because.* So the word *after* may be used as a conjunction, or a preposition, or an adverb ; as, " I went *after* him, *after* I had seen his friend, and not long *after,* I found him." But I can place the noun *time* after the last *after,* and then it will become a preposition : as, " not long *after that time,"* &c. The word *before* may also be used as a preposition, or a conjunction, or an adverb.

When *before* shows the relation between some two words, and governs an object, it is a preposition ;—when it connects two members of a sentence, a conjunction ; and, when it has a reference to time merely, it is an adverb. The same remark applies to *since* and *after*.

Whenever the words *since, after, before, when, whilst, while, whenever,* and *wherever,* are used to connect simple members of sentences, they may be called *adverbial conjunctions ;* because, although they connect as conjunctions, they have a reference to *time* as adverbs.

Caroline. I think we now understand the *conjunction.* Will you explain the *interjection,* which is the last of the ten parts of speech ; and we shall then be able to parse sentences, containing all the parts of speech.

Tutor. INTERJECTIONS are words thrown in between the parts of a sentence to express the sudden passions or emotions of the speaker. The interjections of earnestness and grief, are oh ! ah ! alas ! &c. there are many other interjections expressive of wonder, pity, contempt, disgust, admiration, and salutation. Sometimes a whole phrase is used as an interjection, and we call such *interjectional* phrases : as, *out upon him !—away with him ! Alas, what wonder ! &c.* In parsing an interjection, you merely tell what part of speech it is. I shall now ask you some questions, and then give you a parsing lesson, containing all the parts of speech.

QUESTIONS.

What are conjuctions ?
How many kinds are there ?
What are the principal copulative conjunctions ?
What are the disjunctive ?
What conjunctions connect *sentences* only ?
What conjunctions may connect either *sentences* or members of sentences ?
Which are they that may also connect single words ?

When nouns and pronouns are connected by conjunctions, what rule must be observed ?

Are the words used as conjunctions, ever employed as other parts of speech ?

Give examples.

What is a simple sentence ?

What is a compound sentence ?

What is an interjection ?

When is the word *that* a relative pronoun ?

When a demonstrative adjective pronoun ?

When a demonstrative pronoun merely ?

And when a conjunction ?

EXERCISES IN PARSING.

The boy improves very fast, because he applies well to his studies. Your son behaves so well that he pleases every person that sees him. The snow, falling from the houses, hurt that child very much. You employ all your time in study and exercise ; *that* strengthens the mind, and *this* the body.

NOTE. The prepositions *to* and *for* are frequently understood ; but they govern the objective case then, as well as when expressed, as you will perceive by the following sentences.

He gives a book *to* me. He gives me a book. We lend them assistance. You give me many presents.

Modesty makes large amends for the pain, it gives the persons, who labour under it, by the prejudice, it affords every worthy person in their favour.

NOTE. In this last sentence, you will observe, that the relative *which* is understood twice : the *first* after *pain*, and is governed by *gives*, the *second* after *prejudice*, and is governed by *affords*, according to the latter part of Rule XI.

The friends whom you treat politely, often call at your house ; and they sometimes visit me, and my brothers and sisters. I often see good people bestowing charity on the poor. The rich, giving employment to the needy, afford to the latter, the means of support, and keep them from idleness and dissipation.

9

I will now give you a few general

REMARKS ON CONJUNCTIONS.

The same word is occasionally used both as a conjunction and as an adverb and sometimes, as a preposition. "I rest, *then*, upon this argument :" *then* is here a conjunction : in the following phrase, it is an adverb : "He arrived *then*, and not before." "I submitted ; *for* it was vain to resist :" in this sentence, *for* is a conjunction ; in the next, it is a preposition : "He contended *for* victory only." In the first of the following sentences, *since* is a conjunction ; in the second it is a preposition ; and in the third, an adverb : "*Since* we must part, let us do it peaceably ;" "I have not seen him *since* that time ;" "Our friendship commenced long *since*."

Relative pronouns, as well as conjunctions, serve to connect sentences : as, "Blessed is the man *who* feareth the Lord, *and* keepeth his commandments."

A relative pronoun, possesses the force both of a pronoun and a connective. Nay, the union by relatives is rather closer, than that by mere conjunctions. The latter may form two or more sentences into one ; but, by the former, several sentences may be incorporated into one and the same *clause* of a sentence. Thus, "thou seest a man, *and* he is called Peter," is a sentence consisting of two distinct clauses, united by the copulative *and* : but, "the man *whom* thou seest is called Peter," is a sentence of one clause, and not less comprehensive than the other.

Conjunctions very often unite sentences, when they appear to unite only words ; as in the following instances : "Duty *and* interest forbid vicious indulgences ;" "Wisdom *or* folly governs us." Each of these forms of expression contains two sentences, namely ; "Duty forbids vicious indulgences ; interest forbids vicious indulgences ;" "Wisdom governs us, or folly governs us."

Though the conjunction is commonly used to connect sentences together, yet, on some occasions, it merely connects words, not sentences : as, "The king *and* queen are an amiable pair ;" where the affirmation cannot refer to each ; it being absurd to say, that the *king* or the *queen only*, is an amiable pair. So in the instances, "two *and* two are four ;" "the fifth *and* sixth volumes will complete the set of books." Prepositions also, as before observed, connect words ; but they do it to show the relation which the connected words have to each other : conjunctions when they unite words only, are designed to show the relations which those words, so united, have to other parts of the sentence.

As there are many conjunctions and connective phrases appropriated to the coupling of sentences, that are never employed in joining the members of a sentence ; so there are several conjunctions appropriated to the latter use, which are never employed in the former ; and some that are equally adapted to both those purposes : as, *again, further, besides,* &c. of the first kind ; *than, lest, unless, that, so that,* &c. of the second ; and *but, and, for, therefore,* &c. of the last.

Conjunctions are those parts of language, which, by joining sentences in various ways, mark the connexion, and various dependences, of human thought. And therefore, if our thoughts be really connected and mutually dependent, it is most likely, (as every man in speaking and writing wishes to do justice to his ideas,) that conjunctions will be employed to make that connexion, and those dependences obvious to ourselves, and to others. And where there is, in any discourse, a remarkable deficiency of connecting particles. it may be presumed, either that there is a want of connexion, or that sufficient pains have not been taken to explain it.

Relatives are not so useful in language, as conjunctions. The former make speech more concise ; the latter make it more explicit. Relatives comprehend the meaning of a pronoun and conjunction *copulative ;* conjunctions, while they *couple* sentences, may also express opposition, inference, and many other relations and dependences.

Till men began to think in a train, and to carry their reasonings to a considerable length, it is not probable that they would make use of conjunctions, or of any other connectives. Ignorant people, and children, generally speak in short and separate sentences. The same thing is true of barbarous nations : and hence uncultivated languages are not well supplied with connecting particles. The Greeks were the greatest reasoners that ever appeared in the world ; and their language, accordingly, abounds more than any other in connectives.

Conjunctions are not equally necessary in all sorts of writing. In poetry, where great conciseness of phrase is required and every appearance of formality avoided, many of them would have a bad effect. In passionate language too, it may be proper to omit them : because it is the nature of violent passion, to speak rather in disjointed sentences, than in the way of inference and argument. Books of aphorisms, like the Proverbs of Solomon, have few connectives, because they instruct, not by reasoning, but in detached observations. And narrative will sometimes appear very graceful, when the circumstances are plainly told, with scarcely any other conjunction than the simple copulative *and :* which is frequently the case in the historical parts of Scripture. When narration is full of images or events, the omission of connectives may, by crowding the principal words upon one another, give a sort of picture of hurry and tumult, and so heighten the vivacity of description. But when facts are to be traced down through their consequences, or upwards to their causes ;

when the complicated designs of mankind are to be laid open, or conjectures offered concerning them; when the historian argues either for the elucidation of truth, or in order to state the pleas and principles of contending parties; there will be occasion for every species of connective, as much as in philosophy itself. In fact, it is in argument, investigation, and science, that this part of speech is peculiarly and indispensably necessary.

CONVERSATION XIII.

Tutor. I have now noticed all the different parts of speech, and have shown you some of their relations in sentences; and I have also furnished you with information sufficient to enable you to parse them in those relations. But there are several other relations, which you do not yet understand.

George. If those which remain, are not more difficult than those we have had, I think we shall easily comprehend them.

Tutor. Be patient, and make yourself completely acquainted with whatever I tell you, as we advance, and all difficulties will give way before you.

When I spoke of the conjunction in the last Conversation, I told you that some connect *single words.* When the copulative conjunction *and,* connects two or more actors, you may perceive that the verb, which is used to declare the action, expresses the action of *both* or *all* the actors, and is therefore a *plural* verb: as, the boy *and* his sister *study*—not *studies.* The man *and* horse *walk*—not *walks;* because the verbs *study* and *walk* in each example, express the action of both the nominatives, and it must therefore be plural. But, if I say, the boy *or* his sister, I must use the verb *studies,* in the singular number. The man or horse *walks.*

Caroline. I see the difference very clearly; for when the disjunctive conjunction *or,* is used, the expression does not mean that *both* nominatives act together, but that only one acts; it means that the boy studies, *or* his sister studies ; but that they do not *both study.* And in the other sentence, the meaning is, that either the man walks, *or* the horse walks, but not both.

George. And it is quite plain, that when the verb expresses a single *action* of an individual person or thing, it must be of the singular number, as well as the noun, when that denotes a single person or thing. But when the copulative conjunction is used, the sense is quite different, the verb then expresses the action of all the actors.

Tutor. Very well. I perceive that you begin to understand something of your subject. I will give you a rule concerning this matter.

RULE XV.

When two or more nouns, or nouns and pronouns of the singular number, are connected by a COPULATIVE *conjunction, expressed or understood, they must have verbs, nouns and pronouns in the* PLURAL *number to agree with them ; but when they are connected by a* DISJUNCTIVE *conjunction, they must have verbs, nouns, and pronouns in the* SINGULAR *number to agree with them.*

Caroline. Will you please to illustrate this rule by a few examples, showing us why the *nouns* and *pronouns* must be plural, when other nouns or pronouns are connected by a copulative conjunction, and why they must be singular, when such other nouns or pronouns are connected by a conjunction *disjunctive.*

Tutor. I will. George *and* William, *who obey their* father, *are* dutiful sons. In this sentence, the relative *who* is third person *plural*, because its two antecedents, *George* and *William*, are connected by the copulative conjunction *and;* therefore, the verb *obey* must be *plural*, to agree with *who;* and the adjective pronoun *their*, is plural for the same reason that *who* is ; *are* is plural, to agree with its two nominatives *George* and *William;* and *sons* is plural because it means both George and William.

9*

But let us use the disjunctive *or*. George *or* **William** *who obeys his* father *is* a dutiful *son.* Here you perceive, that the verbs, nouns, and pronouns must be singular.

George.   These examples sufficiently illustrate the rule, and I now perfectly comprehend it.

Tutor.   I will now give an exception to the first part of this rule. When a distributive adjective pronoun belongs to each of the nominatives, the verbs, nouns, and pronouns, must be in the *singular* number! as, every man, and every boy, *exerts himself.* Sometimes an adjective pronoun is used with the first noun, and is *understood* with those that follow: as, every leaf, and twig, and drop of water, *teems* with life.

George.   I see the propriety of this exception to the general rule, because, although several things are referred to, yet each is taken separately, and the verb agrees with each nominative separately. The sense is, that, Every leaf teems, every twig teems, every drop of water teems, &c.

Tutor.   That is right.   And when you parse such sentences, supply a verb for each nominative, as you have now.

I will now give you another rule.

<h3 style="text-align:center">RULE XVI.</h3>

Nouns and pronouns in apposition, must be in the same case.

Caroline.   What is meant by *apposition?*

Tutor.   Apposition, in grammar, means the addition of another name for the same person or thing: as, "*Watts,* the *merchant,* sells goods."

In this sentence you understand, that Watts is the name of the man, and merchant is another name for the same person; therefore *merchant* is in apposition to *Watts,* or another noun in addition to *Watts,* and must be in the same case.   Sometimes several nouns or pronouns are used in addition to the first, and then they are all in apposition to the first.

The propriety of the two nouns' being in the same case, you must readily perceive; because, if

Watts sells goods, the merchant sells goods—for both nouns mean the same person, and, therefore, both are in the nominative case to the verb *sells*.

Again: "I saw *Phelps* the *tailor*." Now it is plain, that when I saw *Phelps*, I saw the *tailor;* for Phelps was the tailor; therefore the noun *tailor*, is in the objective case, and is in *apposition* to Phelps, and is governed by the transitive verb *saw*, according to Rule 16th.

George. This rule will be easily remembered, because the reason of it is plain.

Tutor. It is so; and you will find it of use to you in your writing and conversation, as it will guard you against such errors as the following:— " Love your Maker, *he* that made you." You should honor your parents, *they* that nourish and protect you." "Give the book to my brother, *he* whom you saw here to-day."

In the first of these sentences, *he* is wrong; because it stands for *Maker*, which is in the objective case and governed by *love;* therefore *he* must be changed into *him*, in apposition to *Maker*.

In the second example *they* must be changed into *them*, in apposition to *parents*, and governed by *honor.* In the third example *he* must be changed into *him*, in apposition to brother, and governed by the preposition *to.*

Caroline. I think we shall find no difficulty in remembering the application of this rule; but I hope you will give us some examples of its application in our next parsing lesson, for I find that it is *parsing*, that illustrates the proper connections of the words, and makes us remember them.

Tutor. I will now ask you a few questions, and then I will give you some exercises in parsing.

QUESTIONS.

When nouns and pronouns of the singular number, are connected by a *copulative* conjunction, of what number must verbs, nouns, and pronouns be to agree with them?

Is there any exception to this?

What is it?

What is the rule when nouns and pronouns of the singular number are *disjunctively* connected?

How do you parse nouns and pronouns in *apposition*?

What is meant by apposition?

How do you parse nouns and pronouns, coming together, and signifying different things? See Rule II.

When is an adjective used substantively?

Of what number is it when so used?

How many cases have nouns and pronouns?

What are they?

How do you distinguish them?

In which case does the noun vary?

How does it vary?

How many persons have nouns?

How many have pronouns?

Decline the three persons of the personal pronouns.

How many kinds of adjective pronouns are there?

What are they? Repeat them.

Which of them are declinable?

Decline the relative *who.*

Are *which* and *that* declinable?

How many pa..s of speech may *that* be used for?

When is it a relative?

When is it a demonstrative adjective pronoun?

When is it a demonstrative pronoun merely?

When is it a conjunction?

EXERCISES IN PARSING.

The generous never recount their deeds of charity; nor the brave, their feats of valour. That man whom you see, bestows more benefits on the poor, than any other whom I know. My neighbour has two sons, William and John. Phelps, the tailor, works for me. You honor your parents, them who protect and educate you. John Stiles, the attorney, pleads my cause against Tom Nokes, who pleads for my adversary, the broker. A contented mind and a good conscience make a man happy in all conditions. Prudence and perseverance overcome all obstacles. What thin partitions sense from thought divide! The sun that rolls over our heads, the food that we receive, and the rest that we enjoy, daily admonish us of a superior and superintending power. Idleness and ignorance produce many vices. Either his pride or his folly disgusts us. Every twig, every leaf, and every drop of water, teems with life. None more impatiently suffer injuries, than those that most frequently commit them.

NOTE. When nouns and pronouns of different persons are connected by a copulative conjunction, the verbs must agree in person, with the *second*, in preference to the *third*, and with the *first* in preference to either.

EXAMPLES.

He and thou study well.——He and thou, and I labour much.

In the first sentence *study* is in the second person plural. It is *plural* agreeably to Rule 15th, because its two nominatives are connected by *and*, and the *second* person agreeably to this note. In the second sentence, *labour* is of the *first* person, *plural*, according to the same rule and note.

CONVERSATION XIV.

Tutor. I shall commence this Conversation, by explaining to you what is called the *nominative case independent*. All the nouns and pronouns which you have yet parsed in the nominative case, have had a verb, you know, to agree with them; therefore in parsing such, you have said they were in the nominative case to the verb. But a noun, or pronoun, may be so used, that it can have no verb to agree with it, and still be in the nominative case. This frequently happens, when we make a direct address to a person or thing: as, "George, I wish you would study more." "Caroline, will you give me your book?"

In these sentences, you perceive that the two nouns, George and Caroline, have no verb to agree with them; therefore they cannot be nominatives to any verbs; and you also perceive that they are not in the possessive or objective case; but they must be in one of the three cases. The rule then, for such a construction, is,

RULE XVII.

When a direct address is made, the noun, or pronoun, is in the nominative case INDEPENDENT.

George. The nominative case independent, then, must always be of the second person; because the rule says,—When a *direct address* is made, &c.— and when we make a *direct address*, the person or thing we speak to, is of the *second* person.

Tutor. Right. The nominative independent, is always in the *second* person; but you must observe, that a nominative of the second person is not always independent: it is *independent* only, when it has no verb to agree with it. And what is meant by its being *independent*, is, that it is independent of any verb. All your other nominatives have had verbs to agree with them, and therefore they were *not* independent.

Caroline. Will you give us a few examples to parse under this rule?

Tutor. Yes; you may parse these?

"George, Caroline studies better than you."
"Caroline, you understand this rule quite well."
"Boy, I love you for your good conduct."

I shall give you more examples under this rule, in the next exercises for parsing. There are now remaining four or five rules more, which you must understand, before you can parse *all* the different constructions of the English language; but I shall defer the explanation of these, till I shall have given you the *Moods* and *Tenses* of the verbs, and made you acquainted with the Passive and Neuter verbs; because the remaining rules cannot be so explained, that you can understand them before.

Before I say more, however, I will give you some

EXERCISES IN PARSING.

You, and I, and my cousin, meet here daily.
I saw you yesterday writing a letter.
You see me now teaching you.
Caroline hears George reciting his lesson.
Some persons behave well, others ill.
Two and three make five.
One and one make two.
Two persons perform more work than one.
One likes not ill treatment.
Boys, you do your work very well.
Those who labour with diligence succeed in business; but the idle and vicious come to poverty.

NOTE. The word *what* frequently has the sense of *that which*, and *those which*, and then it must be parsed as a compound pronoun, including both the antecedent and the relative. In this construction, *that* is a demonstrative pronoun. I will illustrate this by a few

EXAMPLES.

I like *what* you dislike. *That is*, I like *that*, *which* you dislike.
What pleases me, displeases you. *What* we have we prize not to the worth, while we enjoy it.

You will find that the prepositions *to* and *for* are frequently understood: as in these

EXAMPLES.

He gave me a book. He bought me a present. That is, He bought *for* me a present. He gave *to* me a book. Her father bought her a present, which she gave her friend.

Modesty makes large amends for the pain it gives the persons who labor under it, by the prejudice it affords every worthy person in their favor.

———

Having explained to you all the different parts of speech, and nearly all their different grammatical relations, I will before I proceed further, give you some

REMARKS ON DERIVATION.

Words are derived from one another in various ways, viz.

1. Substantives are derived from verbs.
2. Verbs are derived from substantives, adjectives, and sometimes from adverbs.
3. Adjectives are derived from substantives.
4. Substantives are derived from adjectives.
5. Adverbs are derived from adjectives.

1. Substantives are derived from verbs: as, from " to love," comes " lover ;" from "to visit, visiter ;" from " to survive, surviver ;" &c.

In the following instances, and in many others, it is difficult to determine, whether the verb was deduced from the noun, or the noun from the verb, viz. " Love, to love ; hate, to hate ; fear, to fear ; sleep, to sleep ; walk, to walk ; ride, to ride ; act, to act ;" &c.

2. Verbs are derived from substantives, adjectives, and sometimes from adverbs ; as, from the substantive *salt* comes, " to salt ;" from the adjective *warm*, " to warm ;" and from the adverb *forward*, " to forward." Sometimes they are formed by lengthening the vowel, or softening the consonant : as, from ' grass, to graze ;" sometimes by adding *en :* as, from " length, to lengthen ;" especially to adjectives : as, from " short, to shorten ;" " bright, to brighten."

3. Adjectives are derived from substantives, in the following manner : Adjectives denoting plenty, are derived from substantives by adding *y ;* as, from " Health, healthy ; wealth, wealthy ; might, mighty," &c.

Adjectives denoting the matter out of which any thing is made, are derived from substantives by adding *en ;* as, from " Oak, oaken ; wood, wooden ; wool, woollen, &c.

Adjectives denoting abundance, are derived from substantives by adding *ful :* as, from "Joy, joyful ; sin, sinful ; fruit, fruitful, &c.

Adjectives denoting plenty, but with some kind of diminution, are derived from substantives, by adding *some :* as, from "Light, lightsome ; trouble, troublesome ; toil, toilsome, &c.

Adjectives denoting want, are derived from substantives, by adding *less :* as, from " Worth, worthless ; from " care, careless ; joy, joyless," &c.

Adjectives denoting likeness, are derived from substantives, by adding *ly :* as, from " Man, manly ; earth, earthly ; court, courtly," &c.

Some adjectives are derived from other adjectives, or from substantives, by adding *ish* to them ; which termination when added to adjectives, imports diminution or lessening the quality ; as, " White, whitish ; i. e. somewhat white. When added to substantives, it signifies similitude, or tendency to a character : as, " Child, childish ; thief, thievish."

Some adjectives are formed from substantives or verbs, by adding the termination *able ;* and those adjectives signify capacity ; as, " Answer, answerable ; to change, changeable."

4. Substantives are derived from adjectives, sometimes by adding the termination *ness :* as, " White, whiteness ; swift, swiftness :" sometimes by adding *th* or *t,* and making a small change in some of the letters : as, " Long, length ; high, height."

5. Adverbs of quality are derived from adjectives, by adding *ly,* or changing *le* into *ly ;* and denote the same quality as the adjectives from which they are derived : as, from " base," comes " basely : " from " slow, slowly ; from " able, ably."

There are so many other ways of deriving words from one another, that it would be extremely difficult, and nearly impossible, to enumerate them. The primitive words of any language are very few ; the derivatives form much the greater number. A few more instances only can be given here.

Some substantives are derived from other substantives, by adding the terminations *hood* or *head, ship, ery, wick, rick, dom, ian, ment,* and *age.*

Substantives ending in *hood* or *head,* are such as signify character or qualities : as, " Manhood, knighthood, falsehood, &c.

Substantives ending in *ship,* are those that signify office, employment, state, or condition : as, " Lordship steward-ship, partnership," &c. Some substantives in *ship,* are derived from adjectives : as, " Hard, hardship," &c.

Substantives which end in *ery,* signify action or habit : as, " Slavery, foolery, prudery, &c. Some substantives of this sort come from adjectives : as, " Brave, bravery," &c.

Substantives ending in *wick, rick,* and *dom,* denote dominion, jurisdiction, or condition : as, " Bailiwick, bishop-rick, kingdom, dukedom, freedom," &c.

Substantives which end in *ian,* are those that signify profession : as, " Physician, musician, &c. Those that end in *ment* and *age,* come generally from the French, and commonly signify the act or habit : as, " Commandment, usage."

Some substantives ending in *ard,* are derived from verbs or adjectives, and denote character or habit : as, " Drunk, drunkard ; dote, dotard."

Some substantives have the form of diminutives; but these are not many. They are formed by adding the terminations, *kin, ling, ing, ock, el,* and the like : as, " Lamb, Lambkin , goose, gosling ; duck, duckling; hill, hillock ; cock, cockerel," &c.

10

That part of derivation which consists in tracing English words to the Greek, Latin, French, and other languages, must be omitted. The best English dictionaries, will, however, furnish some information on this head. The learned Horne Tooke, in his " Diversions of Purley," has given an ingenious account of the derivation and meaning of many of the adverbs, conjunctions, and prepositions: and as you will doubtless be amused, by tracing to their Saxon origin some of these words, I shall present you with a list or specimen of them ; which I presume will be sufficient to excite your curiosity, and induce you to examine the subject more extensively.

ABOUT—is derived from *a*, on, and *bout*, signifying boundary : On the boundary or confines.

AMONG or AMONGST—comes from the passive participle *gemanced*, which is from *gemengan*, to mix .

AND—is from the imperative *an-ad*, which is from the verb, *anan-ad*, signifying to accumulate, to add to : as, " Two and two are four ;" that is, " Two *add* two are four."

SUNDER—comes from the participle *asundred* of the verb *asundrian*, to separate : and this verb is from *Sond*, sand.

ATHWART—is derived from the passive participle *athweoried* of the verb *athweorian*, to wrest.

BEYOND—comes from *be-geond*: *geond*, or *goned*, is the passive participle of the verb *gangan*, to go to pass : Be passed, be gone.

BUT—from the imperative *bot*, of the verb *botan*, to boot, to superadd, to supply : as, " The number three is not an even number, *but* an odd ; that is, not an even number, *superadd*, (it is) an odd number."

BUT—from the imperative, *be-utan*, of the verb *beon-utan*, to be out. It is used by way of exception: as, " She regards nobody, *but* him ;" that is, nobody *be out* him."

IF—comes from *gif*, the imperative of the verb *gifan*, to give : as, if you live honestly, you will live happily ;" that is, " *give* you live honestly."

LEST—from the participle, *lesed*, of the verb *lesan*, to dismiss.

THOUGH—from *thafig*, the imperative of the verb *thafigan*, to allow : as, " Though she is handsome, she is not vain ;" that is, " *Allow, grant*, she is handsome."

UNLESS—comes from *onles*, the imperative of the verb *onlesum*, to dismiss or remove : as, " Troy will be taken unless the palladium be preserved ;" that is, " Remove *the palladium be preserved*, Troy will be taken."

WITH—the imperative of *withan*, to join : as, " A house with a party-wall ;" that is, " A house *join* a party-wall."

WITHOUT—comes from *wyrth-utan*, the imperative of the verb *wyrthan-utan*, to be out : as, " A house without a roof; that is, " A house *be out* a roof."

hastily.—They learn their lesson easily.—Learn I
my lesson ?—Learnest thou thy lesson ?—Learns
he his lesson ?—Learn my lesson ?—Learnest thy
lesson ?—Learns his lesson ?—Learn our lesson ?—
Learn your lesson ?—Learn their lesson ?—I learned grammar.—Thou learnedst thy task well.—
He learned his task thoroughly.—Learned we the
subject sufficiently.—Learned you your exercises
yesterday ?—Learned they their pieces perfectly ?

RULE XVIII.

*The passive participle, unconnected with an aux-
iliary, belongs, like an adjective, to some noun or
pronoun, expressed or understood.*

I see a child well taught.—I saw a boy badly
beaten.—Thou seest me sorely afflicted.—Thou
sawest a letter slovenly written.—He sees a child
wilfully abused.—He saw you ill treated.—Some
pieces of wood, curiously carved, floated ashore.—We,
teaching the class, talk a great deal.—The men, having finished their work, went abroad.—The boys, having learned their lesson, played.—The workmen,
ploughing the ground, broke the plough.—The
men, having ploughed the field left it.—My neighbour bought a field well ploughed.—John Stiles
purchased a farm well cultivated.—He cultivates
one well purchased.

Who does that work ?—Who did this mischief ?
—Who saw that mischief done ?—Whom see I ?—
Whom seest thou now ?—Whom sees he ?—Whom
see ye sometimes ?—Whom saw ye yesterday ?
Which lovest thou most ?—What dost thou to-day ?
I have a book.—Thou hast a pen.—He has money.
—We have gold.—Ye or you have houses.—They
have property.

What has he ?—What book has he—Which
book has he ?—Which road takest thou here ?
Whose house hirest thou ?—Whose child teaches
he ?—Us they teach.—Them we teach.—Her
I instruct.—Thee he cheats.—I who teach you

love them.—Thou who teachest me lovest her.——
He who teaches us, loves them.—We who teach
the boys, love them.—You who teach the girl, love
her.—They who teach the daughter, love her mother.

I, whom you commanded, loved your father once.
Thou, whom he taught, dost well.—Him, whom
you see, I love still.—Whom thou seest, him love
I.—Them whom he whips, I pity.—The book
which I lost you found.—The book I lost you found.
—The money I lost, he spent.—The house you
built, I bought.—I saw to-day, the horse, you sold.
—I taught the boy you sent.—They caught the
thief you suspected.—The boys the boy injures.—
The boy the boys injure.—The boy the boys carries.—The boys the boy carry.—Thee whom they
betray, we love.

I have learned my task.—Thou has learned thy
lesson.—He has learned his exercises.—He hath
learned them.—We have learned very slowly.—The
man has seen his son daily.—The men have seen
their sons thrice.—The parents have clad their children warmly.—I had seen him.—Thou hast seen
them often.—I shall see you to-morrow.—Thou
wilt see me some days hence.—He will see thee
twenty times.—I shall have seen you ten times
to-morrow.—Thou wilt have seen her abused twice,
perhaps thrice, by-and-by. He will have finished
his work to-morrow.

You gave a book to me.—You have given me a
book.—He lent me some money.—He has lent you
a book.—Her father bought her a present, which
she gave her friend.—That man's brother and sister
left him a fortune, which he soon wasted.—Whom
ye ignorantly worship, him declare I unto you.—
Modesty makes large amends for the pain, it gives
the persons who labor under it, by the prejudice, it
affords every worthy person in their favor.

I invited his brother and him to my house.—Him
and his friend I had seen before.—Him whom the

master taught, your brother had taught before.——I shall see him before you arrive.——He will finish his studies first, because he commenced them before you.——I saw her and her sister long since.——I have seen you since I saw her.——I walked before you, and your friend rode before me.——Some people have seen much more of the world than others.——He has seen more years than I.——You labor more than he. ——He came down stairs slowly, but he went briskly up again. —

[125]

CONVERSATION XVI.

OF THE SUBJUNCTIVE MOOD.

Tutor. You now understand the indicative mood, with all its tenses, so well, that you will find the other moods and their tenses very easily acquired.

Caroline. We expected to find the moods and tenses of the verbs somewhat difficult to learn ; but we now begin to think, that they are very easily understood and remembered.

Tutor. If you listen attentively to what I say, and reflect well upon it, I think you will readily comprehend every part of the subject.

I will now proceed to explain the subjunctive mood.

When a verb is preceded by a word or by words, which express a condition, doubt, motive, wish, or supposition, it is in the SUBJUNCTIVE MOOD : as,

He will injure his health, *if* he *walk* in the rain ; I will respect him, *though* he *chide* me ; *on condition that* he *come*, I will consent to stay.

George. I perceive, by your examples, that the third person singular of the verb, in the *subjunctive* mood, present tense, has not the same termination, that it has in the indicative. In the indicative, the verbs, which you have given, viz : *walk, chide, come,* would be *walks, chides, comes.*

11*

Tutor. That is true. The subjunctive mood does not vary the verb in the *present tense.* All the persons are like the first person singular, as you may see by these examples:

Singular.	*Plural.*
If I come.	If we come.
If thou come.	If ye or you come.
If he come.	If they come.

You will conjugate all verbs, in the subjunctive present, in the same manner. But in the subjunctive *imperfect, perfect, pluperfect, first future,* and *second future,* the verb is conjugated just as it is in those tenses of the indicative mood; except that *will* and *wilt* are not used in the subjunctive *second* future, and that a conjunction, expressing a condition, doubt, &c. is used before it, as you have seen, in the examples I have given you. The subjunctive *second* future of the verb *come,* is conjugated thus:

Singular Number.	*Plural Number.*
If I shall have come.	If we shall have come.
If thou shalt have come.	If ye or you shall have come.
If he shall have come.	If they shall have come.

And all others in the same manner.

George. I now see that the difference between the conjugation of the verb in the indicative mood, and in the subjunctive, is only in the *present* tense, and the *second* future. In the *present*, it does not vary on account of the person of its nominative, as it does in the indicative; and in the second future, *will* and *wilt* are not used; but *shall* and *shalt.*

Tutor. That is right.

Caroline. I suppose *any* conjunction, that expresses a condition, doubt, motive, &c. may be used in conjugating the verb in the subjunctive mood, as well as *if.*

Tutor. Certainly. You may use *though, whether, unless, lest,* &c. but these being longer words, are not so convenient in conjugating the verb as *if.*

George. I believe we now know how to form all the tenses of this mood, and we know how it differs from the indicative; but we do not yet know why it is called *subjunctive.*

Tutor. To *subjoin,* means to add at the end; or to add afterwards. *Subjunctive,* means subjoined to something else. Now observe the manner in which the verb is used, when in the subjunctive mood. " He will perform, *if* he *promise ;*" "I shall be satisfied, *though* he *fail, if* he *try* to perform." Here you see that the verbs in the subjunctive mood, are preceded by conjunctions, expressing condition or doubt, and are *subjoined* to other verbs: that is, they are used in the *latter* member of a compound sentence; and the conjunctions connect the two members of the compound sentence together. But sometimes such sentences are inverted, and the member in which the subjunctive mood is used, is placed *first:* as, *If* he *promise,* he will perform;" " *Though* he *fail, if* he *try* to perform, I shall be satisfied." The conjunction, however, connects the two members of the sentence with equal force in both constructions; for, as I told you before, this is an inverted order of the sense, and, by reading the sentence in its proper order, you will perceive, that the conjunction performs its proper office.

Caroline. I suppose, then, from the examples which you have given, that the subjunctive mood cannot be properly used, except in a compound sentence; for a simple sentence contains but *one nominative* and *one verb ;* and the conjunctions, *if, though, unless,* &c. are such as connect only members of compound sentences.

Tutor. That is right, Caroline. But we shall see this more clearly, perhaps, if we make an experiment. If I say, then, " If George study"—"If he spend his time idly"—you perceive the sense is not complete; and, to make it so, I must add another member of a sentence. Let us fill it up. "If George study, *he will improve;*" "If he spend his time idly, *he will not improve.*" Now you see the sense is complete. But these sentences are inverted. Let us read them in the order of the sense. "George will improve, if he study;" "He will not improve, if he spend his time idly."

But now, to make the distinction more plain, if possible, observe the indicative mood, or form: "George *studies;*" "He *spends* his time idly." These are simple sentences, but the sense is complete.

George. Are the conjunctions which express condition, doubt, motive, &c. always written before the verb in the subjunctive?

Tutor. No: sometimes they are understood, and the form of the expression will show you when they are understood: as, "Had he come sooner, I should have seen him;" "Were he rich, he would be liberal;" that is, "*If* he had come," &c.; "*If* he were rich," &c.

Caroline. I believe we comprehend the character and use of the subjunctive mood.

Tutor. I believe you comprehend what I have said; but I have a few words more to say on this subject. There are two forms of the *Present Tense* of the subjunctive mood, which I denominate the *First Form*, and the *Second Form* of the subjunctive present; the *Second Form* is that which I have explained. The *First Form* is that in which the verb retains the personal termination in the second and third persons singular, as it does in the indicative present: as,

SUBJUNCTIVE MOOD.

Present Tense.

FIRST FORM.	SECOND FORM.
If I study.	If I study.
If thou studiest.	If thou study.
If he studies.	If he study.

Plural.	*Plural.*
If we study.	If we study.
If ye or you study.	If ye or you study.
If they study.	If they study.

George. The distinction of these two forms of the present tense of the subjunctive, is very easily remembered, because the *first* is like that of the indicative present, except the conjunction must be prefixed; and the *second* you explained before.

Caroline. But I perceive one difficulty; which is, that I do not know when I must use the *first* form, or when I must use the *second;* and if I know how to conjugate and parse verbs in these two forms of the subjunctive present, but do not know when to use the first form, or when the second, I do not know enough of grammar, with respect to this mood, to make it of much benefit to me; for grammar teaches us to speak and write *correctly.*

Tutor. Very well, Caroline, that is true. I will try to inform you on this point, so that you may be able to use the subjunctive mood correctly.

The *Second Form* of the subjunctive present, as I have given it to you, always has a *future* signification; or a reference to *future* time, as you will perceive by reflecting on the examples which I have used to illustrate it.

The *first form* has no reference to *future* time. Both are preceded by a conjunction, expressed or understood, or by some words which express a condition, doubt, motive, &c. so that, when you take the whole compound sentence together, in which the subjunctive present is used, and find that the expression has a reference to *future* time, you must use the *second form;* otherwise, the *first.* See also sec. XX, page 263.

The truth is, that the second form, having a reference to future time, always has some auxiliary verb understood before it; such as *may, can,* or *should.* Now you will perceive, that, if we conjugate the verb, and use one of these auxiliaries, the *principal* verb cannot vary, in the second and third persons singular : as,

If I *should* go. If I *can* come.
If thou *shouldst* go. If thou *canst* come.
If he *should* go, &c. If he *can* come, &c.

And when I say, "George will improve, if he study;" the phrase means, that George will improve, if he *should* study.

George. I perceive, that that is the meaning; and that the verb must be *study*, and not *studies;* for we cannot say, "If he *should studies;*" and the principal verb must be written in the same manner, when the auxiliary is understood, as it is, when expressed. The reason, therefore, why the verb, in the second form, does not vary, is quite plain. I think I now know how to use the two forms of the subjunctive present.

Caroline. I think I understand too, very clearly, how to use them. For example, if I say, "George will recite his lesson better than I, if he *studies* while I am talking." The phrase does not mean, "If he *should* study," but, "If he *now* studies, or if he is now studying;" therefore, I properly use the *first* form.

Tutor. That is right; and I think now, that you both understand the subjunctive mood; and when you parse a verb in the present tense of this mood, always tell whether it is in the *first* or *second* form.

I will now question you concerning the subject of this Conversation.

QUESTIONS.

When is a verb in the subjunctive mood ?
Why is this mood called *subjunctive ?*
Is this mood ever used in simple sentences ?
What is the difference between the *first* and the *second* form of the subjunctive present ?
How many tenses has this mood ?
In what tenses of the subjunctive mood is the verb conjugated, as it is in the correspondent tenses of the indicative ?

Plural.	*Plural.*
We must	We must.
Ye or you must.	Ye or you must.
They must.	They must.

You will here observe that *must* has no variation on account of *person*, *number*, or *tense*.

WILL.

Singular.	*Singular.*
I will.	I would.
Thou wilt.	Thou wouldst.
He will.	He would.

Plural.	*Plural.*
We will.	We would.
Ye or you will.	Ye or you would.
They will.	They would.

SHALL.

Singular.	*Singular.*
shall.	I should.
Thou shalt.	Thou shouldst.
He shall.	He should.

Plural.	*Plural.*
We shall.	We should.
Ye or you shall.	Ye or you should.
They shall.	They should.

George. I observe that you have given no perfect or passive participle to these verbs.

Tutor. These verbs have no participles ; and they are, therefore, called *defective* verbs.

Caroline. You say, that all these are used in forming the tenses of the potential mood ; but I recollect, that *shall* and *will* were used as auxiliaries, in forming the first and second future tenses of the *indicative* and *subjunctive* moods.

Tutor. They were ; and, when they denote *futurity,* as in these expressions : " I shall see you to-morrow ; or I will meet you ;" meaning at some future time ; they put the verbs in the indicative first future. So, in these phrases, " I shall have seen him ; or if I shall have seen him," &c. the verbs are in the indicative and subjunctive, second future.

But, when these auxiliaries denote inclination or willingness, resolution, or promise, they put the

12

verbs in the potential present : as, " *Will* you give me that book, George ?" that is, " Are you *willing* to give me that book." Again, " Some persons *will* never assist the poor ;" that is, some persons are *unwilling* to assist the poor.

Once more, " *Shall* I hear you recite now ?" " You *shall* recite now." " He *shall* obey me at all times," &c. But *will* and *shall* are not so often used in this sense, as they are in that which denotes futurity.

May, can, must, and their *imperfect tenses,* and the *imperfect* tenses of will and shall, viz. *would* and *should,* are the auxiliaries, which are almost always used to form the potential mood.

I will now give you the irregular verb BEAT, in the four tenses of the potential mood.

POTENTIAL MOOD.

To form the *present* tense, prefix the *present* tense of any of the auxiliaries, which I have just explained, to the verb : as,

PRESENT TENSE.
Singular.
I may or can, &c. beat,
Thou mayst or canst, &c. beat,
He may or can, &c. beat.

Plural.
We may or can, &c. beat,
Ye or you may or can, &c. beat,
They may or can, &c. beat.

To form the *imperfect* tense, prefix the *imperfect* of any of these auxiliaries to the verb : as,

IMPERFECT TENSE.
Singular.
I might, could, would, or should, &c. beat,
Thou mightst, &c. beat,
He might, &c. beat.

Plural.
We might, &c. beat,
Ye or you might, &c. beat,
They might, &c. beat.

To form the *perfect* tense, combine the *present* tense of any of these auxiliaries with *have*, and prefix them both to the perfect participle : as,

PERFECT TENSE.

Singular.
I may or can, &c. have beaten,
Thou mayst, &c. have beaten,
He may, &c have beaten.

Plural.
We may, &c. have beaten,
Ye or you may, &c. have beaten,
They may, &c. have beaten.

To form the pluperfect tense, combine the *imperfect* of any of these auxiliaries with *have*, and prefix them both to the perfect participle : as,

PLUPERFECT TENSE.

Singular.
I might or could, &c. have beaten,
Thou mightst, &c. have beaten,
He might, &c. have beaten.

Plural.
We might, &c. have beaten,
Ye or you might, &c. have beaten,
They might, &c. have beaten.

I have now presented to you the potential mood with its four tenses, and have explained the manner in which they are formed.

George. I now see that all the tenses of this mood are compound tenses, because they are all formed by auxiliaries. I think, with a little reflection, that it will not be difficult to remember the particular form of each.

Caroline. If you please, I will endeavor to tell how each is formed.

Tutor. Let me hear.

Caroline. The potential *present* is formed by prefixing *may, can, must, will,* or *shall,* to any verb ; the *imperfect* is formed by prefixing the *imperfect* tense of these, viz. *might, could, must, would,* or *should,* to any verb ; the *perfect* is formed by prefixing *may have, can have,* or *must have,* &c. to the *perfect participle* of any verb ; and the *pluperfect* is formed by prefixing *might have, could have, would have,* &c. to the *perfect participle* of any verb.

Tutor. You have given them correctly, Caroline ; and to aid you in arranging them distinctly in your mind, I will merely remark, that these auxiliaries, with the exceptions which I made in the first part of this Conversation, respecting *will* and *shall,* may be considered as *signs* of the potential mood.

When you reflect, then, that these signs, in the *present* tense, placed before the *indicative* present, give you the *potential* present ; and, that these signs, in the *imperfect,* placed before the *indicative present also,* give you the *potential imperfect ;* and that *have,* used with the present tense of these signs, and placed before the perfect *participle,* will give you the potential *perfect ;* and that *have,* combined with the *imperfect* tense of them, and placed before the perfect *participle,* will give you the potential *pluperfect ;* you cannot find much difficulty in rendering the tenses of this mood exceedingly familiar.

George. You have said so much about them, that I believe we shall never forget them. We can easily remember this ; that the present and imperfect are formed on the *indicative present,* and the perfect and pluperfect on the *perfect participle.* But you have not yet told us why this mood is called *Potential.*

Tutor. The word *potential,* means *powerful,* or *existing in possibility.* When used as a term in grammar, it denotes the possibility of doing an action. Although this mood does not *always* represent the power or possibility of doing an action, yet it *frequently* does, and we, therefore, call this form of the verb the Potential Mood.

I will here remark to you, that, as the indicative mood is converted into the subjunctive, by the expression of a condition, motive, wish, supposition, &c. being superadded to it ; so the potential mood may, in like manner, be turned into the subjunctive; as will be seen by the following examples : " If I could deceive him, I should abhor it ;" " Though he should increase in wealth, he would not be charitable ;" " Even in prosperity he would gain no esteem, unless he should conduct himself better."

When the verb is changed from the potential into the subjunctive mood, the *tense* is not changed. For example: "I may go," is potential present; "*If* I may go," is subjunctive present ; and, "He would go," potential imperfect ; and, "*If* he would go," subjunctive imperfect, &c.

Caroline. Now I should like to hear some explanation of the infinitive mood.

Tutor. The INFINITIVE MOOD is that form of the verb which simply expresses the action, without a nominative case : as, *to walk, to eat, to speak,* &c. Every verb must have a nominative case, if it is not in the infinitive mood ; but in this mood, you may easily perceive that it cannot have a nominative ; for this form of the verb, as I have shown you, is, *to walk, to go,* &c. and we cannot say, "I *to go,* I *to walk,* he *to run,*" &c. A verb in any mood, except the infinitive, is called a *finite* verb ; because it is *finite,* or limited, in respect to its number and person ; for a verb, when it has a nominative, must agree with it in number and person. Thus, when I say, "I run," run, you know, is of the *first* person singular to agree with *I ;* and, when I say, "They run," run is of the *third* person plural to agree with *they.* It is the nominative, then, you perceive, that gives number and person to the verb. When I say, "To run," run has no nominative, and of course it has neither number nor person, and is, therefore, not a *finite* verb, but a verb in the *infinite form,* or infinitive mood.

When, in a former Conversation, I explained to you simple and compound sentences, I told you, that a simple sentence has but one nominative and one verb. You did not, then, know the difference between a *finite* verb, and a verb in the infinitive mood; or I should have told you, that a *simple sentence is one, which contains but one nominative and one* FINITE *verb.* It may contain other verbs in the infinitive mood, and still it will be a simple sentence.

Caroline. I think you have said, that this mood has but *two* tenses.

Tutor. Yes; the *present* and *perfect.* The present is formed by prefixing *to,* which is called the *sign* of the infinitive mood, before any verb : as, " *To go, to walk, to eat,*" &c. The perfect is formed by prefixing TO HAVE before the perfect participle of any verb : as, " *To have gone, to have walked, to have eaten,*" &c.

But, when a verb is in the infinitive mood, and is placed after *make, need, see, bid, dare, feel, hear, let,* in any of their moods or tenses, or after their participles, the *to* must be omitted: as, "I make him *study;* I hear her *sing;* I see him *run;* I will let him *go;* I dare not *speak,*" &c. In these examples, you perceive, that it would be inelegant to express the *to,* and say, "I heard her *to sing,*" &c.

George. All this is very plain, and easily understood ; but how must we parse a verb in the infinitive mood? for we cannot apply the first rule, as we do, when we parse verbs in other moods, because a verb in this mood has no nominative case.

Tutor. You will tell whether it is *regular* or *irregular; transitive* or *intransitive;* as you do of verbs in other moods; then the mood and tense, and give this

RULE XX.

The infinitive mood may be governed by a verb, noun, adjective, or participle.

Government, is the influence which one verb has over another, in directing its *case,* or *mood.* A verb in the infinitive mood, has no nominative. When a verb, noun, adjective, or participle, then, prevents following verb from having a nominative, it prevents it from being a *finite* verb, and, consequently, causes it to be in the infinitive mood.

Caroline. Will you illustrate this rule by a few examples?

Tutor. I will. When I say, " She sings;" you know that *she* is the nominative to the verb sings. But now I write, " *I will let,*" before that phrase, and you will perceive, that the pronoun *she*, can no longer remain as the nominative to sings, but must be changed into *her*, in the objective case, because *let* is a *transitive* verb, and governs that case; and the *s*, which is the personal termination of the third person singular, of the indicative mood, must be taken off; then the phrase will stand thus: " I will let *her* sing ;" and sing is now in the infinitive mood, and governed by the verb *will let*.

George. I see very clearly, that *will let*, governs *sing ;* or causes *sing* to be in the infinitive mood ; for we cannot say, " I will let she sings."

Tutor. This mood is generally governed by the preceding verb ; but sometimes, by a noun, adjective, or a participle ; and when these govern it, they, in some way or other, prevent the verb from having a nominative. Thus, if I say, " I go," " they work ;" *go* and *work* are finite verbs ; but insert the verbs *intend* and *expect;* " I intend *to go*," "they expect *to work* ;" now, *intend* and *expect* take *I* and *they* for their own nominatives, and put the other verbs into the infinitive mood.

So, when I say, " *Endeavoring* to persuade them," &c. " He is *eager* to learn"—They have a *desire* to improve ;" you see, that a nominative could not be inserted after the participle *endeavoring*, the adjective *eager*, or the noun *desire ;* but, that they govern the verbs that follow them, in the infinitive mood.

I will just remark to you, that the verbs in the infinitive mood, that follow *make, need, see, bid, dare, feel, hear, let,* and their participles, are always governed by them.

And I will also observe, that there are a few verbs besides these, which *sometimes* require the infinitive, that follows them, to be used without the sign *to.*

Caroline. I hope you have now finished your remarks on the infinitive mood; for I wish to hear something about the imperative, which is the last of the moods.

Tutor. The IMPERATIVE MOOD may be very soon disposed of.

It simply expresses a command to a second person; and the person commanded, is its nominative. It is, therefore, always of the *second* person; and, as we cannot command in *past* or *future* time, it is always of the present tense.—The nominative to a verb in this mood, is generally understood, as, "Go;" that is, "Go thou," or, "Go ye." "Come to me, and recite;" that is, "Come thou, or come ye or you," &c.

The verb in the imperative mood, then, is always in the present tense, and always of the second person, either singular or plural. When *one* person is commanded, it is of the singular number, and agrees with *thou,* expressed or understood; when more than one are commanded, it is of the plural number, and agrees with *ye* or *you,* expressed or understood. *Do* is sometimes used as an *auxiliary,* in this mood, as well as in the indicative and subjunctive; as, "*Do* study;" "*Do* thou study, or *do* you study;" "*Do* do the work better," &c. "*Do* let that alone."

When I gave you the potential mood, I made you acquainted with some of the defective verbs.

DEFECTIVE VERBS are those which are used only in some of the moods and tenses, and have no participles.

The principal of them are these :

Present.	Imperfect.	Perf. or Pass. Participles wanting.
May,	might.	————
Can,	could.	————
Will,	would.	————
Shall,	should.	————
Must,	must.	————
Ought,	ought.	————
————,	quoth.	

These are used as auxiliaries except *ought* and quoth ; these two are never used as such. You will observe, that *ought* is the same in both tenses ; you will be able to determine its tense, then, only by the following infinitive ; for it is always followed by a verb in the infinitive mood. When the following infinitive is in the present tense, *ought* is in the present tense : as, " He *ought* to go;" and when followed by the infinitive perfect, *ought* is in the imperfect : as, " He *ought* to have gone."

I will ask you a few questions concerning the subjects of this Conversation.

QUESTIONS.

What are the auxiliaries which form the potential mood ?
How many tenses has this mood ?
How is the present formed ?
How is the imperfect formed ?
How is the perfect formed ?
How is the pluperfect formed ?
What is the meaning of tense ?
When is a tense called compound ?
What is a simple tense ?
Which tenses of the indicative and subjunctive moods are simple, and which compound ?
How many tenses has the infinitive mood ?
How are they formed ?
How does this mood differ from the others ?
Why is it called infinitive ?
Why is the imperative so called ?
Of what person must a verb in the imperative mood *always* be ?
How do you know the tense of the defective verb *ought* ?

EXERCISES IN PARSING.

Study, if you wish to improve.—Behave well, if thou lovest virtue or a good name.—Strive to imitate the virtues, which thou seest exhibited by the good; then thou wilt give evidence of thy own.—He may improve himself, if his industry should increase.—He ought to study more.—He ought to have studied his lesson better.—He can go if he chooses.—The boy must not treat his superiors ill.—My neighbor may have sold his house for aught that I know.—I told him that he might go yesterday, but he would not.—He might have acquired great wealth, if he had desired it.—The man should have returned when he found his enterprise unsuccessful.—We would not serve him then, but we will hereafter.

CONVERSATION XVIII.

OF PASSIVE AND NEUTER VERBS.

When, in the third Conversation, I explained the verb to you, I gave you this definition of it : " *A verb is a word that expresses an action of some creature or thing.*" This definition, although it has been sufficient for our purpose, thus far, is, nevertheless, very incomplete, as you will soon perceive.

VERBS are divided into three sorts, the *Active*, the *Passive*, and the *Neuter* verbs.

The definition of a verb, which has been given by the most respectable grammarians, is this : A verb is a word which signifies to BE, to DO, or to SUFFER : as, I am, I rule, I am ruled."

In this example, AM, is a verb neuter, RULE is a verb active, and AM RULED is a verb passive. According to this definition, then, a verb neuter signifies to BE, or to *exist* merely ; a verb active signifies to DO, or to *act ;* and a verb passive signifies to SUFFER.

This definition of the active verb you understand; but, perhaps, you would hardly know a passive verb, from the definition here given.

George. To *suffer*, means to undergo pain, or inconvenience. Then, when I say, "I suffer pain ; I suffer inconvenience ; I endure pain ;" are not *suffer* and *endure*, passive verbs ?

Tutor. No : these govern objective cases, and any verb that governs an objective case, is a *transitive* verb. You must reflect on what I said about the transitive and intransitive verbs in Conversation **XI**. You may remember, that I called your attention to this subject immediately after giving you an explanation of the preposition.

Caroline To *suffer*, sometimes means to allow, or to permit. If I say, " I *allow*, I *permit*," without using an objective case; as, " I *allow* that he is right," &c. ; are not *these* passive verbs ?

Tutor. No : *allow*, in the sentence you have just given, governs the whole phrase that follows it, as an object. These verbs require an object, without which they make no sense.

Caroline. Then I do not understand the definition that is given of the passive verb.

Tutor. I will endeavor to explain the different kinds of verbs, so that you will be able to distinguish the *active* verb from the *passive*, and the *neuter* from either, without hesitation.

To *nominate*, means to name, or to designate, or to point out by name ; and NOMINATIVE, is derived from the verb to *nominate*, and, when used in grammar, means the creature or thing *named*, or *pointed out ;* so that all nouns, when they are merely *named*, and not connected in sentences, are in the *nominative* case ; that is, they denote things that exist, *named* merely : as, Houses, trees, men, paper, &c.: these words, used in this manner, simply denote things *named ;* or in a state, condition, or *case*, *named* merely, without having any relation with any other things. But, when we frame a sentence, and make a complete sense, *which we can never do with-out a* VERB, the term *nominative,* is used to designate, or point out, the *subject,* concerning which the verb makes some affirmation or declaration, or some *supposed* affirmation or declaration, in contradistinction to the *object of an* action or of a relation.

Every sentence must have in it, at least one *verb* and one *nominative,* expressed or understood. We cannot form a sentence of any kind, which will make a complete sense, without a nominative and a verb. This you will easily perceive, by a few examples. If I say, " The man in the house ;" " The horse in the stable ;" " The books on the table ;" " The laborers in the field," &c. you cannot ascertain what is meant, because there is no affirmation in any of these expressions. But insert the verbs, *eats, drinks, sleeps, is, walks, remains,* in the first two ; and, *are seen, are found, are beheld, will be observed,* in the next two, and you will see, that a complete sense will be formed in each simple sentence, for you will have a *nominative* and *verb* in each.

A nominative to a verb, then, is the word which denotes the person or thing, concerning which the verb makes an affirmation.

The nominatives to verbs may be divided into three classes, viz: those which *produce* the action expressed by the verb ; those which *receive* the action expressed by the verb ; and those which neither produce any action, nor receive any, but are the subjects of the verbs, which simply express the *existence* of these subjects, or their *state* of existence.

The first class, then, are *active* nominatives ; the second are *passive* nominatives ; because *passive* is in direct opposition to active ; it means unresisting, or receiving an action, or an impression, without resistance ; and the third are *neuter* nominatives ; that is, nominatives which neither produce nor receive an action ; because these are connected with verbs which do not express any action, but a mere existence, or state of existence.

To illustrate what I have said, take the following examples :

First, of ACTIVE NOMINATIVES : as, " The box rolls ;" " The horse runs ;" " The men labour ;" " The man writes a letter."

Secondly, of PASSIVE NOMINATIVES : as, " The box is held ;" " The horse is seen ;" " The men are punished ;" " The man is carried."

Thirdly, of NEUTER NOMINATIVES : as, " The box lies on the table ;" " The horse remains in the field ;" " The men stay in the house ;" " The man abides in the city."

Caroline. I think I now understand the difference between the *active, passive,* and *neuter* verbs. When a verb expresses the action of its nominative, it is an active verb ; when it expresses the action received by its nominative, or done to its nominative, it is a passive verb ; and, when it expresses no action *at all,* but the mere existence of its nominative, or its state of existence, it is a verb, neither active, nor passive, and is therefore, called neuter.

George. So the verb takes its character from its nominative. If the verb has an *active* nominative, it is an *active* verb ; if a *passive* nominative, it it is a *passive* verb ; and, if a *neuter* nominative, it is a *neuter* verb.

Tutor. That is right. But I will now give you the conjugation of the neuter verb BE, through all its moods and tenses. When you understand this verb, so that you know it instantly, in all its moods and tenses, you will possess additional means for distinguishing the passive verb ; because this neuter verb BE, is frequently used as an *auxiliary,* as well as a principal verb, and *no passive verb* can be formed without it. You will, therefore, find it of great importance, to make this verb, which is the most irregular one in the English language, exceedingly familiar to you.

The auxiliary and neuter verb *To be,* is conjugated as follows :

To Be.

INDICATIVE MOOD.

Present Tense.

Singular.	Plural.
I am,	We are.
Thou art,	Ye or you are.
He she or it is.	They are.

Imperfect Tense.

Singular.	Plural.
I was,	We were.
Thou wast,	Ye or you were.
He was.	They were.

Perfect Tense.

Singular.	Plural.
I have been,	We have been.
Thou hast been,	Ye or you have been.
He hath or has been.	They have been.

Pluperfect Tense.

Singular.	Plural.
I had been,	We have been.
Thou hadst been,	Ye or you had been.
He had been.	They had been.

First Future Tense.

Singular.	Plural.
I shall or will be,	We shall or will be.
Thou shalt or wilt be,	Ye or you shall or will be.
He shall or will be.	They shall or will be.

Second Future Tense.

Singular.	Plural.
I shall have been,	We shall have been.
Thou wilt have been,	Ye or you will have been.
He will have been.	They will have been.

This neuter verb BE, in the Subjunctive Mood, has *two forms* of the IMPERFECT, as well as of the *present* tense. All other verbs, in the subjunctive mood, have two forms of the *present tense only.*

The two forms of the subjunctive present and imperfect tenses of the neuter verb BE, are these :*

*To understand the proper use of these, see sec. XX.

FIRST FORM.
SUBJUNCTIVE MOOD.
Present Tense.

Singular.	Plural.
If I am,	If we are.
If thou art,	If ye or you are.
If he is.	If they are.

Imperfect Tense.

Singular.	Plural.
If I was,	If we were.
If thou wast,	If ye or you wer
If he was.	If they were.

SECOND FORM.
Present Tense.

Singular.	Plural.
If I be,	If we be.
If thou be,	If ye or you be.
If he be.	If they be.

Imperfect Tense.

Singular.	Plural.
If I were,	If we were.
If thou wert,	If ye or you were.
If he were.	If they were.

The remaining tenses of this mood, are similar to the correspondent tenses of the Indicative Mood, with the exception which I have before given you, viz. that *will* and *wilt* are not used in the second future.

POTENTIAL MOOD.
Present Tense.

Singular.	Plural.
I may or can be,	We may or can be.
Thou mayst or canst be.	Ye or you may or can be.
He may or can be.	They may or can be.

Imperfect Tense.

Singular.	Plural.
I might, could, would, or should be,	We might could, would, or should be,
Thou mightst, couldst, wouldst, or should tst be,	Ye or you might, could, would, or should be,
He might, could, would, or should be.	They might, could, would, or should be.

Perfect Tense.

Singular.	*Plural.*
I may *or* can have been,	We may *or* can have been,
Thou mayst *or* canst have been,	Ye *or* you may *or* can have been.
He may *or* can have been.	They may *or* can have been.

Pluperfect Tense.

Singular.	*Plural.*
I might, could, would, *or* should have been.	We might, could, would, *or* should have been,
Thou mightst, couldst, wouldst, *or* shouldst have been,	Ye *or* you might, could, would, *or* should have been,
He might, could, would, *or* should have been.	They might, could, would, *or* should have been.

INFINITIVE MOOD.

Present Tense. To be. *Perfect.* To have been.

IMPERATIVE MOOD.

Singular.	*Plural.*
Be thou *or* do thou be.	Be ye *or* you, or do ye be.

PARTICIPLES.

Present. Being. *Perfect.* Been.

Compound Perfect. Having been.

I remarked to you, before I gave you the conjugation of this verb, that no passive verb can ever be formed without it. I will now tell you how the passive verb is formed : Add the perfect, or passive *participle*, of any verb that can be made *transitive*, when used in an *active* sense, to this neuter verb BE, and you will have a passive verb, in the same mood and tense that the neuter verb would be in, if the participle were not added. You cannot form a passive verb in any other way.

Caroline. I think I understand it. If I take the word *forsaken*, which is the perfect or passive participle of the active verb *to forsake ;* for this verb can be made *transitive :* as, " I forsake *him ;*" "He forsakes *me*," &c. and place it after the neuter verb *be ;* as, "I am forsaken ; thou art forsaken ; he is forsaken ; I was forsaken, &c. : I have been forsaken, &c. ; I had been forsaken, &c. ; I shall be forsaken, &c. ; I shall have been forsaken," &c. ; I shall have a *passive* verb, from the *active* verb *to forsake*, in all the six tenses of the indicative mood. And I perceive, that the pronoun *I*, when connected with a passive verb, is not an *active*, but a *passive* nominative.

Tutor. I believe, Caroline, that you understand how to form the passive verbs.

George. But there are many active verbs that are *intransitive ;* such as *go, fly, arrive, &c.* Suppose that I should put the perfect participle of an active *intransitive* verb after the neuter verb *be*, and say, "He is gone ;" "He is arrived ;" "The bird is flown," &c. what kind of a verb shall I have then ?

Tutor. A *neuter* verb, in a *passive form.*

Caroline. Is this neuter verb *be,* ever used as an auxiliary connected with the *present* participle ?

Tutor. Yes, very often. What is the rule which you give, when you parse the present participle ?

Caroline. The active participle ending in ing, *when not connected with a verb, refers to some noun, or pronoun, denoting the actor.*

Tutor. That is right ; but when it is added to the neuter verb *be, be* becomes an *auxiliary*, and marks the mood and tense of the verb, and the *participle* becomes the *principal* part of the verb, just as the *passive* participle does when you form a *passive* verb.

George. And what sort of a verb have we, when the *present* participle is added to the neuter verb *be ?*

Tutor. Either an active *transitive* or *intransitive* verb, or a verb neuter. If the participle is derived from a transitive verb, you have an active transitive verb ; if the participle is derived from

13*

an intransitive verb, then you have an intransitive verb; but if it is derived from a verb neuter, you have a neuter verb : as, "I am writing a letter ;" here you see that *am writing*, is a transitive verb from the verb *to write*, and governs letter in the objective case ; "I am running ;" here you see the verb is *active* but *intransitive*, from the verb *to run ;* and, "I am sitting ; I am standing ; I am lying on the bed ;" you now perceive that the verbs are neuter, from the neuter verbs *to sit, to stand, to lie*. And I will remark to you, that this neuter verb *be, is never used as an auxiliary, except with the present or passive participles of other verbs*.

I will now give you the conjugation of the regular verb *to love*, in the passive form.

A passive verb is conjugated by adding the perfect participle to the auxiliary *to be*, through all its changes of number, person, mood, and tense, in the following manner :

To Be Loved.
INDICATIVE MOOD.
Present Tense.

Singular.	*Plural.*
I am loved,	We are loved,
Thou art loved,	Ye or you are loved,
He is loved.	They are loved.

Imperfect Tense.

Singular.	*Plural.*
I was loved,	We were loved,
Thou wast loved,	Ye or you were loved,
He was loved.	They were loved.

Perfect Tense.

Singular.	*Plural.*
I have been loved,	We have been loved,
Thou hast been loved,	Ye or you have been loved,
He hath or has been loved.	They have been loved.

Pluperfect Tense.

Singular.	*Plural.*
I had been loved,	We had been loved,
Thou hadst been loved,	Ye or you had been loved,
He had been loved.	They had been loved.

First Future Tense.

Singular.	Plural.
I shall *or* will be loved,	We shall *or* will be loved,
Thou shalt *or* wilt be loved,	Ye *or* you shall *or* will be loved.
He shall *or* will be loved.	They shall *or* will be loved.

Second Future Tense.

Singular.	Plural.
I shall have been loved,	We shall have been loved,
Thou wilt have been loved,	Ye *or* you will have been loved,
He will have been loved.	They will have been loved.

The passive verb, necessarily, has the same two forms of the subjunctive present and imperfect tenses, that the neuter verb BE has

FIRST FORM.

SUBJUNCTIVE MOOD.

Present Tense.

Singular.	Plural.
If I am loved,	If we are loved,
If thou art loved,	If ye *or* you are loved;
If he is loved.	If they are loved.

Imperfect Tense.

Singular.	Plural.
If I was loved,	If we were loved.
If thou wast loved.	If ye *or* you were loved.
If he was loved,	If they were loved.

SECOND FORM.

Present Tense.

Singular.	Plural.
If I be loved,	If we be loved.
If thou be loved,	If ye *or* you be loved.
If he be loved.	If they be loved.

Imperfect Tense.

Singular.	Plural.
If I were loved,	If we were loved.
If thou wert loved,	If we *or* ye were loved
If he were loved.	If they were loved.

The remaining tenses of this mood are similar to the correspondent tenses of the Indicative Mood, except *will* and *wilt* are not used in the second future.

POTENTIAL MOOD.
Present Tense.

Singular.	Plural.
I may *or* can be loved,	We may *or* can be loved.
Thou mayst *or* canst be loved,	Ye *or* you may *or* can be loved.
He may *or* can be loved,	They may *or* can be loved.

Imperfect Tense.

Singular.	Plural.
I might, could, would, *or* should be loved.	We might, could, would, *or* or should be loved.
Thou mightst, couldst, wouldst, *or* shouldst be loved,	Ye *or* you might, could, would, *or* should be loved.
He might, could, would, *or* should be loved.	They might, could, would, *or* should be loved.

Perfect Tense.

Singular.	Plural.
I may *or* can have been loved,	We may *or* can have been loved.
Thou mayst *or* canst have been loved,	Ye *or* you may *or* can have been loved.
He may *or* can have been loved.	They may *or* can have been loved.

Pluperfect Tense.

Singular.	Plural.
I might, could, would, *or* should have been loved.	We might, could, would, *or* should have been loved.
Thou mightst, couldst, wouldst, *or* shouldst have been loved.	Ye *or* you might, could, would, *or* should have been loved.
He might, could, would, *or* should have been loved.	They might, could, would, *or* should have been loved.

INFINITIVE MOOD.

Present Tense.	Perfect.
To be loved.	To have been loved.

IMPERATIVE MOOD.

Singular.	Plural.
Be thou loved, *or* do thou be loved.	Be ye *or* you loved, *or* do ye be loved.

PARTICIPLES.

Present.	Being loved.
Perfect or Passive.	Loved.
Compound Perfect.	Having been loved.

Now you can take the passive participles of other verbs, and conjugate them in the same manner. Take *beaten, carried, seen, forgotten*, and many others, and use them instead of *loved*, as an exercise to make you familiar with the conjugation of a passive verb.

You will now observe, that, when an auxiliary is joined to the participle of the principal verb, the auxiliary goes through all the variations of person and number, and the participle itself continues invariably the same. When there are two or more auxiliaries joined to the participle, the first of them only is varied according to person and number. The auxiliary *must* admits of no variation.

I will now give you some

EXERCISES IN PARSING.

The man beats the boy.—The boy is beaten by the man.—The horses draw the coach.—The coach is drawn by the horses.—The master teaches the children.—The children are taught by the master. The carpenter built the houses.—The houses were built by the carpenter.—Commerce introduces luxury.—Luxury is introduced by commerce.—That farmer cultivates his farm well.—The farm is well cultivated.—The goods were purchased.—The house was sold.—The ship has been lost.—The money will be found.—The boy will have completed his task before you see him.—The task will have been completed an hour, in ten minutes more.—The lady remains at home.—The book lies on the table.—The desk stands in the corner of the room.—The coach and horses are in the stable.—I am here.—Thou art there.—He is in town.—We are honest.—You are proud.—They are sober.—I was sleepy.—Thou wast angry with him.—He was not eager to learn.—They were guilty.—We were reasonable in our demands.—Ye were found guilty.—I have been on the water frequently.—I have been seen on the water frequently.—I have seen the man.—I have

been seen by the man.—The boy had seen it.—
The boy had been seen.—The letter will be here.
—The letter will be brought hither.—Be honest.
—Be not idle.—Be instructed.—Be carried.—
You like to be carried.—You may be carried —
You ought to be carried.—He ought to have been
carried.—He should have been carried, had I
known his situation.—The house can be enlarged.—He might be convinced —He might have
been convinced.—Being ridiculed and despised, he
still maintained his principles.—Having been ridiculed, he could not endure his chagrin.—Ridiculed, despised, insulted, he became discouraged.—
If I be beaten by him, he will be punished.—If
he has been seen, he has not been caught.—Whether he is at home or not, I have no means of knowing.—If I were beaten as badly as he, I should
complain.—If he was beaten, it is not known.

CONVERSATION XIX.

OF THE AUXILIARY VERBS, & OF THE TENSES.

Tutor. You must, by this time, have have observed the great importance of auxiliary verbs in
the English language; for you have seen, that without them, the verbs would be limited in their moods
and tenses, to the indicative and subjunctive moods,
in the present and imperfect tenses ; the infinitive
mood, present tense ; and the imperative mood.

George. I perceive, that they are of great importance in giving variety, as well as precision, to
the language. For with these, we form the perfect, pluperfect, and two future tenses of the indicative and subjunctive moods ; all the tenses of the
potential mood ; and the perfect of the infinitive.

Tutor. Some of these auxiliaries, I have already
particularly noticed, viz. *may, can, must, will,* and

shall. None of these, except *will*, is ever used as a principal verb, but as an *auxiliary* to some *principal*, either expressed or understood. *Will* is sometimes a principal verb, as I will by-and-by show you. There are four verbs which are sometimes used as auxiliaries, and sometimes as principals. These are, *do, be, have,* and *will.*

Do is used as an auxiliary, in the imperative mood, and in the present and imperfect tenses of the indicative and subjunctive.

Be is used as an auxiliary, in *all* the moods and tenses to form the passive verbs, and neuter verbs in a passive form, by being connected with the passive participles of other verbs; and in forming active and neuter verbs, by being connected with the present participles of other verbs; and, in both instances, serves to mark the *mood* and the *tense* of the verb.

Have is used in forming the perfect, pluperfect, and second future tenses of the indicative and subjunctive moods; the perfect and pluperfect of the potential mood; and the perfect of the infinitive mood.

Will is used in forming the first and second future tenses of the indicative and subjunctive moods; and, *sometimes,* in forming the *present* tense of the potential mood.

Caroline. And when these are used as *principal* verbs, their moods and tenses are formed just as those of other verbs are, are they not?

Tutor. They are. And you perceive, that *have* may be an auxiliary to its own participle: as, in the indicative and subjunctive perfect and pluperfect, "I have had; I had had," and, "If I have had; if I had had," &c. And in the infinitive perfect: as, "To have had." And *do* may be used as an auxiliary to itself: as, "I do do it," in the present; and, "I did do it," in the imperfect; and *will*, as, "He will will it; he will have willed it," &c.

George. I believe we understand the use of the auxiliary verbs now very well, and know which are used as auxiliaries always, and which are used *sometimes* as *such*, and *sometimes* as *principals*.

Tutor. I think you do. But before I dismiss this subject, I will give you some additional

REMARKS ON *DO, BE, HAVE,* AND *WILL.*

The verbs *have, be, will,* and *do,* when they are unconnected with a principal verb, expressed or understood, are not auxiliaries, but principal verbs : as, " We *have* enough" ; " I *am* grateful ;" " He *wills* it to be so ;" " They *do* as they please." In this view, they also have their auxiliaries : as, " I *shall have* enough ;" I *will* be grateful," &c.

The peculiar force of the several auxiliaries will appear from the following account of them.

Do and *did,* mark the action itself, or the time of it, with greater energy and positiveness : as, " I *do* speak truth ;" " I *did* respect him ;" " Here am I, for thou *didst* call me." They are of great use in negative sentences : as, " I *do not* fear ;" " I *did not* write." They are almost universally employed in asking questions : as, " *Does* he learn ?" " *Did* he not write ?" They sometimes also supply the place of another verb, and make the repetition of it, in the same or a subsequent sentence, unnecessary, as, " You attend not to your studies as he *does* :" (i. e. as he attends, &c.) " I shall come if I can : but if I *do not,* please to excuse me ;" (i. e. if I come not.)

Let, not only expresses permission, but entreating, exhorting, commanding : as, " Let us know the truth ;" " Let me die the death of the righteous ;" " Let not your hearts be too much elated with success ;" " Let your inclinations submit to your duty."

May and *might* express the possibility or liberty of doing a thing ; *can* and *could,* the power : " as, " It may rain ;" " I may write or read ;" " He might have improved more than he has ;" " He can write much better than he could last year."

Must is sometime called in for a helper, and denotes necessity : as, " We *must* speak the truth, whenever we do speak, and we *must not* prevaricate."

Will, in the first person singular and plural, intimates resolution and promising ; in the second and third person, only foretels : as " I *will* reward the good, and will punish the wicked ;" " We will remember benefits, and be grateful ;" " Thou wilt, or he will repent of that folly ;" " You or they will have a pleasant walk."

Shall, on the contrary, in the first person, simply foretels ; in the second and third persons, promises, commands, or threatens : as, " I shall go abroad ;" " We shall dine at home ;" " Thou shalt, or you shall, inherit the land ;" " Ye shall do justice and love mercy ;" " They shall account for their misconduct." The following passage is not translated according to the distinct and proper meaning of the words *shall* and *will* : " Surely goodness and mercy shall follow me all the days of my life ; and I will dwell in the house of the Lord forever." " It ought to be, " *Will* follow me." and " I *shall* dwell."—The foreigner who, as it is said, fell into the Thames, and cried out ; " I *will* be drowned, no body *shall* help me ;" made a sad misapplication of these auxiliaries.

These observations respecting the import of the verbs *will* and *shall*, must be understood of explicative sentences ; for when the sentence is interrogative, just the reverse, for the most part, takes place : thus, " I *shall* go ; you *will* go ;" express event only : but, " *will* you go ?" imports intention ; and " *shall* I go ?" refers to the will of another. But, " He *shall* go " and " *shall* he go ?" both imply will, expressing or referring to a command.

When the verb is put in the subjunctive mood, the meaning of these auxiliaries likewise undergoes some alteration ; as the learner will readily perceive by a few examples : " He *shall* proceed," " If he *shall* proceed ;" " You *shall* consent," " If you *shall* consent." These auxiliaries are sometimes interchanged, in the indicative and subjunctive moods, to convey the same meaning of the auxiliary : as, " He *will* not return," " If he *shall* not return ;" " He *shall* not return," " If he *will* not return."

Would primarily denotes inclination of will ; and *should*, obligation : but they both vary their import, and are often used to express simple events.

Were is frequently used for *would be*, and *had*, for *would have* : as, " It *were* injustice to deny the execution of the law to any individual ; that is, " it *would be* injustice." " Many acts which *had* been blamable in a peaceable government, were employed to detect conspiracies ;" that is, "which *would have* been blamable."

Sometimes that form of the auxiliary verbs *shall, will,* &c. which is generally conditional, is elegantly used to express a very slight assertion, with a modest diffidence. Thus we say, " I *should* think it would be proper to give up the point ;" that is, " I am rather inclined to think."

Some writers still use *shall* and *will, should* and *would,* as they were formerly used ; that is, in a sense quite contrary to that in which they are generally used at present. The following expressions are instances of this incorrect practice : " We would have been wanting to ourselves, if we had complied with the demand ;" "We *should :*" "We *will* therefore briefly unfold our reasons ;" " We *shall :*" " He imagined, that, by playing one party against the other, he *would* easily obtain the victory over both ?" " He *should* easily," &c.

In several familiar forms of expression, the word *shall* still retains its original signification, and does not mean, to promise, threaten, or engage, in the third person, but the mere futurition of an event : as, " This is as extraordinary a thing as one shall hear of."

You now know, very well, how to form all the tenses, in all the different moods ; but *to use them with propriety*, is quite another affair, and requires much reflection and critical attention. To aid you in understanding this, I will give you the following

REMARKS ON THE TENSES.

TENSE, being the distinction of time, might seem to admit only of the present, past, and future : but to mark it more accurately, it is made to consist of six variations, viz.

THE PRESENT,   THE PERFECT,
THE IMPERFECT,   THE PLUPERFECT, and
THE FIRST AND SECOND FUTURE TENSES.

The PRESENT TENSE represents an action or event, as passing at the time in which it is mentioned : as, " I rule ; I am ruled ; I think ; I fear."

The present tense likewise expresses a character, quality, &c. at present existing : as " He is an able man ;" " She is an amiable woman." It is also used in speaking of actions continued, with occasional intermissions, to the present time : as, " he frequently rides ;" " He walks out every morning ;" " He goes into the country every summer." We sometimes apply this tense even to persons long since dead : as, " Seneca reasons and moralizes well ;" " Job speaks feelingly of his afflictions."

The present tense, preceded by the words, *when, before, after, as soon as*, &c. is sometimes used to point out the relative time of a future action : as, " *When* he arrives he will hear the news ;" " He will hear the news *before* he arrives, or *as soon as* he arrives, or, at farthest, *soon after* he arrives ;" " The more she *improves*, the more amiable she will be."

In animated historical narrations, this tense is sometimes substituted for the imperfect tense : as. " He *enters* the territory of the peaceable inhabitants : he *fights* and *conquers*, *takes* an immense booty, which he *divides* amongst his soldiers, and *returns* home to enjoy a vain and useless triumph."

Every point of space or duration, how minute soever it may be, has some degree of extension. Neither the present, nor any other, instant of time, is wholly unextended. Nay, we cannot conceive, as Dr. Beattie justly observes, an unextended instant : and that which we call the *present*, may in fact admit of very considerable extension.—While I write a letter, or read a book, I say, that I *am* reading or writing it, though it should take up an hour, a day, a week, or a month ; the whole time being considered as present, which is employed in the present action.—So, while I build a house, though that should be the work of many months, I speak of it in the present time, and say that I *am building* it. In like manner, in contradistinction to the century past, and to that which is to come, we may consider the whole space of a hundred years as time present, when we speak of a series of actions, or of a state of existence, that is co-extended with it ; as in the following example : " In this century *we are* more neglectful of the ancients, and *we are* consequently more ignorant, than they *were* in the last, or, perhaps, than others *will be* in the next. Nay, the entire term of man's probationary state in this world, when opposed to that eternity which is before him, is considered as present time by those who say, " In this state *we see* darkly as through a glass ; but in a future life, our faith *will be* lost in vision, and *we shall know* even as we are known."

———

The **Imperfect Tense** represents the action or event, either as past and finished, or as remaining unfinished at a certain time past : as, " I loved her for her modesty and virtue ;" "They were travelling post when he met them."

The first example in the preceding paragraph, shows that the action was past and finished, though the precise time of it was not defined. In this point of view, the tense may be said to be *imperfect :* the time of the action is not exactly and perfectly ascertained.—In the second instance, the action is represented as past, but not finished ; and it may therefore with propriety be denominated *imperfect.*

It is proper to observe, on this occasion, that in such sentences as the following—"He wrote to him yesterday ;" " They behaved themselves at that period very properly ;" the precise time of the action is not denoted, by the tense of the verb itself ; but by the addition of the words *yesterday* and *at that period.*

———

The **Perfect Tense** not only refers to what is past, but also conveys an allusion to the present time : as, " I have finished my letter ;" " I have seen the person that was recommended to me."

In the former example, it is signified that the finishing of the letter, though past, was at a period immediately preceding the present time. In the latter instance, it is uncertain whether the person mentioned was seen by the speaker a long or

short time before.   The meaning is, " I have seen him sometime in the course of a period which includes, or comes to, the
present time."   In both instances, " The finishing of the letter," and " The seeing of the person," comprehend periods,
each of which extends to the time present.   We have no idea
of any certain portion of time intervening, between the time
of action and the time of speaking of it.   The sentence, " I
have written a letter," implies that " I have, or possess, the
finished action of writing a letter."   Under these views of
the subject, it appears that the term *perfect* may be properly
applied to this tense ; as the action is not only finished, but
the period of its completion is especially referred to, and ascertained.

When the particular time of any occurrence is specified, as
prior to the present time, this tense is not used ; for it would
be improper to say, " I *have seen* him yesterday ;" or, " I
have finished my work last week."   In these cases the imperfect is necessary ; as, " I *saw* him yesterday ;" " I *finished*
my work last week."   But when we speak indefinitely of any
thing past, as happening or not happening in the day, year, or
age, in which we mention it, the perfect must be employed :
as, " I *have been* there this morning ;" " I *have travelled*
much this year ;" " We *have escaped* many dangers through
life."   In referring, however, to such a division of the day as
is past before the time of our speaking, we use the imperfect :
as, " They *came* home early this morning ;" " He *was* with
them at three o'clock this afternoon."

The perfect tense, and the imperfect tense, both denote a
thing that is past ; but the former denotes it in such a manner, that there is still actually remaining some part of the
time to slide away, wherein we declare the thing has been
done ; whereas the imperfect denotes the thing or action past,
in such a manner, that nothing remains of that time in which
it was done: If we speak of the present century, we say,
" Philosophers *have made* great discoveries in the present century : but if we speak of the last century, we say, " Philosophers *made* great discoveries in the last century."   " He *has*
been much afflicted this year ;" " I *have* this week *read* the
king's proclamation ;" " I *have heard* great news this morning ;" in these instances, " He *has been*," " I *have read*," and
" *heard*," denote things that are past ; but they occurred in
this year, in this week, and to-day ; and still there remains a
part of this year, week, and day, whereof I speak.

In general, the perfect tense may be applied wherever the
action is connected with the present time, by the actual existence, either of the author, or of the work, though it may
have been performed many centuries ago ; but if neither the
author nor the work remains, it cannot be used.   We may say,
" Cicero *has written* orations ;" but we cannot say, " Cicero
has written poems ;" because the orations are in being, but

the poems are lost. Speaking of priests in general, we may say, "They *have* in all ages *claimed* great powers;" because the general order of the priesthood still exists; but if we speak of the Druids, as a particular order of priests, which does not now exist, we cannot use this tense. We cannot say, "The Druid priests *have claimed* great powers;" but must say, "The Druid priests *claimed* great powers;" because that order is now totally extinct.

The perfect tense, preceded by the words, *when, after, as soon as,* &c. is often used to denote the relative time of a future action: as, "*When* I have finished my letter, I will attend to his request:" "I will attend to the business, *as soon as* I have finished my letter."

The PLUPERFECT TENSE represents a thing, not only as past, but also prior to some other point of time, specified in the sentence: as, "I had finished my letter before he arrived."

The term used to designate this tense, may, in some degree at least, be justified by observing that the time of the action or event, is *more than* or *beyond* the time of some other action or event to which it refers, and which is in the *perfect,* or the *imperfect tense.* Thus, in the sentences, "I *have seen* him, but I *had written* to him before;" "Though he *had not then agreed* to the proposal, he *has* at length *consented* to it;" "I *saw* him after I *had written* to him;" "He *decided* indeed very culpably, but he *had been* vehemently *urged* to it;" the pluperfect extends not only beyond, and precedent to, the time signified in the perfect tense, but also that denoted by the imperfect.

The first FUTURE TENSE represents the action as yet to come, either with or without respect to the precise time: as, "The sun will rise to-morrow;" "I shall see them again."

The SECOND FUTURE intimates that the action will be fully accomplished, at or before the time of another future action or event: as, "I shall have dined at one o'clock;" "The two houses will have finished their business, when the king comes to prorogue them."

It is to be observed, that in the subjunctive mood, the event being spoken of under a condition or supposition, or in the form of a wish, and therefore as doubtful and contingent, the verb itself in the present, and the auxiliary both of the present and past imperfect times, often carry with them somewhat of a future tense: as, "If he come to-morrow, I may speak of them;" "If he should, or would come to-morrow, I might, would, could, or should speak to him." Observe also, that the auxiliaries *should* and *would,* in the imperfect times, are used to express the present and future as well as the past: as, "It is my desire, that he should, or would, come now, or to-morrow;" as well as, "It was my desire, that he

14*

should or would come yesterday." So that, in this *mood*, the precise time of the verb is very much determined by the nature and drift of the sentence.

In treating of the tenses, there are two things to which attention ought principally to be turned,—the *relation* which the several tenses have to one another, in respect of *time;* and the *notice* which they give of an action's being *completed* or *not completed.*

The present, past, and future tenses, may be used either *definitely* or *indefinitely*, both with respect to *time and action.* When they denote customs or habits, and not individual acts, they are applied indefinitely : as, " Virtue *promotes* happiness;" " the old Romans *governed* by benefits more than by fear;" " I *shall* hereafter *employ* my time more usefully." In these examples, the words, *promotes, governed*, and *shall employ*, are used indefinitely, both in regard to action and time ; for they are not confined to individual actions, nor to any precise points of present, past or future, time. When they are applied to signify particular actions, and to ascertain the precise points of time to which they are confined, they are used definitely ; as in the following instances : " My brother *is writing ;*" " He *built* the house last summer, but did not *inhabit* it till yesterday." " He *will write* another letter to-morrow."

The different tenses also represent an action as *complete* or *perfect*, or as *incomplete* or *imperfect*. In the phrases, "I am writing," " I was writing," " I shall be writing," imperfect, unfinished actions are signified. But the following examples, " I wrote," " I have written," " I had written," "I shall have written, all denote complete, perfect action.

The distinction of the tenses into *definite* and *indefinite*, may be more intelligible to you by the following explanation and arrangement.

PRESENT TENSE.

Indefinite. This form of the present tense denotes action or being, in present time, without limiting it with exactness to a given point. It expresses also facts which exist generally at all times, general truths, attributes which are permanent, habits, customary actions, and the like, without the reference to a specific time : as, " Hope *springs* eternal in the human breast ; Virtue *promotes* happiness ; Man *is* imperfect and dependent ; The wicked *flee* when no man pursueth ; Plants *rise* from the earth ; sometimes he *works*, but he often *plays* : Birds *fly* ; Fishes *swim.*"

Definite. This form expresses the present time with precision ; and it usually denotes action or being, which corresponds in time with another action : as, " He *is meditating*; I *am writing*, while you *are waiting.*

IMPERFECT TENSE.

Indefinite. This form of the imperfect tense represents action past and finished, and often with the precise time undefined: as, "Alexander *conquered* the Persians ; Scipio was as virtuous as brave."

Definite. This form represents an action as taking place and unfinished, in some specified period of past time; as, "I *was standing* at the door, when the procession passed."

PERFECT TENSE.

Indefinite. This form of the perfect tense represents an action completely past, and often at no great distance, but not specified : as, "I have accomplished my design ;" "I have read the History of England."

Definite. This form represents an action as just finished : as, "I have been reading a History of the revolution ;" "I have been studying hard to-day."

PLUPERFECT TENSE.

Indefinite. This form of the pluperfect tense, expresses an action which was past at or before some other past time specified : as, "He *had received* the news before the messenger arrived."

Definite. This form denotes an action to be just past, at or before another past time specified : as, "I had been waiting an hour when the messenger arrived."

FIRST FUTURE TENSE.

Indefinite. This form of the first future, simply gives notice of an event to happen hereafter : as, "Charles *will go* to London ;" "I think we *shall have* a fine season."

Definite. This form expresses an action, which is to take place, and be unfinished, at a specified future time : as, "He *will be preparing* for a visit, at the time you arrive."

SECOND FUTURE TENSE.

Indefinite. This form of the second future, denotes an action which will be past at a future time specified : as, "They *will have accomplished* their purpose, at the time they proposed."

Definite This form represents an action, which will be just past at a future specified time : as, "The scholars *will have been studying* an hour, when the tutor comes to examine them."

You will observe, that in this scheme, all the *definite* tenses are formed by the participle of the present tense, and the substantive verb *to be*

There are other modes of expressing future time: as, "I am going to write;" "I am about to write." These have been called the *Inceptive* future, as they note the commencement of an action, or an intention to commence an action without delay.

The substantive verb followed by a verb in the infinitive mood, forms another method of indicating future time: as, "Ferdinand *is to command* the army." "On the subject of style, I *am* afterwards *to discourse*." "Eneas went in search of the seat of an empire, which *was*, one day, *to govern* the world." The latter expression has been called a future past: that is, *past* as to the narrator; but *future* as to the event, at the time specified.

From the preceding representation of the different tenses, it appears, that each of them has its distinct and peculiar province; and that though some of them may sometimes be used promiscuously, or substituted one for another, in cases where great accuracy is not required, yet there is a real and essential difference in their meaning.—It is also evident, that the English language contains the six tenses which I have enumerated. Grammarians who limit the number to two, or at most to three, namely, the present, the imperfect, and the future, do not reflect that the English verb is mostly composed of principal and auxiliary; and that these several parts constitute one verb. Either the English language has no regular future tense, or its future is composed of the auxiliary and the principal verb. If the latter be admitted, then the auxiliary and principal united, constitute a tense, in one instance; and, from reason and analogy, may doubtless do so, in others, in which minuter divisions of time are necessary, or useful. What reason can be assigned for not considering this case, as other cases, in which a whole is regarded as composed of several parts, or of principal and adjuncts? There is nothing heterogeneous in the parts: and precedent, analogy, utility, and even necessity, authorize the union.

I will now question you concerning the subjects of this and the preceding Conversation.

QUESTIONS.

When is a verb in the subjunctive mood?

How does a verb differ in this mood from one in the indicative? Which tenses have two forms?

What is the difference between the first form and the second of the subjunctive mood, present tense?

When must the second form be used?

When is a verb called regular?

When must the first form of the subjunctive present be used?

How are the four tenses of the potential mood formed?

How does the infinitive mood differ from other moods?

Why is it called infinitive?

Why does not the second form of the subjunctive present, vary the verb in the second and third persons singular, as the indicative does?

How do you know the imperfect tense of verbs, from the perfect or passive participle, when they are both spelled alike?

When must *to* be omitted before the infinitive mood?

How are all the passive verbs formed?

Why are passive verbs so called?

What is the meaning of neuter?

When is a verb neuter?

How many classes of nominatives are there?

Can you explain them?

What verbs are sometimes auxiliaries, and sometimes principals?

What auxiliaries are never used as principals?

In what moods and tenses is *do* used as an auxiliary?

In what tenses is *have* used as an auxiliary? and how?

What is it *always* prefixed to, when an auxiliary?

Can you give a definition of *tense*, and of the six tenses?

CONVERSATION XX.

Tutor. You are now quite familiar with nearly all the regular constructions of the language; but there are a few, which I have not yet presented to you. These I will endeavor to explain in this Conversation. A few more rules, properly explained, will enable you to parse any word, in a regularly constructed sentence, in the English language. The first, which I shall give you this morning, is this,

RULE XXI.

Any INTRANSITIVE, PASSIVE, *or* NEUTER *verb, must have the same case after it as before it, when both words refer to, and signify the same thing.*

George. I think that I already understand this rule, for no verbs except *transitive*, govern the *objective* case. When nouns or pronouns, then, follow *intransitive*, *passive*, or *neuter* verbs, they cannot be governed by them. And, when *both words refer to,*

and signify the same thing, the latter is in apposition
to the former, and must be in the same case, according to the sixteenth rule in Conversation XIII.

Tutor. That is true.

Caroline. Then what is the use of this twenty-
first rule, if the sixteenth would enable us to parse
all the words to which this applies ?

Tutor. This rule will serve as a further illustration of that, and bring under your consideration
many erroneous constructions, with which you have
not yet been made sufficiently familiar, and which
might escape your notice, if they were not more
particularly considered.

I will first direct your attention to the neuter
verb *to be*, and give you many examples and illustrations, which you must *parse*, and then you will
remember them. The nouns and pronouns *before*
and *after* the verbs, and which you will perceive to
be in *apposition*, I will mark in Italics.

" *I* am *he* whom they invited ;" " *It* may be (or
might have been) *he*, but *it* cannot be (or could not
have been) *I* ;" " *It* is impossible to be *they* ;" " *It*
seems to have been *he*, who conducted himself so
wisely ;" " *It* appears to be *she* that transacted the
business ;" " I understood *it* to be *him* ;" " I believe
it to have been *them* ;" " We at first took *it* to be
her ; but were afterwards convinced that *it* was not
she." " He is not the person *who* it seemed *he* was."
" He is really the person *who he* appeared to be."
" She is not now the woman *whom* they represented
her to have been." " *Whom* do you fancy *him* to be ?"
" *He* desired to be their *king* ?" " They desired
him to be their *king*."

By these examples, it appears that this substantive verb has no government of case, but serves, in
all its forms, as a conductor to the cases ; so that
the two cases which, in the construction of the sentence, or member of the sentence, are the *next* before
and after it, must always be alike. In the sentence,
" I understood it to be him," the words *it* and *him*

are in apposition ; that is, " they refer to the same thing, and are in the same case."—If this rule be considered as applying to simple sentences, or to the simple members of compound sentences, the difficulties respecting it, will be still further diminished.

The following sentences contain deviations from the rule, and exhibit the pronoun in a wrong case : " It might have been *him*, but there is no proof of it ;" " Though I was blamed, it could not have been *me* ;" " I saw one whom I took to be *she* ;" " She is the person *who* I understood it to have been ;" " *Who* do you think me to be ?" " *Whom* do men say that I am ?" " And *whom* think ye that I am ?"

In the last example, the natural arrangement is " Ye think that I am whom ;" where, contrary to the rule, the nominative *I* precedes, and the objective case *whom* follows the verb. The best method of discovering the proper case of the pronoun, in such phrases as the preceding, is, to turn them into declarative expressions, and to substitute the personal pronoun for the interrogative, or relative pronoun ; as the interrogative, or relative pronoun must be in the same case as the personal pronoun would be in, if substituted for it. Thus, the question, " Whom do men say that I am ?" if turned into a declarative sentence, with the personal pronoun, would be, " Men do say that I am he :" consequently the interrogative must be in the same case as *he* ; that is, the nominative *who*, and not *whom*. In the same manner, in the phrase, " Who should I see but my old friend ?" if we turn it into a declarative one, as, " I should see him, my old friend," we shall perceive that the interrogative is governed by the verb ; as *him* and *my friend* are in the objective case, and that it ought to be in the same case ; that is, *whom*, and not *who*.

When the verb *to be* is *understood*, it has the same case before and after it, as when it is *expressed* : as,

" *He* seems the *leader* of the party ;" " *He* shall continue *steward ;*" " They appointed *me executor ;*" " I supposed *him* a *man* of learning ;" that is, " He seems *to be* the leader of the party," &c.

Passive verbs which signify *naming*, and others of a similar nature have the same case before and after them : as, " *He* was called *Cæsar ;*" " *She* was named *Penelope ;*" " *Homer* is styled the *prince* of poets;" " *James* was created a *duke ;*" " The general *was* saluted *emperor ;*" " The *professor* was appointed *tutor* to the prince;" " He caused *himself* to be proclaimed *king ;*" " The senate adjudged *him* to be declared a *traitor*."

From the observations and examples which have been produced, under this rule, it is evident that certain other neuter verbs, besides the verb *to be,* require the same case, whether it be the nominative or the objective, before and after them. The verbs to become, to wander, to go, to return, to expire, to appear, to die, to live, to look, to grow, to seem, to roam, and several others, are of this nature. "After this event, *he* became *physician* to the king ;" "*She* wanders an *outcast ;*" " He forced *her* to wander an *outcast ;*" " *He* went out *mate*, but *he* returned *captain ;*" " And *Swift* expires a *driv'ler* and a *show ;*" " This conduct made *him* appear an *encourager* of every virtue ;" " *Hortensius* died a *martyr ;*" "The gentle *Sidney* lived the shepherd's *friend*."

All the examples under this rule, and all others of a similar construction, may be explained on the principle, that nouns and pronouns are in the same case, when they signify the same thing, the one merely describing or elucidating the other.

So also in the following : "The Author of my being formed *me man*, and made me accountable to him." "They desired me to call *them brethren*." " He seems to have made *him what* he was."

We sometimes meet with such expressions as these : " They were asked a question ;" " They were offered a pardon ;" " He had been left a great estate by his father." In these phrases, verbs passive are improperly made to govern the objective case. This license is not to be approved. The expressions should be: "A question was put to them;" "A pardon was offered to them;" "His father left him a great estate."

Caroline. I think that we shall find these remarks and examples of service to us, and, that we shall not, after this, say, "It was *him*; it was *her*; it was *them*; *who* do you think him to be? nor, *whom* does he think that I am?" &c.

RULE XXII.

The infinitive mood, or part of a sentence, is sometimes the subject of a verb, and is, therefore, its nominative.

Every nominative to a verb which you have hitherto parsed, has been either a noun or a pronoun. But you will now find, that a *verb in the infinitive mood*, may be used *substantively*, and form the nominative to a verb. A few examples, which you must parse, will be sufficient to illustrate this rule. I will give you the following:

To err, is human. *To be*, contents his natural desire. *To play* is pleasant. *Promising without due consideration*, often produces a breach of promise. *To mourn without measure*, is folly; *not to mourn at all*, insensibility. *Reading books*, improved his mind. *Letting him escape*, was a fault.

When a nominative is composed of a verb in the infinitive mood only; as, *to err*, *to be*, &c. in parsing it, you will say, "It is a verb in the infinitive mood, used substantively, of the third person singular, and forms the nominative to the verb," whatever it may be. Then repeat Rule XXII.

When a part of the sentence is the nominative, you will call it *a substantive phrase*, third person singular, &c.

As a verb in the infinitive mood, or a substantive phrase, composed of part of a sentence, may be the

15

nominative to a verb, so each of them may be used substantively, as the *object* of a verb: as, "They love *to play;*" "They begin *to see;*" "Learn of the mole *to plough,* the worm *to weave;*" "I endeavoured to prevent *letting him escape;*" "I love *to read good books.*"

In these sentences *him* is governed by the participle *letting,* and *books,* by *to read.* But the **two** phrases, "*letting him escape,*" and "*to read good books,*" are governed by the preceding verbs, *to prevent,* and *love.* So a substantive phrase is frequently governed by a preposition: as, "A breach of promise is often produced by *promising without due consideration.*" "The atrocious crime of *being a young man,* I shall neither attempt to palliate nor deny."

When you analyze such phrases as these last **two,** you will find that you cannot parse the participle, as referring to any subject or actor, according to the sixth rule, because there is no subject or actor known in the sentence: but you will merely say it is a present participle from such a verb, and composes a part of the substantive phrase. Take, for instance, the phrase, "Promising without due consideration," &c. and you will find, that the participle has no reference to any actor in the sentence, but expresses the action generally.

The next and last rule that I shall give you for parsing, is,

RULE XXIII.

When a noun or pronoun has no verb to agree with it, but is placed before a participle, independently on the rest of the sentence, it must be in the NOMINATIVE CASE *absolute.*

This rule presents to you another instance, in which a noun or pronoun must be in the *nominative case,* without having a verb to agree with it.

If you now observe the *nominative case independent,* according to the seventeenth rule, and the *nom-*

inative case absolute, which we have now under consideration, you will see that the two constructions are very different. The nominative case independent, always denotes the person spoken to, and is of the *second* person; the nominative case absolute, may be of *any* of the three persons, and is always connected with a *participle*, expressed or understood: as, "*I being* badly *wounded*, they sent for a surgeon;" *He being* badly *wounded*, they sent," &c. In these sentences, you perceive that the pronouns *I* and *he*, have no verbs to agree with them; that they are placed before the *participle*, *being wounded*; and stand independently on the rest of the sentence? they are, therefore, in the nominative *absolute*, according to the rule.

But, "*I being* badly *wounded*, was carried home;" "*He being* badly *wounded*, soon died," are constructions very different from the others. In these sentences, you see that the pronoun *I* has the verb *was carried*, to agree with it; and, that *he* has the verb *died* to agree with it. But the rule *begins* by saying, "When a noun or pronoun has *no verb* to agree with it," &c.

Sometimes the noun, or pronoun, and the participle are both understood: as, "Conscious of his own weight and importance, the aid of others was not solicited." Here the words, *he being*, are understood; that is, "*He being* conscious of his own weight," &c.

I will here say a word respecting a particular construction of the infinitive mood. You know, that it is *generally* governed by a *verb*, noun, adjective, or participle: and, that it is *sometimes* used *substantively*, and forms the nominative to a verb. I will now show you, that it is sometimes used in neither of these constructions: as, "*To confess* the truth, I was in fault;" "*To enjoy* present pleasure, he sacrificed his future reputation." These are called the infinitive mood *absolute;* because in such constructions, the verb in the infinitive mood has no regular dependence on any governing word.

The nominative case *independent*, the nominative *absolute*, and the *infinitive mood absolute*, must always be separated from the body of the sentence by a comma.

have now given you all the rules necessary for the parsing of any regularly constructed sentence in the English language.

You may now practise on the following

EXERCISES IN PARSING.

That it is our duty to promote the purity of our minds and bodies, admits not of any doubt in a rational and well informed mind.—To mourn without measure, is folly.—To err is human; to forgive, divine.—Continue, my dear children, to make virtue your principal study.—To you, my worthy benefactors, I am greatly indebted, under Providence, for all that I enjoy.—Come then, companions of my toils, let us take fresh courage, persevere, and hope to the end.—The rain having ceased, the men pursued their journey.—The goods being considerably damaged, the merchant sold them very low.—The sun being risen, the day became fine.—Shame being lost, all virtue is lost.—That having been discussed long ago, there is no occasion to resume it.—I wish that he would lend me that book, that you sold him.—I think that, that man that you saw, is the wisest one, that ever lived.—If he do but go, I shall be satisfied.—If he did go, I care not.—Let him take heed, that he violate not the laws.—Admonish thy friend, that he speak not rashly.—The ship rolls.—I see the ship roll.—She sings.—I hear her sing.—He comes.—I bade him come.—They study.—The master makes them study.—I like him both on his own account, and on that of his parents.—Young men are subtle arguers; the cloak of honor covers all their faults, as that of passion, all their follies.—What is the reason that our language is less refined, than that of France?—What you do, do well.—What you like, I dislike.—He praises that

which you praise.—He praises what you praise.—
He extols that which he sees.—He extols what he
sees.—That, which reason weaves, is undone by
passion.—What reason weaves by passion is undone.
What they cannot but purpose, they postpone.—I
went myself.—I hurt myself.—They did it themselves.—They went themselves.—He esteems himself too highly.—He understood the matter in the
same manner himself.—The man, being dismissed
from office, had no means of support.—The man,
being dismissed from office, his family suffered.—
The man's being dismissed from office, was a misfortune to his family.—You sit next to your sister.—
My house is opposite to yours.—Pursuant to orders,
the company met this morning.—Agreeably to my
request, he came this evening.—He will be remu-
nerated according to his disbursement.—Notwithstanding his disappointments, he finally succeeded.

Tutor. I will now give you some remarks on a
figure of rhetoric, called ELLIPSIS, which will assist
you very much in understanding the grammatical
connexion of words in a sentence.

When a sentence is written out *in full*, you now
find no difficulty in parsing it; but frequently there
are words, and sometimes a whole clause of a sentence, omitted in speaking or writing, which are
understood in the mind, as necessary to express the
complete sense. In such instances, you will find it
necessary to supply the words that are omitted, remembering at the same time, that the words which
are written, have the same grammatical connexion
with those that are understood, that they would have,
if they were all on the paper. You will soon begin
the correcting of false syntax, and then you will find
the remarks I am about to make of considerable advantage, because there are many errors which you
will not discover, till you fill up the ellipsis, but
which you will then, immediately perceive; and you
will, by the same means, see the propriety of the
corrections.

15*

To avoid disagreeable repetitions, and to express our ideas in few words, an ellipsis, or omission of some words, is frequently admitted. Instead of saying, "He was a learned man, he was a wise man, and he was a good man;" we make use of the ellipsis, and say, "He was a learned, wise, and good man."

When the omission of words would obscure the sentence, weaken its force, or be attended with an impropriety, they must be expressed. In the sentence; "We are apt to love who love us," the word *them* should be supplied. "A beautiful field and trees," is not proper language; because, when we fill up the ellipsis, it would be, "A beautiful field and a beautiful trees;" for, when conjunctions connect two or more nouns, the same words that are applied to the first, belong also to the others, unless such connexion is broken by *expressing different* words. It should be, "Beautiful fields and trees;" or, "A beautiful field and fine trees."

Almost all compounded sentences, are more or less elliptical; some examples of which may be seen under the different parts of speech.

1. The *noun* is frequently omitted in the following manner. "The laws of God and man;" that is, "the laws of God and the laws of man." In some very emphatical expressions, the ellipsis should not be used: as, "Christ the power of God, and the wisdom of God;" which is more emphatical than, "Christ the power and wisdom of God."

2. The ellipsis of the *verb* is used in the following instances. "The man was old and crafty;" that is, "the man was old, and the man was crafty." "She was young, and beautiful and good;" that is, "She was young, she was beautiful, and she was good." "Thou art poor, and wretched, and miserable, and blind, and naked." If we would fill up the ellipsis in the last sentence, *thou art* ought to be repeated before each of the adjectives.

If, in such enumeration, we choose to point out one property above the rest, that property must be placed last, and the ellipsis supplied : as, " She is young and beautiful, and she is good."

" I went to see and hear him ;" that is, " I went to see him, and I went to hear him." In this instance, there is not only an ellipsis of the governing verb, *went*, but likewise of the sign of the infinitive mood, which is governed by it.

Do, did, have, had, shall, will, may, might, and the rest of the auxiliaries of the compound tenses, are frequently used alone, to spare the repetition of the verb : as, " He regards his word, but thou dost not ;" i. e. " does not regard it." " We succeeded, but they did not :" " did not succeed." " I have learned my task, but you have not ;" " have not learned." " They must, and they shall be punished :" that is, " they must be punished."

The auxiliary verbs are often very properly omitted before the principal verb : as, " I have seen and heard him frequently ;" not, " I *have* heard :" "He will lose his estate, and incur reproach ;" not " he *will* incur." But when any thing is emphatically expressed, or when opposition is denoted, this ellipsis should be avoided : as, " I have seen, and I have heard him too ;" " He was admired, but he was not beloved."

3. The ellipsis of the *article* is thus used : " A man, woman, and child ;" that is, " a man, a woman, and a child." " A house and garden ;" that is, " A house and a garden." "The sun and moon ;" that is, " the sun and the moon." " The day and hour ;" that is, " the day and the hour." In all these instances, the article being once expressed, the repetition of it becomes unnecessary. There is, however, an exception to this observation, when some peculiar emphasis requires a repetition ; as in the following sentence : " Not only the year, but the day and the hour." In this case the ellipsis of the last article would be improper. When a differ-

ent form of the article is requisite, the article is also properly repeated; as, " *a* house and *an* orchard ;" instead of, " a house and orchard."

4. The ellipsis of the *adjective* is used in the following manner. " **A** delightful garden and orchard ;" that is, " a delightful garden and a delightful orchard." " **A** little man and woman ;" that is, " **A** little man and a little woman." In such elliptical expressions as these, the adjective ought to have exactly the same signification, and to be quite as proper, when joined to the latter substantive as the former ; otherwise the ellipsis should not be admitted.

Sometimes the ellipsis is improperly applied to nouns of different numbers : as, " A magnificent house and gardens." In this case it is better to use another adjective : as, " A magnificent house and fine gardens."

5. In the following example, the pronoun and participle are omitted : " Conscious of his own weight and importance, the aid of others was not solicited." Here the words *he being* are understood ; that is, " He being conscious of his own weight and importance." This clause constitutes the case absolute, or, the nominative absolute; which is not so obvious before, as after the ellipsis is supplied.

6. The ellipsis of the *adverb* is used in the following manner. " He spoke and acted wisely ;" that is, " He spoke wisely, and he acted wisely." " Thrice I went and offered my service ;" that is, " Thrice I went and thrice I offered my service."

7. The following is the ellipsis of the *pronoun.* " I love and fear him ;" that is, " I love him, and I fear him." " My house and lands ;" that is, " my house and my lands." In these instances the ellipsis may take place with propriety ; but if we would be more express and emphatical, it must not be used ; as, " His friends and his foes." " My sons and my daughters."

In some of the common forms of speech, the relative pronoun is usually omitted : as, " This is the man they love ;" instead of, "This is the man *whom* they love." "These are the goods they bought ;" for, "These are the goods *which* they bought."

In complex sentences, it is much better to have the relative pronoun expressed : as, it is more proper to say, "The posture in which I lay," than, "In the posture I lay :" "The horse on which I rode, fell down ;" than, "The horse I rode fell down."

The antecedent and the relative connect the parts of a sentence together ; and, to prevent obscurity and confusion. they should answer to each other with great exactness. " We speak that we do know, and testify that we have seen." Here the ellipsis is manifestly improper, and ought to be supplied : as, "We speak that *which* we do know, and testify that *which* we have seen."

8. The ellipsis of the *preposition*, as well as of the verb, is seen in the following instances : " He went into the abbeys, halls, and public buildings ;" that is, " He went into the abbeys, he went into the halls, and he went into the public buildings." "He also went through all the streets, and lanes of the city ; that is, " Through all the streets, and through all the lanes," &c. " He spoke to every man and woman there," that is, " to every man and to every woman." " This day, next month, last year ;" that is, " on this day, in the next month, in the last year." " The Lord do that which seemeth him good ;" that is, " which seemeth *to* him.

9. The ellipsis of the *conjunction* is as follows : "They confess the power, wisdom goodness, and love, of their Creator ;" i. e. " the power, *and* wisdom, *and* goodness, *and* love of," &c. " Though I love him, I do not flatter him," that is, "Though I love him, *yet* I do not flatter him."

There is a very common ellipsis of the conjunction *that* : as, "He told me he would proceed im-

mediately ;" "I desire he would not be too hasty ;"
"I fear it comes too much from the heart :" instead
of "He told me *that* he would proceed immediately ;" "I desired *that* he would not be too hasty ;"
"I fear *that* it comes too much from the heart."—
This ellipsis is tolerable in conversation, and in
epistolary writing : but it should be sparingly in-
dulged, in every other species of composition. The
French do not use this mode of expression : they
avoid the ellipsis on such occasions.

10. The ellipsis of the *interjection* is not very
common : it, however, is sometimes used : as, "Oh!
pity and shame !" that is, "Oh pity ! Oh shame !"

As the ellipsis occurs in almost every sentence in
the English language, numerous examples of it
might be given : but only a few more can be admitted here.

In the following instance, there is a very considerable one : "He will often argue, that if this part
of our trade were well cultivated, we should gain
from one nation, and if another, from another ;" that
is, "He will often argue, that if this part of our
trade were well cultivated, we should gain from one
nation, and if another part of our trade were well
cultivated, we should gain from another nation."

Sometimes a considerable part of a sentence is
properly omitted, when we presume that the nominative case and its whole regimen may be readily
understood : as, "Nature has given to animals one
time to act, and another to rest ;" instead of saying : "Nature has given to animals one time to act,
and nature has given to animals another time to rest."

The following instances, though short, contain
much of the ellipsis, "Wo is me ;" i. e. "wo is to
me."   "To let blood ;" i. e. "to let out blood."
"To let down :" i. e. "to let it fall or slide down."
"To walk a mile ;" i. e. "to walk through the
space of a mile."   "To sleep all night ;" i. e. "to
sleep through all the night."   "To go a fishing ;"
"To go a hunting ;" i. e. "to go on a fishing
voyage or business ;" "to go on a hunting party."

"I dine at two o'clock;" i. e. "at two of the
clock." By sea, by land, on shore;" i. e. "by
the sea, by the land, on the shore."

After the word *notwithstanding*, when used as a
conjunction disjunctive, or a *preposition*, we frequently omit the whole succeeding member of the
sentence; and in this use of *notwithstanding*, we
have a striking proof of the value of abbreviations
in language. For example: "Moses said, Let no
man leave of it till the morning: *notwithstanding*
they harkened not unto him." Here *notwithstanding* appears without the clause, to which it belongs;
and to complete the sense in words, it would be necessary to repeat the whole preceding clause, or the
substance of it.—"Moses said, let no man leave of
it until the morning. *Notwithstanding this command of Moses*, or, *notwithstanding Moses said that
which has been recited*, they harkened not unto Moses."
"Folly meets with success in this world: but it is
true *notwithstanding*, that it labors under disadvantages." This passage, at length, would read thus:
"Folly meets with success in this world: but it is
true, *notwithstanding folly meets with success in this
world*, that it labors under disadvantages."

It is not unusual to apply a pronoun, *this*, *that*,
which, or *what*, to represent nearly the whole of a
sentence; as, "Bodies which have no taste, and no
power of affecting the skin, may, notwithstanding
this, act upon organs which are more delicate."
Here *this* stands for, "*they have no taste, and no
power to affect the skin*," and is governed by the
preposition *notwithstanding*.

11. The examples that follow are produced to
show the impropriety of ellipsis in some particular
cases. "The land was always possessed, during
pleasure, by those intrusted with the command;"
it should be, "those *persons* intrusted;" or, "those
who were intrusted." "If he had read further, he would
have found several of his objections might have been
spared:" that is, "he would have found *that* several
of his objections," &c. "There is nothing men are

more deficient in, than knowing their own characters." It ought to be, "nothing *in which* men ;"
and, "than *in* knowing." "I scarcely know any
part of natural philosophy would yield more variety
and use :" it should be, "*which* would yield," &c.
"In the temper of mind he then was ;" i. e. "*in
which* he then was." "The little satisfaction and
consistency, to be found in most of the systems
of divinity I have met with, made me betake
myself to the sole reading of the Scriptures ;" it
ought to be, "*which are* to be found," and "*which*
I have met with." He desired they might go to
the altar together, and jointly return their thanks to
whom only they were due ; i. e. "He desired *that*
they might go to the altar together, and jointly return
their thanks *to him* to *whom* only they were due."

CONVERSATION XXI.

Tutor. In most languages, there are some verbs
which are defective with respect to persons. These
are denominated *impersonal* verbs. They are used
only in the third person, because they refer to a
subject peculiarly appropriated to that person : as,
"It rains, it snows, it hails, it lightens, it thunders."
But as the word *impersonal* implies a total absence
of persons, it is improperly applied to those verbs
which have a person : and hence it is manifest, that
there is no such thing in the English, nor indeed, in
any language, as a sort of verbs really impersonal.
The plea urged to prove the existence of impersonal verbs is, in substance, as follows : and you
will perceive that it is not wholly destitute of
plausibility. There are certain verbs which do not
admit for their subject any thing that has life, or
any thing that is strictly definable : such as, "It
snows, it hails, it freezes, it rains, it lightens, it
thunders." In this point of view, and with this
explanation, it is supposed by some grammarians,

that our language contains a few impersonal verbs; that is, verbs which declare the existence of some action or state, but which do not refer it to any animate being, or any determinate particular subject.

The whole number of verbs in the English language, regular and irregular, simple and compounded, taken together, is about 4300 The number of irregular verbs, the defective included, is about 177.

The whole number of words, after deducting proper names, and the inflections of our verbs and nouns, does not exceed forty thousand.

George. What you have just said of *impersonal* verbs, reminds me of a sentence, which I saw the other day. It was this: "There needs no ghost come from the grave to tell us this." I could not parse *needs.*

Tutor. *Needs* is frequently used in this manner: as, "There *needs* more assistance;" "There *needs* one more to make up the number;" and Pope says, "There *needs* but thinking right, and meaning well."

It is, doubtless, a contraction of *need is,* the nominative and the verb: as, "There *need is* of no ghost," &c. or "There is need of," &c. "There *need is* of more assistance." *Needs* is sometimes used as an adverb: as, "Offences must *needs* come," &c.; "He *needs* would show his master what his art could do;" that is, *necessarily.*

Before you commence the correcting of false syntax, it is proper, that you should be exercised more in parsing. I will give you a few lessons in which you will find some constructions more difficult than any which you have yet had; but comprehend the sense of the author, supply the ellipsis, and you will not find much difficulty.

EXERCISES IN PARSING.

A few instances of the same word's constituting several of the parts of speech.

Calm was the day, and the scene delightful.
We may expect a calm after a storm.

To prevent passion is easier than to calm it.

Better is a little with content, than a great deal with anxiety.

The gay and dissolute think little of the miseries, which are stealing softly after them.

A little attention will rectify some errors.

Though he is out of danger, he is still afraid.

He labored to still the tumult.

Fair and softly go far.

The fair was numerously attended.

His character is fair and honourable.

Damp air is unwholesome.

Guilt often casts a damp over our sprightliest hours

Soft bodies damp the sound much more than hard ones.

Though she is rich and fair, yet she is not amiable.

They are yet young, and must suspend their judgment yet a while.

Many persons are better than we suppose them to be.

The few and the many have their prepossessions.

Few days pass without some clouds.

The hail was very destructive.

Hail virtue! source of every good.

We hail you as friends.

Much money is corrupting.

Think much, and speak little.

He has seen much of the world, and been much caressed.

His years are more than hers, but he has not more knowledge.

The more we are blessed, the more grateful we should be.

The desire of getting more is rarely satisfied.

He has equal knowledge, but inferior judgment.

She is his inferior in sense, but his equal in prudence.

Every being loves its like.

We must make a like space between the lines.

Behave yourselves like men.

We are too apt to like pernicious company.
He may go or stay as he likes.
They strive to learn.
He goes to and fro.
To his wisdom we owe our privilege.
The proportion is ten to one.
He has served them with his utmost ability.
When we do our utmost, no more is required.
I will submit, for I know submission brings peace.
It is for our health to be temperate.
Oh! for better times.
I have a regard for him.
He is esteemed, both on his own account, and on that of his parents.
Both of them deserve praise.
Yesterday was a fine day.
I rode out yesterday.
I shall write to-morrow.
To-morrow may be brighter than to-day.

Promiscuous Exercises in Parsing.

PROSE.

DISSIMULATION in youth, is the forerunner of perfidy in old age. Its first appearance is the fatal omen of growing depravity, and future shame.

If we possess not the power of self-government, we shall be the prey of every loose inclination, that chances to arise. Pampered by continual indulgence, all our passions will become mutinous and headstrong. Desire, not reason, will be the ruling principle of our conduct.

Absurdly we spend our time in contending about the trifles of a day, while we ought to be preparing for a higher existence.

How little do they know of the true happiness of life, who are strangers to that intercourse of good offices and kind affections, which, by a pleasing charm, attaches men to one another, and circulates rational enjoyment from heart to heart.

If we view ourselves, with all our imperfections and failings, in a just light, we shall rather be surprised at our enjoying so many good things, than discontented, because there are any which we want.

True cheerfulness makes a man happy in himself, and promotes the happiness of all around him. It is the clear and calm sunshine of a mind illuminated by piety and virtue.

Wherever views of interest, and prospects of return, mingle with the feelings of affections, sensibility acts an imperfect part, and entitles us to a small share of commendation.

Let not your expectations from the years that are to come, rise too high ; and your disappointments will be fewer, and more easily supported.

To live long, ought not to be your favorite wish, so much as to live well. By continuing too long on earth, we might only live to witness a greater number of melancholy scenes, and to expose ourselves to a wider compass of human wo.

How many pass away some of the most valuable years of their lives, tossed in a whirlpool of what cannot be called pleasure, so much as mere giddiness and folly ?

Look around you with attentive eye, and weigh characters well, before you connect yourselves too closely with any who court your society.

The true honor of man consists not in the multitude of riches, or the elevation of rank ; for experience shews, that these may be possessed by the worthless, as well as the deserving.

Beauty of form has often betrayed its possessor. The flower is easily blasted. It is short lived at the best ; and trifling, at any rate, in comparison with the higher and more lasting beauties of the mind.

A contented temper opens a clear sky, and brightens every object around us. It is in sullen and dark shade of discontent, that noxious passions, like venomous animals, breed and prey upon the heart.

Thousands whom indolence has sunk into contemptible obscurity, might have come forward to usefulness and honor, if idleness had not frustrated the effects of all their powers.

Sloth is like the slowly flowing, putrid stream, which stagnates in the marsh, breeds venomous animals, and poisonous plants; and infects with pestilential vapour the whole country round it.

Disappointments derange, and overcome vulgar minds. The patient and the wise, by a proper improvement, frequently make them contribute to their high advantage.

Whatever fortune may rob us of, it cannot take away what is most valuable, the peace of a good conscience, and the cheering prospect of a happy conclusion to all the trials of life in a better world.

Be not overcome by the injuries you meet with, so as* to pursue revenge; by the disasters of life, so as to sink into despair; by the evil examples of the world, so as to follow them into sin. Overcome injuries, by forgiveness; disasters, by fortitude; evil examples, by firmness of principle.

Sobriety of mind is one of those virtues, which the present condition of human life strongly inculcates. The uncertainty of its enjoyments, checks presumption; the multiplicity of its dangers, demands perpetual caution. Moderation, vigilance, and self-government, are duties incumbent on all, but especially on such as are beginning the journey of life.

The charms and comforts of virtue are inexpressible; and can only be justly conceived by those who possess her. The consciousness of Divine approbation and support, and the steady hope of future happiness, communicate a peace and joy, to which all the delights of the world bear no resemblance.

---

*As, following so, sometimes governs the infinitive mood. See sec. xv. rule XX. Read all that is written under this rule.

If we knew how much the pleasures of this life deceive and betray their unhappy votaries: and reflected on the disappointments in pursuit, the dissatisfaction in enjoyment, or the uncertainty of possession, which every where attend them; we should cease to be enamoured with these brittle and transient joys; and should wisely fix our hearts on those virtuous attainments which the world can neither give nor take away.

POETRY.

ORDER is Heaven's first law : and this confess'd,
Some are, and must be, greater than the rest ;
More rich, more wise ; but who infers from hence,
That such are happier, shocks all common sense.

Needful austerities our wills restrain ;
As thorns fence in the tender plant from harm.

Reason's whole pleasure, all the joys of sense,
Lie in three words, health, peace, and competence :
But health consists with temperance alone ;
And peace, O virtue ! peace is all thy own.

On earth nought precious is obtain'd,
   But what is painful too ;
By travel and *to* travel born,
   Our sabbaths are but few.

Who noble ends by noble means obtains,
Or failing, smiles in exile or in chains,
Like good Aurelius let him reign, or bleed
Like Socrates, that man is great indeed.

Our hearts are fasten'd to this world,
   By strong and endless ties ;
But ev'ry sorrow cuts a string,
   And urges us to rise.

Oft pining cares in rich brocades are dress'd,
And diamonds glitter on an anxious breast.

Teach me to feel another's wo,
   To hide the fault I see ;
That mercy I to others show ;
   That mercy show to me.
This day be bread, and peace my lot ;
   All else beneath the sun
Thou know'st if best bestow'd or not ;
   And let thy will be done.

Vice is a monster of so frightful mien,
As, to be hated, needs but to be seen:
Yet seen too oft, familiar with her face,
We first endure, then pity, then embrace.

If nothing more than purpose in thy power,
Thy purpose firm, is equal to the deed ;
Who does the best his circumstance allows,
Does well, acts nobly ; angels can no more.

In faith and hope the world will disagree;
But all mankind's concern is charity.

To be resign'd when ill's betide,
Patient when favors are denied,
    And pleas'd with favors given ;
Most surely this is Wisdom's part,
This is that incense of the heart,
    Whose fragrance smells to Heav'n.

All fame is foreign but of true desert ;
Plays round the head, but comes not to the heart ;
One self-approving hour whole years outweighs
Of stupid starers, and of loud huzzas ;
And more true joy Marcellus exil'd feels,
Than Cæsar with a senate at his heels.

Far from the madding crowd's ignoble strife,
    Their sober wishes never learn'd to stray ;
Along the cool sequester'd vale of life,
    They kept the noiseless tenor of their way.

What nothing earthly gives, or can destroy,
The soul's calm sunshine, and the heartfelt joy,
Is virtue's prize.

Pity the sorrows of a poor old man,
Whose trembling limbs have borne him to your door;
Whose days are dwindled to the shortest span ;
O give relief, and Heaven will bless your store.

Who lives to nature, rarely can be poor ;
Who lives to fancy, never can be rich.

When young, life's journey I began,
    The glitt'ring prospect charm'd my eyes ;
I saw, along th' extended plain,
    Joy after joy successive rise.
But soon I found 'twas all a dream,
    And learn'd the fond pursuit to shun,
Where few can reach the purpos'd aim,
    And thousands daily are undone.

'Tis greatly wise to talk with our past hours,
And ask them what report they bore to Heav'n.
All nature is but art unknown to thee ;
All chance, direction which thou can'st not see ;
All discord, harmony not understood ;
All partial evil, universal good.

Heaven's choice is safer than our own ;
  Of ages past inquire ;
What the most formidable fate ;
  "To have our own desire."

  Two Principles in human nature reign ;
Self-love to urge, and Reason to restrain :
Nor this a good, nor that a bad we call,
Each works its end, to move or govern all ;
And to their proper operation still,
Ascribe all Good, to their improper, Ill.
  Self-love, the spring of motion, acts the soul ;
Reason's comparing balance rules the whole.
Man but for* that, no action could attend,
And, but for this, were active to no end :
Fix'd like a plant on his peculiar spot,
To draw nutrition, propagate, and rot :
Or, meteor-like, flame lawless through the void,
Destroying others, by himself destroy'd.
  Most strength the moving principle requires ;
Active its task, it prompts, impels, inspires.
Sedate and quiet the comparing lies,
Form'd but to check, delib'rate and advise.
Self-love still stronger as its objects nigh ;
Reason's at distance, and in prospect lie :
That sees immediate good by present sense :
Reason, the future and the consequence.
Thicker than arguments, temptations throng,
At best more watchful this, but that more strong.
The action of the stronger to suspend,
Reason still use, to reason still attend.
Attention, habit and experience gains,
Each strengthens Reason, and Self-love restrains.
Let subtle schoolmen teach these friends to fight,
More studious to divide than to unite :
And Grace and Virtue, Sense and Reason split,
With all the rash dexterity of wit.
Wits, just like fools, at war about a name,
Have full as oft no meaning, or the same.
Self-love and Reason to one end aspire,

---

  * *But for*, must here be taken together as a compound preposition,
equivalent to *without*. We cannot parse them separately, without
perverting the sense of the author.

Pain their aversion, Pleasure their desire :
But greedy That, its object would devour,
This taste the honey, and not wound the flow'r :
Pleasure, or wrong, or rightly understood,
Our greatest evil, or our greatest good.

Whate'er the passion, knowledge, fame, or pelf,
Not one will change his neighbour with himself.
The learn'd is happy nature to explore,
The fool is happy that he knows no more ;
The rich is happy in the plenty giv'n,
The poor contents him with the care of Heav'n.
See the blind beggar dance, the cripple sing,
The sot a hero, lunatic a king ;
The starving chymist in his golden views
Supremely blest, the poet in his muse.
See some strange comfort ev'ry state attend,
And pride bestow'd on all, a common friend ;
See some fit passion ev'ry age supply,
Hope travels thro' nor quits us when we die.
Behold the child, by nature's kindly law,
Pleas'd with a rattle, tickled with a straw ;
Some livelier plaything gives his youth delight,
A little louder, but as empty quite :
Scarfs, garters, gold, amuse his riper stage,
And beads and prayer-books are the toys of age :
Pleas'd with this bauble still, as that before ;
Till tir'd he sleeps, and life's poor play is o'er.
Meanwhile opinion gilds with varying rays
Those painted clouds that beautify our days ;
Each want of happiness by hope suppli'd,
And each vacuity of sense by pride :
These build as fast as knowledge can destroy ;
In folly's cup still laughs the bubble joy ;
One prospect lost, another still we gain ;
And not a vanity is giv'n in vain ;
Ev'n mean self-love becomes, by force divine,
The scale to measure others' wants by thine.
See! and confess, one comfort still must rise :
'Tis this, 'Tho' man's a fool, yet GOD is WISE.

Whether with Reason or with instinct blest ;
Know, all enjoy that pow'r which suits them best ;
To bliss alike by that direction tend,
And find the means proportion'd to their end,
Say, where full Instinct is th' uneering guide,
What pope or council can they need beside ?
Reason, however able, cool at best,
Cares not for service, or but serves when prest,
Stays till we call, and then not often near ;
But honest Instinct comes a volunteer.

Sure never to o'ershoot, but just to hit ;
While still too wide or short is human wit,
Sure by quick Nature, happiness to gain,
Which heavier Reason labors at in vain.
This too, serves always, Reason never long :
One must go right, the other may go wrong.
See then the acting and comparing pow'rs,
One in their nature, which are two in ours !
And Reason raise o'er Instinct as you can,
In this, 'tis God directs, in that 'tis Man.
Who taught the nations of the field and flood
To shun their poison, and to choose their food?
Prescient, the tides or tempests to withstand,
Build on the wave, or arch beneath the sand ?
Who made the Spider parallels design,
Sure as *De Moivre*, without rule or line ?
Who bid the Stork, *Columbus* like, explore
Heav'ns not his own, and worlds unknown before ?
Who calls the council, states the certain day,
Who forms the phalanx, and who points the way?

ADDITIONAL REMARKS.

OF SYNTAX.

SECTION I.

The third part of Grammar is SYNTAX, which treats of the agreement and construction of words in a sentence.

A sentence is an assemblage of words, forming a complete sense.

Sentences are of two kinds, simple and compound.

A simple sentence has in it but one subject, and one finite verb: as, "Life is short."

A compound sentence consists of two or more simple sentences, connected together: as, "Life is short, and art is long." "Idleness produces want, vice, and misery."

As sentences themselves are divided into simple and compound, so the members of sentences may be divided likewise into simple and compound members: for whole sentences, whether simple or compounded, may become members of other sentences, by means of some additional connexion; as in the following example: "The ox knoweth his owner, and the ass his master's crib: but Israel doth not know, my peop e do not consider." This sentence consists of two compounded members, each of which is subdivided into two simple members, which are properly called clauses.

There are three sorts of simple sentences; the *explicative*, or explaining; the *interrogative*, or asking; the *imperative*, or commanding.

An explicative sentence is, when a thing is said to be or not to be, to do or not to do, to suffer or not to suffer, in a direct manner: as "I am; thou writest; Thomas is loved." If the sentence be negative, the adverb *not* is placed after the auxiliary, or after the verb itself when it has no auxiliary: as, "I did not touch him;" or, "I touched him not."

In an interrogative sentence, or when a question is asked, the nominative case follows the principal verb, or the auxiliary: as, "Was it he?" "Did Alexander conquer the Persians?"

In an imperative sentence, when a thing is commanded to be, to do, to suffer, or not, the nominative case likewise follows the verb or the auxiliary: as, "Go, thou traitor!" "Do thou go:" "Haste ye away:" unless the verb *let* be used; as, "Let us be gone."

A phrase is two or more words rightly put together, making sometimes part of a sentence, and sometimes a whole sentence.

The principal parts of a simple sentence are, the subject, the attribute, and the object.

The subject is the thing chiefly spoken of; the attribute is the thing or action affirmed or denied of it; and the object is the thing affected by such action.

The nominative denotes the subject, and usually goes before the verb or attribute; and the word or phrase, denoting the object, follows the verb: as, "A wise man governs his passions." Here, *a wise man* is the subject; *governs*, the attribute, or thing affirmed; and *his passions*, the object.

Syntax principally consists of two parts, *Concord* and *Government*.

Concord is the agreement which one word has with another, in gender, number, case, or person.

Government is that power which one part of speech has over another, in directing its mood, tense, or case.

I shall now proceed to recapitulate all the rules, and give some illustrations, and notes under each, and then add exercises in false syntax, for you to correct and parse.

If you attend well to the illustrations, and the notes, you will be able to make the proper corrections, in all similar constructions.

RULE I.

A verb must agree with its nominative case in number and person.

The following are a few instances of the violation of this rule. "What signifies good opinions, when our practise is bad?" "what *signify*." "There's two or three of us, who have seen the work:" "there *are*." "We may suppose there was more imposters than one;" "there *were* more." "I have considered what have been said on both sides in this controversy:" "what *has* been said." "If thou would be healthy, live temperately:" "if thou *wouldst*." "Thou sees how little has been done:" "thou *seest*." "Though thou cannot do much for the cause, thou may and should do something:" *canst not, mayst,* and *shouldst*." "Full many a flower are born to blush unseen;" "*is* born." "A conformity of inclinations and qualities prepare us for friendship:" "*prepares* us." "A variety of blessings have been conferred upon us;" "*has* been." "In piety and virtue consist the happiness of man:" "*consists*." "To these precepts are subjoined a copious selection of rules and maxims:" "*is* subjoined."

1. Every verb, except in the infinitive mood, or the participle, ought to have a nominative case, either expressed or implied: as, "Awake; arise;" that is, "Awake ye; arise ye."

I shall here add some examples of inaccuracy, in the use of the verb without its nominative case. "As it hath pleased him of his goodness to give you safe deliverance, and hath preserved you in the great danger," &c. The verb "*hath preserved*," has here no nominative case; for it cannot be properly supplied by the preceding word, "*him*," which is in the objective case. It ought to be, "and as *he hath preserved* you;" or rather, "and *to preserve* you." "If the calm in which he was born, and lasted so long, had continued;" "and *which* lasted," &c. "These we have extracted from an historian of undoubted credit, and are the same that were practised," &c.: "and *they are* the same." "A man whose inclinations led him to be corrupt, and had great abilities to manage the business;" "and *who* had," &c. "A cloud gathering in the north; which we have helped to raise, and may quickly break in a storm upon our heads;" "and *which* may quickly."

2. Every nominative case, except the case absolute, and when an address is made to a person, should belong to some verb, either expressed or implied: as, "Who wrote this book?" "James;" that is, "James wrote it." "To whom thus Adam," that is, "spoke." "Who invented the telescope?" "Galileo;" that is, "Galileo invented the telescope."

One or two instances of the improper use of the nominative case, without any verb, expressed or implied, to answer it, may be sufficient to illustrate the usefulness of the preceding observation.

"*Which rule*, if it had been observed, a neighboring prince would have wanted a great deal of that incense, which hath been offered up to him." The pronoun *it* is here the nominative case to the verb "observed;" and *which rule*, is left by itself, a nominative case without any verb following it. This form of expression, though improper, is very common. It ought to be, "*If this rule* had been observed," &c. "*Man*, though he has a great variety of thoughts, and such from which others as well as himself might receive profit and delight, yet they are all within his own breast. In this sentence, the nominative *man* stands alone and unconnected with any verb, either expressed or implied. It should be, "*Though man* has great variety," &c.

3. When a verb comes between two nouns, either of which may be understood as the subject of the affirmation, it may agree with either of them; but some regard must be had to that which is more naturally the subject of it, as also to that which stands next to the verb: as, "His meat *was* locusts and wild honey;" "A great cause of the low state of industry *were* the restraints put upon it;" "The wages of sin *is* death."

17

In such instances as those which follow, either of the clauses may be considered as the nominative to the verb. "To show how the understanding proceeds herein, *is* the design of the following discourse." This sentence may be inverted without changing a single word: "The design of the following discourse *is*, to show how the understanding proceeds herein." "To fear no eye, and to suspect no tongue, *is* the great prerogative of innocence." This sentence may be inverted: but, according to the English idiom, the pronoun *it* would in that case, precede the verb: as, "*It* is the prerogative of innocence, to fear no eye, and to suspect no tongue."

The nominative case is commonly placed before the verb; but sometimes it is put after the verb, if it is a simple tense; and between the auxiliary, and the verb or participle, if a compound tense: as,

1st, When a question is asked, a command given, or a wish expressed: as, "Confidest thou in me?" "Read thou;" "Mayst thou be happy!" "Long live the King!"

2d, When a supposition is made, without the conjunction *if:* as, "Were it not for this;" "Had I been there."

3d, When a verb neuter is used: as, "On a sudden appeared the king." "Above it stood the seraphim."

4th, When the verb is preceded by the adverbs, *here, there, then, thence, thus,* &c.: as, "Here am I;" "There was he slain;" "Then cometh the end;" "Thence ariseth his grief;" "Hence proceeds his anger;" "Thus was the affair settled."

5th, When a sentence depends on *neither* or *nor*, so as to be coupled with another sentence: as, "Ye shall not eat of it, neither shall ye touch it, lest ye die."

6th, When an emphatical adjective introduces a sentence: as, "Happy is the man, whose heart does not reproach him."

You can now correct the following

EXERCISES IN FALSE SYNTAX.

DISAPPOINTMENTS sinks the heart of man; but the renewal of hope give consolation.

The smiles that encourage severity of judgment, hides malice and insincerity.

He dare not act contrary to his instructions.

Fifty pounds of wheat contains forty pounds of flour.

The mechanism of clocks and watches, were totally unknown a few centuries ago.

The number of inhabitants in Great Britain and Ireland, do not exceed sixteen millions.

Nothing but vain and foolish pursuits delight some persons.

A variety of pleasing objects charm the eye.

So much both of ability and merit are seldom found.

In the conduct of Parmenio, a mixture of wisdom and folly were very conspicuous.

He is an author of more credit than Plutarch, or any other, that write lives too hastily.

The inquisitive and curious is generally talkative.

Great pains has been taken to reconcile the parties.

I am sorry to say it, but there was more equivocators than one.

The sincere is always esteemed.

Has the goods been sold to advantage? and did thou embrace the proper season?

There is many occasions in life, in which silence and simplicity is true wisdom.

The generous never recounts minutely the actions they have done; nor the prudent those they will do.

He need not proceed in such haste.

The business that related to ecclesiastical meetings, matters and persons, were to be ordered according to the king's direction.

In him were happily blended true dignity with softness of manners.

The support of so many of his relations, were a heavy tax upon his industry; but thou knows he paid it cheerfully.

What avails the best sentiments, if persons do not live suitably to them?

Reconciliation was offered, on conditions as moderate as was consistent with a permanent union.

Not one of them whom thou sees clothed in purple, are completely happy.

And the fame of this person, and of his wonderful actions, were diffused throughout the country.

The variety of the productions of genius, like that of the operations of nature, are without limit.

In vain our flocks and fields increase our store,
When our abundance make us wish for more.

Thou should love thy neighbor as sincerely as thou loves thyself.

Has thou no better reason for censuring thy friend and companion?

Thou who art the Author and Bestower of life, can doubtless restore it also: but whether thou will please to restore it, or not, that thou only knows.

O thou my voice inspire,
Who touch'd Isaiah's hallowed lips with fire.

Accept these grateful tears: for thee they flow;
For thee that ever felt another's wo.

Just to thy word, in ev'ry thought sincere;
Who knew no wish but what the world might hear.

The following examples are adapted to the notes under
RULE I.

1. If the privileges to which he has an undoubted right, and he has long enjoyed, should now be wrested from him, would be flagrant injustice.

These curiosities we have imported from China, and are similar to those which were some time ago brought from Africa.

Will martial flames for-ever fire thy mind,
And never, never be to Heav'n resign'd ?

2. Two substantives, when they come together, and do not signify the same thing, the former must be in the genitive case.

Virtue, however it may be neglected for a time, men are so constituted as ultimately to acknowledge and respect genuine merit.

SECTION II.

RULE II.

When two nouns come together, signifying different things, the former implying possession, must be in the possessive case, and governed by the latter.

The preposition *of* joined to a substantive, is frequently equivalent to the possessive case : as, " A Christian's hope," " The hope of a Christian." But it is only so, when the expression can be converted into the regular form of the possessive case. We can say, " The reward of virtue," and " Virtue's reward ;" but though it is proper to say, " A crown of gold," we cannot convert the expression into the possessive case, and say, " Gold's crown."

Substantives govern pronouns as well as nouns, in the possessive case : as, " Every tree is known by *its* fruit ;" "Goodness brings *its* reward ;" " That desk is *mine.*"

The genitive *its* is often improperly used for *'tis* or *it is :* as, " Its my book ;" instead of, " It is my book."

The pronoun *his*, when detached from the noun to which it relates, is to be considered, not as a possessive adjective pronoun, but as the genitive case of the personal pronoun : as, " This composition is *his.*" " Whose book is that ?" " *His.*" If we use the noun itself, we should say, " This composition is John's." " Whose book is that ?" " Eliza's." The position will be still more evident, when we consider that both the pronouns, in the following sentence, must have a similar construction : " Is it *her* or *his* honor that is tarnished ?" " It is not *hers*, but *his*."

Sometimes a substantive in the genitive or possessive case stands alone, the latter one by which it is governed being understood : as, " I called at the bookseller's," that is, 'at the bookseller's *shop*."

1. If several nouns come together in the genitive case, the apostrophe with *s* is annexed to the last, and understood in the rest : as, " John and Eliza's books :" " This was my father, mother, and uncle's advice." But when any words intervene, perhaps on account of the increased pause, the sign of the possessive should be annexed to each : as, " They are John's as well as Eliza's books ;" " I had the physician's, the surgeon's, and the apothecary's assistance." The following distinction, on this point, appears to be worthy of attention. When any subject or subjects are considered as the common property of two or more persons, the sign of the possessive case is affixed only to the name of the last person : as, "This is Henry, William, and Joseph's estate." But when several subjects are considered, as belonging separately to distinct individuals, the names of the individuals have the sign of the possessive case annexed to each of them : as, " These are Henry's, William's and Joseph's estates."—It is, however, better to say, " It was the advice of my father, mother, and uncle ;" " I had the assistance of the physician, the surgeon, and the apothecary ;" " This estate belongs in common to Henry, William, and Joseph."

2. In poetry, the additional *s* is frequently omitted, but the apostrophe retained, in the same manner as in substantives of the plural number ending in *s* : as, " The wrath of Peleus' son." This seems not so allowable in prose ; which the following erroneous examples will demonstrate : " Moses' minister ;" " Phinehas' wife ;" " Festus came into Felix' room." " These answers were made to the witness' questions." But in cases which would give too much of the hissing sound, or increase the difficulty of pronunciation, the omission takes place even in prose : as, " For righteousness' sake ;" " For conscience' sake."

3. Little explanatory circumstances are particularly awkward between a genitive case, and the word which usually follows it : as, " She began to extol the farmer's, as she called him, excellent understanding " It ought to be, " the excellent understanding of the farmer, as she called him."— The word in the genitive case is frequently placed improperly : as, " This fact appears from Dr. Pearson of Birmingham's experiments." It should be, " from the experiments of Dr. Pearson of Birmingham."

4. When a sentence consists of terms signifying a name and an office, or of any expressions by which one part is descriptive or explanatory of the other, it may occasion some doubt

17*

to which of them the sign of the genitive case should be annexed : or whether it should be subjoined to them both. Thus, some would say, "I left the parcel at Smith's the bookseller ; others, " at Smith the bookseller's ;" and perhaps others, " at Smith's the bookseller's." The first of these forms is most agreeable to the English idiom ; and if the addition consists in two or more words, the case seems to be less dubious : as, "I left the parcel at Smith's, the bookseller and stationer " The point will be still clearer, if we supply the ellipsis in these sentences, and give the equivalent phrases, at large : thus, " I left the parcel at the house of Smith the bookseller." "I left it at Smith the house of the bookseller." " I left it at the house of Smith the house of the bookseller." By this process, it is evident, that only the first mode of expression is correct and proper. But as this subject requires a little further explanation, to make it intelligible to the learners, I shall add a few observations calculated to unfold its principles.

A phrase in which the words are so connected and dependent, as to admit of no pause before the conclusion, necessarily requires the genitive sign at or near the end of the phrase : as, " Whose prerogative is it ? It is the king of Great Britain's ;" " That is the duke of Bridgwater's canal ;" " The bishop of Landaff's excellent book :" "The Lord mayor of London's authority ;" " The captain of the guard's house."

When words in apposition follow each other in quick succession, it seems also most agreeable to our idiom, to give the sign of the genitive a similar situation ; especially if the noun which governs the genitive be expressed : as, " The emperor Leopold's ;" " Dionysius the tyrant's ;" " For David my *servant's* sake ;" "Give me John the *Baptist's* head ;" "Paul the *apostle's* advice." But when a pause is proper, and the governing noun not expressed : and when the latter part of the sentence is extended ; it appears to be requisite that the sign should be applied to the first genitive, and understood to the other : as, " I reside at lord Stormont's, my old patron and benefactor ;" " Whose glory did he emulate ? He emulated Cæsar's, the greatest general of antiquity." In the following sentences, it would be very awkward to place the sign, either at the end of each of the clauses, or at the end of the latter one alone : as, " These psalms are David's, the king, priest, and prophet of the Jewish people ;" " We staid a month at lord Lyttelton's, the ornament of his country, and the friend of every virtue." The sign of the genitive case may very properly be understood at the end of these members, an ellipsis at the latter part of the sentences being a common construction in our language ; as the learner will see by one or two examples : " They wished to submit, but he did not ;" that is, " he did not *wish to submit* ;" " He said it was their concern, but not his ;" that is, " *not his concern.*"

If we annex the sign of the genitive to the end of the last clause only, we shall perceive that a resting place is wanted, and that the connecting circumstance is placed too remotely, to be either perspicuous or agreeable : as, " Whose glory did he emulate ? He emulated Cæsar, the greatest general of *antiquity's*." " These psalms are David, the king, priest, and prophet of the Jewish *people's*." It is much better to say, " This is *Paul's* advice, the Christian hero, and great apostle of the Gentiles," than, " This is Paul the Christian hero, and great apostle of the *Gentiles'* advice." On the other hand, the application of the genitive sign to both or all of the nouns in apposition, would be generally harsh and displeasing, and perhaps in some cases incorrect : as, " The emperor's Leopold's ;" " King's George's ;" " Charles's the second's ;" " The parcel was left at Smith's, the bookseller's and stationer's." The rules which I have endeavored to elucidate, will prevent the inconveniences of both these modes of expression ; and they appear to be simple, perspicuous, and consistent with the idiom of the language.

5. The English genitive has often an unpleasant sound ; so that we daily make more use of the participle *of* to express the same relation. There is something awkward in the following sentences, in which this method has not been taken. " The general in the army's name, published a declaration." " The commons' vote." " The Lord's house." " Unless he is very ignorant of the kingdom's condition." It were certainly better to say, " In the name of the army ;" " The votes of the commons ;" " The house of lords ;" " The condition of the kingdom." It is also rather hard to use two English genitives with the same substantive : as, "Whom he acquainted with the pope's and the king's pleasure." " The pleasure of the pope and the king," would have been better.

We sometimes meet with three substantives dependent on one another, and connected by the preposition *of* applied to each of them : as, " The severity of the distress of the son of the king, touched the nation ;" but this mode of expression is not to be recommended. It would be better to say, " The severe distress of the king's son, touched the nation." We have a striking instance of this laborious mode of expression, in the following sentence : " *Of* some *of* the books *of* each *of* these classes *of* literature, a catalogue will be given at the end of the work."

6. In some cases, we use both the genitive termination and the preposition *of* : as, " It is a discovery of Sir Isaac Newton's." Sometimes indeed, unless we throw the sentence into another form, this method is absolutely necessary, in order to distinguish the sense, and to give the idea of property, strictly so called, which is the most important of the relations expressed by the genitive case : for the expressions, " This picture of my friend," and " This picture of my friend's," sug-

gest very different ideas. The latter only is that of property in the strictest sense. The idea would, doubtless, be conveyed in a better manner, by saying, "This picture belongs to my friend."

When this double genitive, as some grammarians term it, is not necessary to distinguish the sense, and especially in a grave style, it is generally omitted. Except to prevent ambiguity, it seems allowable only in cases which suppose the existence of a plurality of subjects of the same kind. In the expressions, "A subject of the emperor's;" "A sentiment of my brother's;" more than one subject and one sentiment, are supposed to belong to the possessor. But when this plurality is neither intimated, nor necessarily supposed, the double genitive, except as before mentioned, should not be used : as, "This house of the governor is very commodious;" "The crown of the king was stolen;" "That privilege of the scholar was never abused." But after all that can be said for this double genitive, as it is termed, some grammarians think, that it would be better to avoid the use of it, altogether, and to give the sentiment another form of expression.

7. When an entire clause of a sentence, beginning with a participle of the present tense, is used as one name, or to express one idea or circumstance, the noun on which it depends may be put in the genitive case; thus instead of saying, "What is the reason of this person dismissing his servant so hastily ?" that is, "What is the reason of this person, in dismissing his servant so hastily ?" we may say, and perhaps ought to say, "What is the reason of this person's dismissing of his servant so hastily ?" Just as we say, "What is the reason of this person's hasty dismission of his servant ?" So also, we say, "I remember it being reckoned a great exploit;" or more properly, "I remember it's being reckoned," &c. The following sentence is correct and proper : "Much will depend on the *pupil's composing*, but more on *his reading* frequently." It would not be accurate to say, "Much will depend on the *pupil composing*," &c. We also properly say; "This will be the effect *of the pupil's composing* frequently; instead of, "*Of the pupil composing* frequently." The participle, in such constructions, does the office of a substantive; and it should therefore have a correspondent regimen.

Now correct and parse the following

EXERCISES IN FALSE SYNTAX.

My ancestors virtue is not mine.

His brothers offence will not condemn him.

I will not destroy the city for ten sake.

Nevertheless, Asa his heart was perfect with the Lord.

A mothers tenderness and a fathers care, are natures gift for mans advantage.

A mans manner's frequently influence his fortune.

Wisdoms precepts' form the good mans interest and happiness.

The following examples are adapted to the notes and observations under RULE II.

1. It was the men's, women's, and children's lot to suffer great calamities.

Peter's, John's, and Andrew's occupation, was that of fishermen.

This measure gained the king, as well as the people's approbation.

Not only the counsel's and attorney's, but the judge's, opinion also, favored his cause.

2. And he cast himself down at Jesus feet.

Moses rod was turned into a serpent.

For Herodias sake, his brother Philips wife.

If ye suffer for righteousness's sake, happy are ye.

Ye should be subject for conscience's sake.

3. The very justly condemned the prodigal's, as he was called, senseless and extravagant conduct.

They implicitly obeyed the protector's, as they called him, imperious mandates.

4. I bought the knives at Johnson's, the cutler's.

The silk was purchased at Brown's, the mercer's and haberdasher's.

Lord Feversham the general's tent.

This palace had been the grand sultan's Mahomet's.

I will not for David's thy father's sake.

He took refuge at the governor, the king's representative's.

Whose works are these ? They are Cicero, the most eloquent of men's.

5 The world's government is not left to chance.

She married my son's wife's brother.

This is my wife's brother's partner's house.

It was necessary to have both the physician's and the surgeon's advice.

The extent of the prerogative of the king of England is sufficiently ascertained.

6. This picture of the king's does not much resemble him.

These pictures of the king were sent to him from Italy.

This estate of the corporation's is much encumbered.

This is the eldest son of the king of England's.

7. What can be the cause of the parliament neglecting so important a business ?

Much depends on this rule being observed.

The time of William making the experiment at length arrived.

It is very probable that this assembly was called to clear some doubt which the king had, about the lawfulness of the Hollanders their throwing off the monarchy of Spain, and their withdrawing entirely their allegiance to that crown.

If we alter the situation of any of the words, we shall presently be sensible of the melody suffering.

Such will ever be the effect of youth associating with vicious companions.

SECTION III.

RULE III.

Transitive verbs govern the objective case.

In English, the nominative case denoting the subject, usually goes before the verb ; and the objective case, denoting the object, follows the verb transitive ; and it is the order that determines the case in *nouns ;* as, " Alexander conquered the Persians." But the *pronoun* having a proper form for each of those cases, is sometimes, when it is in the objective case, placed before the verb ; and, when it is in the nominative case, follows the object and verb : as, " *Whom* ye ignorantly worship, *him* declare I unto you."

This position of the pronoun sometimes occasions its proper case and government to be neglected : as in the following instances : " Who should I esteem more than the wise and good ?" " By the character of those who you choose for your friends, your own is likely to be formed." " Those are the persons who he thought true to his interest." " Who should I see the other day but my old friend ?" " Whosoever the court favors." In all these places it ought to be *whom,* the relative being governed in the objective case by the verbs " esteem, choose, thought," &c. " He, who under all proper circumstances, has the boldness to speak truth, choose for thy friend ;" It should be, " *him* who," &c.

Verbs neuter do not act upon, or govern, nouns and pronouns. " He *sleeps ;* they *muse,*" &c. are not transitive. They are therefore, not followed by an objective case, specifying the object of an action. But when this case or an object of action, comes after such verbs, though it may carry the appearance of being governed by them, it is generally affected by a preposition or some other word understood : as, " He resided many years [that is, *for* or *during* many years] in that street ;" " He rode several miles [that is, *for* or *through* the space of several miles] on that day ;" " He lay an hour [that is, *during* an hour] in great torture." In the phrases, " To dream a dream," "To live a virtuous life," "To run a race," "To walk the horse," "To dance the child," the verbs certainly assume a transitive form, and may not, in these cases, be improperly denominated transitive verbs.

Part of a sentence, as well as a noun or pronoun, may be said to be in the objective case, or to be put objectively, governed by the active verb : as, " We sometimes see *virtue in distress :* but we should consider *how great will be her ultimate reward*." Sentences or phrases under these circumstances may be termed *objective sentences* or *phrases.*

1. Some writers, however, use certain neuter and intransitive verbs as if they were transitive, putting after them the objective case, agreeably to the French construction of reciprocal verbs ; but this custom is so foreign to the idiom of the English tongue, that it ought not to be adopted or imitated. The following are some instances of this practice. " *Repenting* him of his design." " The king soon found reason *to repent* him of his provoking such dangerous enemies." " The popular lords did not fail to *enlarge* themselves on the subject." " The nearer his successes *approached* him to the throne." " Go *flee* thee away into the land of Judah." " I think it by no means a fit and decent thing to *vie* charities," &c. " They have spent their whole time and pains, to *agree* the sacred with the profane chronology."

2. " Transitive verbs are sometimes as improperly made intransitive : as, " I must *premise* with three circumstances." " Those that think to *ingratiate with* him by calumniating me." " They should be, " premise three circumstances ;" " ingratiate themselves with him."

3. The neuter and intransitive verb is varied like the transitive ; but having in some degree the nature of the passive, it admits, in many instances, of the passive form, retaining still the neuter signification, chiefly in such verbs as signify some sort of motion, or change of place or condition : as, " I am come ; I was gone ; I am grown ; I was fallen."— The following examples, however, appear to be erroneous, in giving the intransitive verbs a passive form, instead of a transitive one. " The rule of our holy religion, from which we *are* infinitely *swerved*." " The whole obligation of that law and covenant *was* also *ceased*." " Whose number *was* now *amounted* to three hundred." " This mareschal, upon some discontent, *was entered* into a conspiracy against his master." " At the end of a campaign, when half the men *are deserted* or killed." " They should be, " *have* swerved, *had* ceased," &c.

4. *Let* governs the objective case : " Let *him* beware ; " Let *us* judge candidly ;" " Let *them* not presume ; " Let *George* study his lesson."

Now correct and parse the following

EXERCISES IN FALSE SYNTAX.

They who opulence has made proud, and who luxury has corrupted, cannot relish the simple pleasures of nature.

You have reason to dread his wrath, which one day will destroy ye both.

Who have I reason to love so much as this friend of my youth.

Ye, who were dead, hath he quickened.

Who did they entertain so freely.

The man who he raised from obscurity, is dead.

Ye, as I have I known of all the families of the earth.

He and they we know, but who are you?

She that is idle and mischievous, reprove sharply.

Who did they send to him on so important an errand?

That is the friend who you must receive cordially, and who you cannot esteem too highly.

He invited my brother and I to see and examine his library.

He who committed the offence, you should correct, not I who am innocent.

We should fear and obey the Author of our being, even He who has power to reward or punish us for ever.

They who he had most injured, he had the greatest reason to love.

The examples which follow, are suited to the notes and observations under RULE III.

1. Though he now takes pleasure in them, he will one day repent him of indulgences so unwarrantable.

The nearer his virtues approached him to the great example before him, the humbler he grew.

It will be very difficult to agree his conduct with the principles he professes.

2. To ingratiate with some, by traducing others, marks a base and despicable mind.

I shall premise with two or three general observations.

3. If such maxims, and such practices prevail, what has become of decency and virtue?

I have come according to the time proposed; but I have fallen upon an evil hour.

The mighty rivals are now at length agreed.

The influence of his corrupt example was then entirely ceased. He was entered into the connexion, before the consequences were considered.

4. Whatever others do, let thou and I act wisely.
Let them and we unite to oppose this growing evil.

SECTION IV.

RULE IV.

The article refers to a noun or pronoun, expressed or understood, to limit its signification.

It is the nature of both the articles to determine or limit the thing spoken of. *A* determines it to be one single thing of the kind, leaving it still uncertain which: *the* determines which it is, or of many, which they are.

The following passage will serve as an example of the different uses of *a* and *the*, and of the force of the substantive without any article. " *Man* was made for society, and ought to extend his good will to all men : but *a man* will naturally entertain a more particular kindness for *the men*, with whom he has the most frequent interoourse ; and enters into a still closer union with *the man* whose temper and disposition suit best with his own."

There is in some instances, a peculiar delicacy in the application or omission of the indefinite article. This will be seen in the following instances. We commonly say ; " I do not intend to turn critic on this occasion :" not "turn *a* critic." On the other hand, we properly add the article in this phrase ; "I do not intend to become *a* critic in this business ;" not "to become critic." It is correct to say, with the article, " He is in *a* great hurry ;" but not, " in great hurry." And yet, in this expression, " He is in great haste," the article should be omitted : it would be improper to say, " He is in *a* great haste." A nice discernment, and accurate attention to the best usage, are necessary to direct us, on these occasions.

As the articles are sometimes misapplied, it may be of some use to exhibit a few instances : " And I persecuted this way unto *the* death." The apostle does not mean any particular sort of death, but death in general : the definite article therefore is improperly used : it ought to be "unto death," without any article.

" When he, the Spirit of Truth, is come, he will guide you into all truth ;" that is, according to this translation, "into all truth whatsoever, into truth of all kinds ;" very different from the meaning of the evangelist, and from the original, " into all *the* truth ;" that is, " into all evangelical truth, all truth necessary for you to know."

" Who breaks a butterfly upon *a* wheel ?" it ought to be " *the* wheel," used as an instrument for the particular purpose of torturing animals. "The Almighty hath given reason to *a* man to be a light unto him :" it should rather be, " to *man*," in general. " This day is salvation come to this house, forasmuch as he is also *the* son of Abraham :" it ought to be, " *a* son of Abraham."

These remarks may serve to show the great importance of the proper use of the article, and the excellence of the English language in this respect ; which by means of its two articles, does most precisely determine the extent of signification of common names.

1. A nice distinction of the sense is sometimes made by the use or omission of the article *a*. If I say, " He behaved with *a* little reverence ;" my meaning is positive. If I say, " He behaved with little reverence ;" my meaning is negative. And these two are by no means the same, or, to be used in the same cases. By the former, I rather praise a person ; by the latter, I dispraise him. For the sake of this distinction, which is a very useful one, we may better bear the seeming impropriety of the article *a* before nouns of number. When I say, " There were few men with him ;" I speak diminutively, and mean to represent them as inconsiderable : whereas, when I say, " There were *a* few men with him ;" I evidently intend to make the most of them.

2. In general, it may be sufficient to prefix the article to the former of two words in the same construction ; though the French never fail to repeat it in this case. " There were many hours, both of the night and day, which he could spend, without suspicion, in solitary thought." It might have been " of *the* night and *of the* day." And, for the sake of emphasis, we often repeat the article in a series of epithets. " He hoped that this title would secure him *an* ample and *an* independent authority."

3. In common conversation, and in familiar style, we frequently omit the articles, which might be inserted with propriety in writing, especially in a grave style. " At worst, time might be gained by this expedient." " At *the* worst," would have been better in this place. " Give me here John Baptist's head." There would have been more dignity in saying, " John *the* Baptist's head :" or, " The head of John *the* Baptist."

The article *the* has sometimes a different effect, in distinguishing a person by an epithet. " In the history of Henry the fourth, by Father Daniel, we are surprised at not finding him *the* great man." " I own I am often surprised that he should have treated so coldly, a man so much *the* gentleman."

This article is often elegantly put, after the manner of the French, for the possessive adjective pronoun : as, " He looks him full in *the* face ;" that is, in *his* face." In his presence they were to strike *the* forehead on the ground ;" that is, "*their foreheads.*"

We sometimes, according to the French manner, repeat the same article, when the adjective, on account of any clauss depending upon it, is put after the substantive. "Of all the considerable governments among the Alps, a commonwealth is a constitution *the* most adapted of any to the poverty of those countries." "With such a specious title as that of blood, which with the multitude is always a claim, *the* strongest, and the most easily comprehended."

" They are not the men in the nation *the* most difficult to be replaced."

The definite article is likewise used to distinguish between things, which are individually different, but have one generic name, and things which are, in truth, one and the same, but are characterized by several qualities. If we say, "The ecclesiastical and secular powers concurred in this measure," the expression is ambiguous, as far as language can render it such. The reader's knowledge, as Dr. Campbell observes, may prevent his mistaking it ; but if such modes of expression be admitted, where the sense is clear, they may inadvertantly be imitated in cases where the meaning would be obscure, if not entirely misunderstood. The error might have been avoided, either by repeating the substantive, or by subjoining the substantive to the first adjective, and prefixing the article to both adjectives ; or by placing the substantive after both adjectives, the article being prefixed in the same manner : as, " The ecclesiastical powers, and the secular powers ;" or better, "The ecclesiastical powers, and the secular ;" or " The ecclesiastical, and the secular powers." The repetition of the article shows, that the second adjective is not an additional epithet to the same subject, but belongs to a subject totally different, though expressed by the same generic name. " The lords spiritual and temporal," is a phraseology objectionable on the same principle, though now so long sanctioned by usage, that we scarcely dare question its propriety. The subjects are different, though they have but one generic name. The phrase should, therefore, have been, " The spiritual and the temporal lords." —On the contrary, when two or more adjectives belong as epithets, to one and the same thing, the other arrangement is to be preferred : as, " The high and mighty States." Here both epithets belong to one subject. " The States high and mighty," would convey the same idea.

The indefinite article has sometimes, the meaning of *every* or *each* : as, " They cost five shillings a dozen ;" that is, " every dozen."

" A man he was to all the country dear,
" And passing rich with forty pounds a year."
                                        Goldsmith.

that is, " every year."

There is a particular use of the indefinite article, which deserves attention, as ambiguity may, by this means, be, in some cases, avoided.   Thus, if we say, " He is a better soldier than scholar," the article is suppressed before the second term, and the expression is equivalent to, " He is more warlike than learned ;" or, " He possesses the qualities, which form the soldier, in greater degree than those, which constitute the scholar."   If we say, " He would make a better soldier than a scholar," the article is prefixed to the second term, and the meaning is, " He would make a better soldier than a scholar would make ;" that is, " He has more of the constituent qualities of a soldier, than are to be found in any literary man." These two phraseologies are frequently confounded, which seldom fails to produce uncertainty of meaning.   In the former case, the subject, as possessing different qualities in various degrees, is compared with itself ; in the latter, it is compared with something else.

You are now prepared to correct and parse the following

EXERCISES IN FALSE SYNTAX.

The fire, the air, the earth, and the water, are four elements of the philosophers.

Reason was given to a man to control his passions.

We have within us an intelligent principle, distinct from body and from matter.

A man is the noblest work of creation.

Wisest and best men sometimes commit errors.

Beware of drunkenness ; it impairs understanding ; wastes an estate ; destroys a reputation ; consumes the body ; and renders the man of the brightest parts the common jest of the meanest clown.

He is a much better writer than a reader.

The king has conferred on him the title of a duke.

There are some evils of life, which equally affect prince and people.

We must act our part with a constancy, though reward of our constancy be distant.

We are placed here under a trial of our virtue.

The virtues like his are not easily acquired.   Such qualities honor the nature of a man.

Purity has its seat in the heart ; but extends its influence over so much of outward conduct, as to form the great and material part of a character.

The profligate man is seldom or never found to be the good

husband, the good father, or the beneficent neighbor.

True charity is not the meteor, which occasionally glares; but the luminary, which in its orderly and regular course, dispenses benignant influence.

The following sentences exemplify the notes and observations under RULE IV.

1. He has been much censured for conducting himself with a little attention to his business.

So bold a breach of order, called for little severity in punishing the offender.

His error was accompanied with so little contrition and candid acknowledgment, that he found a few persons to intercede for him.

There were so many mitigating circumstances attending his misconduct, particularly that of his open confession, that he found few friends who were disposed to interest themselves in his favor.

As his misfortunes were the fruit of his own obstinacy, a few persons pitied him.

2. The fear of shame, and desire of approbation, prevent many bad actions.

In this business he was influenced by a just and generous principle.

He was fired with a desire of doing something, though he knew not yet, with distinctness, either end or means.

3. At worst, I could but incur a gentle reprimand.

At best his gift was a poor offering, when we consider his estate.

SECTION V.

RULE V.

Every adjective belongs to some noun or pronoun, express-ed or understood.

1. Adjectives are sometimes improperly applied as adverbs : as, ''Indifferent honest ; excellent well ; miserable poor,'' instead of '' Indifferently honest ; excellently well ; miserably poor.'' '' He behaved himself conformable to that great example ;'' '' *conformably.*'' ''Endeavor to live hereafter suitable to persons in your station ;'' '' *suitably.*'' '' I can never think so very mean of him ;'' '' *meanly.*'' '' He describes this river agreeable to the common reading ;'' '' *agreeably.*'' ''Agreeable to my promise, I now write ;'' '' *agreeably.*

18*

" Thy exceeding great reward."   When united to an adjective, or adverb not ending in *ly*, the word *exceeding* has *ly* added to it; as, "exceedingly dreadful, exceedingly great ;" " exceedingly well, exceedingly more active :" but when it is joined to an adverb or adjective, having that termination, the *ly* is omitted : as, " Some men think exceeding clearly, and reason exceeding forcibly :" " She appeared on this occasion, exceeding lovely :" " He acted in this business *bolder* than was expected :" " They behaved the *noblest*, because they were disinterested."   They should have been, " *more boldly ; most nobly.*"—The adjective pronoun *such* is often misapplied : as, " He was such an extravagant young man, that he spent his whole patrimony in a few years :" " it should be, " *so extravagant a young man.*"   " I never before saw such large trees :" " *saw trees so large.*"   When we refer to the species or nature of a thing, the word *such* is properly applied : as, " Such a temper is seldom found :" but when degree is signified, we use the word *so :* as, " So bad a temper is seldom found."

Adverbs are likewise improperly used as adjectives; as, " The tutor addressed him in terms rather warm, but suitably to his offence ;" " *suitable.*"   " They were seen wandering about solitarily and distressed ;" " *solitary.*"   " He lived in a manner agreeably to the dictates of reason and religion ;" " *agreeable.*"   " The study of syntax should be previously to that of punctuation ;" "*previous.*"*

* Young persons who study grammar, find it difficult to decide, in particular constructions, whether an adjective, or an adverb, ought to be used.   A few observations on this point, may serve to inform their judgment, and direct their determination.—They should carefully attend to the definitions of the adjective and the adverb; and consider whether, in the case in question, *quality* or *manner*, is indicated.   In the former case, an adjective is proper; in the latter, an adverb.   A number of examples will illustrate this direction, and prove useful on other occasions.

She looks cold.—She looks coldly on him.
He feels warm—He feels warmly the insult offered to him.
He became sincere and virtuous—He became sincerely virtuous.
She lives free from care—He lives freely at another's expense.
Harriet always appears neat—She dresses neatly.   [utation.
Charles has grown great by his wisdom—He has grown greatly in rep-
They now appear happy—They now appear happily in earnest.
The statement seems exact—The statement seems exactly in point.

The verb *to be*, in all its moods and tenses, generally requires the word immediately connected with it to be an adjective, not an adverb; and consequently, when this verb can be substituted for any other, without varying the sense or the construction, that other verb must also be connected with an adjective.   The following sentences elucidate

2. Double comparatives and superlatives should be avoided : such as. "A worser conduct ;" "On lesser hopes ;" "A more serener temper ;" "The most straitest sect ;" "A more superior work." They should be, "worse conduct ;" "less hopes ;" "a more serene temper ;" "the straitest sect ;" a superior work."

3. Adjectives that have in themselves a superlative signification, do not properly admit of the superlative or comparative form superadded : such as, "Chief, extreme, perfect, right, universal, supreme," &c. ; which are sometimes improperly written, "Chiefest, extremest, perfectest, rightest, most universal, most supreme," &c. The following expressions are therefore improper. "He sometimes claims admission to the *chiefest* offices ;" "The quarrel became so *universal* and national ;" "A method of attaining the *rightest* and greatest happiness." The phrases, so perfect, so right, so extreme, so universal, &c. are incorrect ; because they imply that one thing is less perfect, less extreme, &c. than another, which is not possible.

4. Inaccuracies are often found in the way in which the degrees of comparison are applied and construed. The following are examples of wrong construction in this respect : "This noble nation hath of all others, admitted fewer corruptions." The word *fewer* is here construed precisely as if it were the superlative. It should be, "This noble nation hath admitted fewer corruptions than any other." We commonly say, "This is the weaker of the two ;" or, "The weakest of the two ;" but the former is the regular mode of expression, because there are only two things compared. "The vice of covetousness is what enters deepest into the soul of any other." "He celebrates the church of England as the most perfect of all others." Both these modes of expression are faulty : we should not say, "The best of any man," or, "The

these observations : "This is agreeable to our interest ; That behavior was not suitable to his station ;

                                                 is
Rules should be conformable to sense ;" "The rose smells sweet ; How
                 is   is
sweet the hay smells! How delightful the country appears! How pleas-
               are   are   was
ant the fields look! The clouds look dark; How black the sky looked!
    is   were   is
The apple tastes sour ; How bitter the plums tasted! He feels happy." In all these sentences, we can, with perfect propriety, substitute some tenses of the verb *to be*, for the other verbs. But in the following sentences we cannot do this : "The dog smells disagreeably ; George feels exquisitely ; How pleasantly she looks at us !"

The directions contained in this note are offered as useful, not as complete and unexceptionable. Anomalies in language every where encounter us ; but we must not reject rules, because they are attended with exceptions.

best of any other man," for " the best of men." The sentences may be corrected by substituting the comparative in the
room of the superlative. "The vice, &c. is what enters
deeper into the soul than any other." "He celebrates, &c.
as more perfect, or less imperfect, than any other." It is also possible to retain the superlative, and render the expression
grammatical, "Covetousness, of all vices, enters the deepest
into the soul." "He celebrates, &c. as the most perfect of
all churches." These sentences contain other errors, against
which it is proper to caution the learner. The words *deeper*
and *deepest*, being intended for adverbs, should have been
more deeply, most deeply. The phrases *more perfect*, and
most perfect, are improper ; because perfection admits of no
degrees of comparison. We may say *nearer* or *nearest* to
perfection, or more or less imperfect.

5. In some cases, adjectives should not be separated from
their substantives, even by words which modify their meaning, and make but one sense with them ; as, "A large enough
number surely." It should be, a " number large enough."
" The lower sort of people are good enough judges of one not
very distant from them."

The adjective is usually placed before its substantive : as,
" A *generous* man ;" " How *amiable* a woman !" The instances in which it comes after the substantive, are the following :

1st. When something depends upon the adjective ; and
when it gives a better sound, especially in poetry, as, " A man
generous to his enemies ;" " Feed me with food *convenient*
for me ;" " A tree three feet *thick* ;" " A body of troops fifty
thousand *strong* ;" " The torrent tumbling through rocks
abrupt."

2d, When the adjective is emphatical : as, " Alexander the
Great ;" " Lewis the *Bold* ;" "Goodness *infinite* ;" "Wisdom
unsearchable."

3d, When several adjectives belong to one substantive : as,
" A man just, wise, and charitable ;" " A woman modest,
sensible, and virtuous."

4th, When the adjective is preceded by an adverb : as, "A
boy regularly studious ;" " A girl unaffectedly modest."

5th, When the verb *to be*, in any of its variations, comes
between a substantive and an adjective, the adjective may frequently either precede or follow it ; as, "The man is *happy* ;"
or, " *happy* is the man who makes virtue his choice :" "The
interview was *delightful* ;" or, " *delightful* was the interview."

6th, When the adjective expresses some circumstance of a
substantive placed after an active verb : as, " Vanity often
renders its possessor *despicable*." In an exclamatory sentence, the adjective generally precedes the substantive ; as,
" How *despicable* does vanity often render its possessor !"

There is sometimes great beauty, as well as force, in placing the adjective before the verb, and the substantive immediately after it: as, " Great is the Lord ! just and true are thy ways, thou King of saints !"

Sometimes the word *all* is emphatically put after a number of particulars comprehended under it. " Ambition, interest, honor, *all* concurred." Sometimes a substantive, which likewise comprehends the preceding particulars, is used in conjunction with this adjective pronoun : as, " Royalists, republicans, churchmen, sectaries, courtiers, patriots, *all parties*, concur in the illusion."

An adjective pronoun, in the plural number, will sometimes properly associate with a singular noun : as, " Our desire, your intention, their resignation." This association applies rather to things of an intellectual nature, than to those which are corporeal. It forms an exception to the general rule.

A substantive with its adjective is reckoned as one compounded word ; whence they often take another adjective, and sometimes a third, and so on : as, " An old man ; a good old man ; a very learned, judicious, good old man."

Though the adjective always relates to a substantive, it is, in many instances, put as if it were absolute ; especially where the noun has been mentioned before, or is easily understood, though not expressed : " I often survey the green fields, as I am very fond of *green* ;" " The wise, the virtuous, the honored, famed, and great," that is, " persons ;" " The twelve," that is, " apostles ;" " Have compassion on the *poor* : be feet to the *lame*, and eyes to the *blind*."

Substantives are often used as adjectives. In this case, the word so used is sometimes unconnected with the substantive to which it relates ; sometimes connected with it by a hyphen ; and sometimes joined to it, so as to make the two words coalesce. The total separation is proper, when either of the two words is long, or when they cannot be fluently pronounced as one word : as, " an adjective pronoun, a silver watch, a stone cistern :" the hyphen is used, when both the words are short, and are readily pronounced as a single word: as, "coal-mine, corn-mill, fruit-tree ;" the words coalesce, when they are readily pronounced together ; have a long established association ; and are in frequent use ; as, " honeycomb, gingerbread, inkhorn, Yorkshire."

Sometimes the adjective becomes a substantive, and has another adjective joined to it : as, " The chief good ;" " The vast immense of space."

Some adjectives of number are more easily converted into substantives, than others. Thus we more readily say, " A million of men," than " a thousand of men." On the other hand, it will hardly be allowable to say, " A million men," whereas, " a thousand men," is quite familiar. Yet in the plural number, a different construction seems to be required. We say, " some hundreds," or " thousands," as well as "millions of men." Perhaps, on this account the words *millions*, *hundreds*, and *thousands*, will be said to be substantives.

When an adjective has a preposition before it, and the substantive is understood, the words assume the nature of an adverb, and may be considered as an adverbial phrase ; as, " In general, in particular, in common," &c. ; that is, " Generally, particularly, commonly."

Enow was formly used as the plural of *enough* : but it is now obsolete.

Now correct and parse the following

EXERCISES IN FALSE SYNTAX.

1. She reads proper, writes very neat, and composes accurate.

He was extreme prodigal, and his property is now near exhausted.

They generally succeeded ; for they lived comformable to the rules of prudence.

We may reason very clear, and exceeding strong, without knowing that there is such a thing as a syllogism.

He had many virtues, and was exceeding beloved.

The amputation was exceeding well performed, and saved the patient's life.

He came agreeable to his promise, and conducted himself suitable to the occasion.

He speaks very fluent, reads excellent, but does not think very coherent.

He behaved himself submissive, and was exceeding careful not to give offence.

They rejected the advice and conducted themselves exceedingly indiscreetly.

He is a person of great abilities, and exceeding upright : and is like to be a very useful member of the community.

The conspiracy was the easier discovered, from its being known to many.

Not being fully acquainted with the subject, he could affirm no stronger than he did.

He was so deeply impressed with the subject, that few could speak nobler upon it.

We may credit his testimony, for he says express, that he saw the transaction.

Use a little wine for thy stomach's sake, and thine often infirmities.

From these favorable beginnings, we may hope for a soon and prosperous issue.

He addressed several exhortations to them suitably to their circumstances.

Conformably to their vehemence of thought, was their vehemence of gesture.

We should implant in the minds of youth, such seeds and principles of piety and virtue, as are likely to take the soonest and deepest root.

Such an amiable disposition will secure universal regard.

Such distinguished virtues seldom occur.

2. 'Tis more easier to build two chimneys than to maintain one.

The tongue is like a race-horse ; which runs the faster the lesser weight it carries.

The pleasures of the understanding are more preferable than those of the imagination, or of sense.

The nightingale sings : hers is the most sweetest voice in the grove.

The Most Highest hath created us for his glory, and our own happiness.

The Supreme Being is the most wisest, and most powerfullest and the most best of beings.

3. Virtue confers the supremest dignity on man ; and should be his chiefest desire.

His assertion was more true than that of his opponent ; nay, the words of the latter were most untrue.

His work is perfect ; his brother's more perfect ; and his father's the most perfect of all.

He gave the fullest and the most sincere proof of the truest friendship.

3. A talent of this kind would, perhaps, prove the likeliest of any other to succeed.

He is the strongest of the two, but not the wisest.

He spoke with so much propriety, that I understood him the best of all others, who spoke on the subject.

Eve was the fairest of all her daughters.

4. He spoke in a distinct enough manner to be heard by the whole assembly.

Thomas is equipped with a new pair of shoes, and a new pair of gloves ; he is the servant of an old rich man.

The two first in the row are cherry trees, the two others are pear trees.

SECTION VI.

RULE VI.

The participle ending in ing, *when not connected with the auxiliary verb* TO BE, *refers to some noun or pronoun, denoting the subject or actor.*

In Conversation VII. I made all the remarks on this rule, that can be of any benefit to you in parsing or writing the participle in this connexion.

RULE VII.

Participles of TRANSITIVE *verbs govern the objective case.*

1. The present participle, with the definite article *the* before it, becomes a substantive, and must have the preposition *of* after it: as, "These are the rules of, grammar, by the observing of which, you may avoid mistakes." It would not be proper to say, "by the observing which;" nor, "by observing of which;" but the phrase, without either article or preposition, would be right; as, "by observing which." The article *a* or *an*, has the same effect: as, "This was a betraying of the trust reposed in him."

This rule arises from the nature and idiom of our language, and from as plain a principle as any on which it is founded; namely, that a word which has the article before it, and the possessive preposition *of* after it, must be a noun: and, if a noun, it ought to follow the construction of a noun, and not to have the regimen of a verb. It is the participial termination of this sort of words that is apt to deceive us, and make us treat them as if they were of an amphibious species, partly nouns and partly verbs.

The following are a few examples of the violation of this rule. "He was sent to prepare the way by preaching of repentance;" it ought to be, "by *the* preaching of repentance;" or, "by preaching repentance." "By the continual mortifying our corrupt affections," it should be, "by the continual mortifying *of*," or, "by continually mortifying our corrupt affections." "They laid out themselves towards *the* advancing and promoting the good of it;" "towards advancing and promoting the good." "It is *an* overvaluing ourselves, to reduce every thing to the narrow measure of our capacities;" "it is overvaluing ourselves," or, "*an* overvaluing *of* ourselves." "Keeping of one day in seven," &c. it ought to be, "*the* keeping *of* one day;" or, "keeping one day."

A phrase in which the article precedes the present participle, and the possessive preposition follows it, will not, in every instance, convey the same meaning, as would be conveyed by the participle without the article and preposition. "He expressed the pleasure he had in the hearing of the philosopher," is capable of a different sense from, "He expressed the pleasure he had in hearing the philosopher." When, therefore, we wish, for the sake of harmony or variety, to substitute one of these phraseologies for the other, we should previously consider, whether they are perfectly similar in the sentiments they convey.

2. The same observations, which have been made respecting the effect of the article and participle, appear to be applicable to the pronoun and participle, when they are similarly associated: as, "Much depends on *their observing of* the rule, and error will be the consequence of *their neglecting of* it," instead of "*their observing* the rule and *their neglecting* it." We shall perceive this more clearly, if we substitute a noun for the pronoun: as, "Much depends upon *Tyro's observing of* the rule," &c.; which is the same as, "Much depends on Tyro's observance of the rule." But, as this construction sounds rather harshly, it would, in general, be better to express the sentiment in the following, or some other form: "Much depends on the *rule's being observed*; an error will be the consequence of *its being neglected*:" or—"on observing the rule; and—of neglecting it." This remark may be applied to several other modes of expression, which, though they are contended for as strictly correct, are not always the most eligible, on account of their unpleasant sound.

We sometimes meet with expressions like the following: "*In forming of* his sentences, he was very exact;" "*From calling of* names, he proceeded to blows." But this is incorrect language; for prepositions do not, like articles and pronouns, convert the participle itself into the nature of a substantive; as we have shown above in the phrase, "By observing which." And yet the participle with its adjuncts, may be considered as a substantive phrase in the objective case, governed by the preposition or verb, expressed or understood: as, "By *promising much, and performing but little,* we become despicable." "He studied to avoid *expressing himself too severely.*"

3. As the perfect participle and the imperfect tense, are sometimes different in their form, care must be taken that they be not indiscriminately used. It is frequently said, "He begun," for "he began:" "He run," for "he ran;" "He drunk," for "he drank;" the participle being here used instead of the imperfect tense: and much more frequently the imperfect tense instead of the participle: as, "I had wrote," for "I had written;" "I was chose," for "I was chosen;" "I have eat," for "I have eaten." "His words were interwove with sighs;" "were *interwoven.*" "He would have spoke;" "*spoken.*" "He hath bore witness to his faithful servant;" "*borne.*" "By this means he over-run his guide;" "*over-ran.*" "The sun has rose;" "*risen.*" "His constitution has been greatly shook, but his mind is too strong to be shook by such causes;" "*shaken,*" in both places. "They were verses wrote on glass:" "*written.*" "Philosophers have often mistook the source of true happiness:" it ought to be "*mistaken.*"

19

The participle ending in *ed*, is often improperly contracted, by changing *ed* into *t*: as, "In good behaviour, he is not *surpast* by any pupil of the school." "She was much distrest." They ought to be, "*surpassed*," "*distressed*."

When a substantive is put absolutely, and is not the subject of any following verb, it remains connected with the participle, and is called the *case absolute*, or the *nominative absolute*: as, "The *painter being* entirely *confined* to that part of time he has chosen, the picture comprises but very few incidents." Here, the *painter* is the subject of no verb, as the verb *comprises*, which follows, agrees with *picture*. But when the substantive preceding the participle is the subject of the subsequent verb, it loses its absoluteness, and is like every other nominative: as, "The *painter*, *being* entirely *confined* to that part of time which he has chosen, *cannot exhibit* various stages of the same action." In this sentence we see that *the painter* is the nominative to the verb *can exhibit*. In the following sentence, a still different construction takes place; "The painter's *being entirely confined to that part of time which he has chosen*, deprives him of the power of exhibiting various stages of the same action." In this sentence, if we inquire for the nominative case, by asking, what deprives the painter of the power of exhibiting various stages of the same action, we shall find it to be the words marked in italics; and this *state* of things belonging to the painter governs it in the possessive case, and forms the compound nominative to the verb *deprives*.

In the sentence, "What do you think of my horse's running to-day?" it is implied that the horse did actually run. If it is said, "What think you of my horse running to-day?" it is intended to ask, whether it be proper for my horse to run to-day. This distinction, though frequently disregarded, deserves attention; for it is obvious, that ambiguity may arise, from using the latter only of these phraseologies, to express both meanings.

The active participle is frequently introduced without an obvious reference to any noun or pronoun: as, "Generally *speaking*, his conduct was very honorable:" "*Granting* this to be true, what is to be inferred from it?" "It is scarcely possible to act otherwise, *considering* the frailty of human nature." In these sentences, there is no noun expressed or implied, to which *speaking*, *granting*, and *considering*, can be referred. The most natural construction seems to be, that a pronoun is to be understood: as, "*We* considering the frailty of human nature," &c.; "*I* granting this to be true," &c.

The word *the*, before the active participle, in the following sentences, and in all others of a similar construction, is improper, and should be omitted: "This style may be more properly called *the* talking upon paper than writing:" "*The advising*, or *the* attempting, to excite such disturbances, is unlawful :" " *The* taking from another what is his, without his knowledge or allowance, is called stealing." They should be ; " May be called talking upon paper ;" " Advising or attempting to excite disturbances ;" " Taking from another what is his," &c.

In some of these sentences, the infinitive mood might very properly be adopted : as, " To advise or attempt ;" " To take from another," &c.

You can now proceed to correct and parse the following

EXERCISES IN FALSE SYNTAX.

Esteeming theirselves wise, they became fools.

Suspecting not only ye, but they also, I was studious to avoid all intercourse.

I could not avoid considering, in some degree, they as enemies to me ; and he as a suspicious friend.

From having exposed hisself too freely in different climates, he entirely lost his health.

The examples which follow, are suited to the notes and observations under RULE VII.

1. By observing of truth, you will command esteem, as well as secure peace.

He prepared them for this event, by the sending to them proper information.

A person may be great or rich by chance ; but cannot be wise or good, without the taking pains for it.

Nothing could have made her so unhappy, as the marrying a man who possessed such principles.

The changing times and seasons, the removing and setting up of kings, belong to Providence alone.

The middle station of life seems to be the most advantageously situated for gaining of wisdom. Poverty turns our thoughts too much upon the supplying our wants ; and riches upon the enjoying our superfluities.

Pliny, speaking of Cato the Censor's disapproving the Grecian orators, expressed himself thus.

Propriety of pronunciation is the giving to every word that sound, which the most polite usage of the language appropriates to it.

The not attending to this rule, is the cause of a very common error.

This was in fact a converting the deposite to his own se.

2. There will be no danger of their spoiling their faces, or of their gaining converts.

For his avoiding that precipice, he is indebted to his friend's care.

It was from our misunderstanding the directions, that we lost our way.

n trncing of his history, we discover little that is worthy of imitation.

By reading of books written by the best authors, his mind became highly improved.

3. By too eager pursuit, he run a great risk of being disappointed.

He had not long enjoyed repose, before he begun to be weary of having nothing to do.

He was greatly heated, and drunk with avidity.

Though his conduct was, in some respects, exceptionable, yet he dared not to commit so great an offence, as that which was proposed to him.

A second deluge learning thus o'er-run :
And the monks finish'd what the Goths begun.

If some events had fell out very unexpectedly, I should have been present.

He would have went with us, had he been invited.

He returned the goods which he had stole, and made all the reparation in his power.

They have chose the part of honor and virtue.

His vices have weakened his mind, and broke his health.

He had mistook his true interest, and found himself forsook by his former adherents.

The bread that has been eat is soon forgot.

No contentions have arose amongst them since their reconciliation.

The cloth had no seam, but was wove throughout.

The French language is spoke in every state in Europe.

His resolution was too strong to be shook by slight opposition.

He was not much restrained afterwards, having took improper liberties at first.

He has not yet wore off the rough manners, which he brought with him.

You who have forsook your friends, are entitled to no confidence.

They who have bore a part in the labour, shall share the rewards.

When the rules have been wantonly broke, there can be no plea for favour.

He writes as the best authors would have wrote, had they writ on the same subject.

He heapt up great riches, but past his time miserably.

He talkt and stampt with such vehemence, that he was suspected to be insane.

SECTION VII.

RULE VIII.

Adverbs qualify verbs, adjectives, participles, and other adverbs.

Adverbs, though they have no government of case, tense, &c. require an appropriate situation in the sentence, viz. for the most part, before adjectives, after verbs active or neuter, and frequently between the auxiliary and the verb : as, "He made a *very sensible* discourse ; he *spoke unaffectedly* and *forcibly ; and was attentively heard* by the whole assembly."

A few instances of erroneous positions of adverbs may serve to illustrate the rule. "He must not expect to find study agreeable always ;" "*always* agreeable." "We always find them ready when we want them ;" "we find them *always* ready," &c. "Dissertations on the prophecies which have remarkably been fulfilled ;" "which have been *remarkably*." "Instead of looking contemptuously down on the crooked in mind or body, we should look up thankfully to God, who hath made us better :" "instead of looking down *contemptuously*, &c. we should *thankfully look up*," &c. "If thou art blessed naturally with a good memory, continually exercise it;" "*naturally blessed*," &c. "exercise it *continually*."

Sometimes the adverb is placed with propriety before the verb, or at some distance after it ; sometimes between the two auxiliaries ; and sometimes after them both : as in the following examples. "Vice *always* creeps by degrees, and *insensibly* twines around us those concealed fetters, by which we are at last *completely* bound." "He encouraged the English Barons to carry their opposition *farther*." "They compelled him to declare that he would abjure the realm *for ever* ;" instead of, "to carry further their opposition ;" and "to abjure for ever the realm." "He has *generally* been reckoned an honest man :" "The book may *always* be had at such a place ;" in preference to "has been generally :" and "may be always." "These rules will be *clearly* understood, after they have been *diligently* studied," are preferable to, "These rules will *clearly* be understood, after they have *diligently* been studied."

When adverbs are emphatical, they may introduce a sentence, and be separated from the word to which they belong : as, "*How completely* this most amiable of human virtues, *had taken possession* of his soul !" This position of the adverb is most frequent in interrogative and exclamatory phrases.

From the preceding remarks and examples, it appears that no exact and determinate rule can be given for the placing of adverbs, on all occasions. The general rule may be of considerable use: but the easy flow and perspicuity of the phrase, are the things which ought to be chiefly regarded.

The adverb *there* is often used as an expletive, or as a word that adds nothing to the sense: in which case it precedes the verb and nominative noun: as, "There is a person at the door;" "There are some thieves in the house:" which would be as well, or better, expressed by saying, "A person is at the door;" "Some thieves are in the house." Sometimes, it is made use of to give a small degree of emphasis to the sentence: as, "*There* was a man sent from God, whose name was John." When it is applied in its strict sense, it principally follows the verb and the nominative case; as, "The man stands *there*."

1. The adverb *never* generally precedes the verb; as, "I never was there:" "He never comes at a proper time." When an auxiliary is used, it is placed indifferently, either before or after this adverb: as, "He was never seen (or never was seen) to laugh from that time." *Never* seems to be improperly used in the following passages. "Ask me never so much dowry and gift." "If I make my hands never so clean." "Charm he never so wisely." The word "*ever*" would be more suitable to the sense.—*Ever* is sometimes improperly used for *never*, as, "I seldom or ever see him now." It should be, "I seldom or *never*;" the speaker intending to say, "that rarely, or rather at no time, does he see him now;" not "rarely," or, "at any time."

2. In imitation of the French idiom, the adverb of place *where*, is often used instead of the pronoun relative and a preposition. "They framed a protestation, *where*, they repeated all their former claims," i. e. "*in which* they repeated." "The king was still determined to run forwards, in the same course *where* he was already, by his precipitate career, too fatally advanced;" i. e. "*in which* he was." But it would be better to avoid this mode of expression.

The adverbs *hence*, *thence*, and *whence*, imply a preposition; for they signify, "from this place, from that place, from what place." It seems, therefore, strictly speaking, to be improper to join a preposition with them, because it is superfluous: as, "This is the leviathan, from whence the wits of our age are said to borrow their weapons;" "an ancient author prophecies from hence." But the origin of these words is little attended to, and the preposition *from* is so often used in construction with them, that the omission of it, in many cases, would seem stiff, and be disagreeable.

The adverbs *here*, *there*, *where*, are often improperly applied to verbs signifying motion, instead of the adverbs *hither*, *thither*, *whether*: as, "He came *here* hastily;" "They rode *there* with speed." They should be, "He came *hither*:" "They rode *thither*," &c.

3. We have some examples of adverbs being used for substantives: "In 1687, he erected it into a community of regulars, since *when*, it has begun to increase in those countries as a religious order ;" i. e. "since *which time*." "A little while and I shall not see you ;" i. e. "a *short time*." "It is worth their while ;" i. e. "it deserves their time and pains." But this mode of expression rather suits familiar than grave style. The same may be said of the phrase, "To do a thing *anyhow* ;" i. e. "in any manner ;" or, "*somehow* ;" i. e. "in some manner." "Somehow, worthy as these people are, they are under the influence of prejudice."

Such expressions as the following, though not destitute of authority, are very inelegant, and do not suit the idiom of our language ;" "The *then* ministry," for, "the ministers of that time ;" "The above discourse," for, "the preceding discourse."

4. Two negatives, in English, destroy one another, or are equivalent to an affirmative : as, "*Nor* did they *not* perceive him ;" that is, "they did perceive him." "His language though inelegant, is *not ungrammatical*," that is, "It is grammatical."

It is better to express an affirmation, by a regular affirmative, than by two separate negatives, as in the former sentence : but when one of the negatives is joined to another word, as in the latter sentence, the two negatives form a pleasing and delicate variety of expression.

Some writers have improperly employed two negatives instead of one : as in the following instances : "I never did repent of doing good, nor shall not now ;" "*nor shall I now*." "Never no imitator grew up to this author :" "*never did any*," &c. "I cannot by no means allow him what his argument must prove ;" "I cannot by *any* means," &c. or, "*I can by no means*." "Nor let no comforter approach me :" "Nor let *any* comforter, &c. "Nor is danger ever apprehended in such a government, no more than we commonly apprehend danger from thunder or earthquakes :" it should be, "*any more*." "Ariosto, Tasso, Galileo, *no more* than Raphael, were *not* born in Republics." It would be better thus, "Neither Ariosto, Tasso, nor Galileo, any more than Raphael, was born in a republic."

Now correct and parse the following

EXERCISES IN FALSE SYNTAX.

He was pleasing not often, because he was vain.

William nobly acted, though he was unsuccessful.

We may happily live, though our possessions are small.

From whence we may date likewise the period of this event.

It cannot be impertinent or ridiculous therefore to remonstrate.

He offered an apology, which being not admitted, he became submissive.

These things should be never separated.

Unless he have more government of himself, he will be always discontented.

Never sovereign was so much beloved by the people.

He was determined to invite back the king, and to call together his friends.

So well educated a boy gives great hopes to his friends.

Not only he found her employed, but pleased and tranquil also.

We always should prefer our duty to our pleasure.

It is impossible continually to be at work.

The heavenly bodies are in motion perpetually.

Having not known, or having not considered, the measures proposed, he failed of success.

My opinion was given on rather a cursory perusal of the book.

It is too common with mankind, to be engrossed, and overcome totally, by present events.

When the Romans were pressed with a foreign enemy, the women contributed all their rings and jewels voluntarily, to assist the government.

The following sentences exemplify the notes and observations under RULE VIII.

1. They could not persuade him though they were never so eloquent.

If some persons' opportunities were never so favorable, they would be too indolent to improve them.

2. He drew up a petition, where he too freely represented his own merits.

His follies had reduced him to a situation where he had much to fear, and nothing to hope.

It is reported that the prince will come here to-morrow.

George is active ; he walked there in less than an hour.

Where are you all going in such haste ?

Whither have they been since they left the city ?

3. Charles left the seminary too early, since when he has made very little improvement.

Nothing is better worth the while of young persons, than the acquisition of knowledge and virtue.

4. Neither riches nor honors, nor no such perishing goods, can satisfy the desires of an immortal spirit.

Be honest, nor take no shape nor semblance of disguise.

We need not, nor do not confine his operations to narrow limits.

I am resolved not to comply with the proposal, neither at present, nor at any other time.

There cannot be nothing more insignificant than vanity.

Nothing never affected her so much as this misconduct of her child.

Do not interrupt me yourselves, not let no one disturb my retirement.

These people do not judge wisely, nor take no proper measures to effect their purpose.

The measure is so exceptionable, that we cannot by no means permit it.

I have received no information on the subject, neither from him nor from his friend.

Precept nor discipline is not so forcible as example.

The king nor the queen was not at all deceived in the business.

SECTION VIII.

RULE IX.

Pronouns must agree with the nouns for which they stand in number and gender; as,

"The king and the queen had put on *their* robes;" "The moon appears, and *she* shines, but the light is not *her* own."

Of this rule there are many violations to be met with; a few of which may be sufficient to put the learner on his guard. "*Each* of the sexes should keep within *its* particular bounds, and content *themselves* with the advantages of *their* particular districts:" better thus: "The sexes should keep within *their* particular bounds," &c. "Can any *one*, on *their* entrance into the world, be fully secure that *they* shall not be deceived?" "on *his* entrance," and "that *he* shall." "*One* should not think too favorably of *ourselves;*" "of *one's self.*"

1. Personal pronouns being used to supply the place of the nouns, are not employed in the same part of a sentence as the noun which they represent; for it would be improper to say, "The king *he* is just;" "I saw *her* the queen;" "The men *they* were there;" "Many words *they* darken speech;" "My banks *they* are furnished with bees." These personals are superfluous, as there is very seldom any occasion for a substitute in the same part where the principal word is present. The nominative case *they*, in the following sentence, is also superfluous: "Who instead of going about doing good, *they* are perpetually intent upon doing mischief."

This rule is often infringed, by the case absolute's not being properly distinguished from certain forms of expression apparently similar to it. In this sentence, "The candidate being chosen, the people carried him in triumph," the word *candidate* is in the absolute case.   But in the following sentence, "The candidate, being chosen, was carried in triumph by the people," *candidate* is the nominative to the verb *was carried* ; and therefore it is not in the case absolute.   Many writers, however, apprehending the nominative in this latter sentence, as well as in the former, to be put absolutely, often insert another nominative to the verb, and say, "The candidate being chosen, *he* was carried in triumph by the people ;" "The general approving the plan, *he* put it in execution. The error in each of these two sentences, is, that there are two nominatives used, where one would have been sufficient, and consequently that *he* is redundant.

2. *It is* and *it was*, are often, after the manner of the French, used in a plural construction, and by some of our best writers : as, "*It is* either a few great men who decide for the whole, or *it is* the rabble that follow a seditious ringleader ;" "*It is* they that are the real authors, though the soldiers are the actors of the revolutions ;" "*It was* the heretics that first began to rail," &c. ; '*Tis these* that early taint the female mind."   This license in the construction of *it is* (if it be proper to admit it at all,) has, however, been certainly abused in the following sentence, which is thereby made a very awkward one.   "*It is* wonderful the very few accidents, which, in several years, happen from this practice."   The word *accidents* is not in apposition to *it* following the neuter verb *be ;* it is a nominative without a verb, without being the nominative independent, or absolute.   The sentence should be, " It is wonderful that so few accidents happen," &c.

3. The interjections *O ! Oh !* and *Ah !* require the objective case of a pronoun in the first person after them : as, "O me ! Oh me ! Ah me !" But the nominative case in the second person : as, "O thou persecutor !" "Oh ye hypocrites !" "O thou, who dwellest," &c. ; because the first person is governed by a preposition understood ; as, "Ah *for* me !" or, "*O what will become of* me !" &c. ; and the second person is in the nominative independent, there being a direct address.

The neuter pronoun, by an idiom peculiar to the English language, is frequently joined in explanatory sentences, with a noun or pronoun of the masculine or feminine gender : as, " It was I ;" " It was the man or woman that did it."

The neuter pronoun *it* is sometimes omitted and understood ; thus we say, " As appears, as follows ;" for "As it appears, as it follows ;" and " May be," for " It may be."

The neuter pronoun *it* is sometimes employed to express ;

1st, The subject of any discourse or inquiry : as, "*It* happened on a summer's day ;" " Who is *it* that calls on me ?"

2d, The state of condition of any person or thing : as, " How is *it* with you ?"

3d, The thing, whatever it be, that is the cause of any effect or event, or any person considered merely as a cause: as, "We heard her say *it was not he* ;" " The truth is, *it was I* that helped her."

You may now correct and parse the following

EXERCISES IN FALSE SYNTAX.

The male amongst birds seems to discover no beauty, but in the colour of its species.

Take handfuls of ashes of the furnace, and let Moses sprinkle it towards heaven, in the sight of Pharaoh ; and it shall become small dust.

Rebecca took goodly raiment, which were with her in the house, and put them upon Jacob.

The fair sex, whose task is not to mingle in the labours of public life, has its own part assigned it to act.

The Hercules man of war foundered at sea ; she over-set, and lost most of her men.

The mind of man cannot be long without some food to nourish the activity of his thoughts.

I do not think any one should incur censure for being tender of their reputation.

The following examples are adapted to the notes and observations under RULE IX.

1. Whoever entertains such an opinion, he judges erroneously.

The cares of this world they often choke the growth of virtue.

Disappointments and afflictions, however disagreeable, they often improve us.

2. It is remarkable his continual endeavours to serve us, notwithstanding our ingratitude.

It is indisputably true his assertion, though it is a paradox.

3. Ah! unhappy thee, who art deaf to the calls of duty, and of honour.

Oh! happy we, surrounded with so many blessings.

SECTION IX.

[RULE X.

Every adjective pronoun belongs to some noun or pronoun expressed or understood.

The adjective pronouns this *and* that *and their plurals* these *and* those, *and* other *and* another, *and the* numeral adjectives, *must* agree *in* number *with the nouns to which they belong.*

A few instances of the breach of the latter part of this rule are here exhibited. " I have not travelled this twenty years ;" *" thece* twenty." " I am not recommending these kind of sufferings ;" *" this* kind." " Those set of books was a valuable present ;" *" that set."*

1. The word *means* in the singular number, and the phrases, " *By this means,*" " *By that means,*" are used by our best and most correct writers ; namely, Bacon, Tillotson, Atterbury, Addison, Steele, Pope, &c.* They are, indeed, in so general and approved use, that it would appear awkward, if not affected, to apply the old singular form, and say, " By this *mean ;* by that *mean ;* it was by a *mean ;*" although it is more agreeable to the general analogy of the language. " The word *means,* (says Priestley,) belongs to the class of words, which do not change their termination on account of number ; for it is used alike in both numbers."

The word *amends* is used in this manner in the following sentences ; " Though he did not succeed, he gained the ap-

---

* " *By this means* he had had them the more at vantage, being tired and harrassed with a long march."—BACON.

" *By this means* one great restraint from doing evil would be taken away."—" And *this* is *an* admirable *means* to improve men in virtue."—" *By that means* they have rendered their duty more difficult."—TILLOTSON.

" It renders us careless of approving ourselves to God, and by *that means* securing the continuance of his goodness.—" A good character, when established, should not be rested in as an end, but employed as *a means* of doing still further good."—ATTERBURY.

" *By this means* they are happy in each other."—" He by *that means* preserves his superiority."—ADDISON.

" Your vanity *by this means* will want its food."—STEELE.

" *By this means* alone, their greatest obstacles will vanish."—POPE.

" Which *custom* has proved the most effectual *means* to ruin the nobles."—DEAN SWIFT.

" There *is* no *means* of escaping the persecution."—" Faith is not only a *means* of obeying, but a principal act of obedience."—Dr. YOUNG.

" He looked on money as *a* necessary *means* of maintaining and increasing power."—Lord LITTLETON's HENRY II.

" John was too much intimidated not to embrace *every means* afforded for his safety."—GOLDSMITH.

" Lest *this means* should fail."—" By *means* of *ship-money* the late king," &c.—" The *only means* of securing a durable peace."—HUME.

" *By this means* there was nothing left to the Parliament of Ireland," &c.—BLACKSTONE.

" *By this means* so many slaves escaped out of the hands of their masters."—Dr. ROBERTSON.

" *By this means* they bear witness to each other."—BURKE.

" *By this means* the wrath of man was made to turn against itself."—Dr. BLAIR.

" A magazine, which has by *this means,* contained," &c.—" Birds, in general procure their food by *means* of their *beak.*"—Dr. PALEY.

probation of his country; and with *this amends* he was content." "Peace of mind is *an* honorable *amends* for the sacrifices of interest." "In return he received the thanks of his employers, and the present of a large estate; *these* were ample *amends* for his labors." "We have described the rewards of vice: the good man's *amends are* of a different nature."

It can scarcely be doubted, that this word *amends* (like the word *means*) had formerly its correspondent form in the singular number, as it is derived from the French *amende*, though now it is exclusively established in the plural form. If, therefore, it is alleged, that *mean* should be applied in the singular, because it is derived from the French *moyen*, the same kind of argument may be advanced in favor of the singular *amende:* and the general analogy of the language may also be pleaded in support of it.

Campbell, in his "Philosophy of Rhetoric," has the following remark on the subject before us: "No persons of taste will, I presume, venture so far to violate the present usages, and consequently to shock the ears of the generality of readers, as to say, "By this *mean*, by that *mean*."

Lowth and Johnson seem to be against the use of *means* in the singular number. They do not, however, speak decisively on the point; but rather dubiously, and as if they knew that they were questioning eminent authorities, as well as general practice. That they were not decidedly against the application of this word to the singular number, appears from their own language: "Whole sentences, whether simple or compound, may become members of other sentences, by *means* of some additional *connexion*."

"There is no other method of teaching that of which any one is ignorant, but by *means* of *something* already known." "Neither grace of person nor vigor of understanding, is to be regarded otherwise than as *a means* of happiness."

The practice of the best and most correct writers, or a great majority of them, corroborated by general usage, forms, during its continuance, the standard of language; especially, if, in particular instances, this practice continue, after objection and due consideration. Every connexion and application of words and phrases, thus supported, must therefore be proper, and entitled to respect, if not exceptionable in a moral point of view.

" Sermo constat ratione, vetustate, auctoritate, consuetudine.
" Consuetudo vero certissima loquendi magistra."
QUINCTILIAN.

.........................." Si volet usus
" Quem penes arbitrium est, et jus, et norma loquendi."
HORACE.

On this principle many forms of expression, not less deviating from the general analogy of the language, than those before mentioned, are to be considered as strictly proper and justifiable. Of this kind are the following : " *None* of them *are* varied to express the gender :" and yet *none* originally signified *no one.* " He *Himself* shall do the work :" here, what was first appropriated to the objective, is now properly used as the nominative case. " *You* have behaved yourselves well ;" in this example the word *you* is put in the nominative case plural, with strict propriety ; though formerly it was confined to the objective case, and *ye* exclusively used for the nominative.

With respect to anomalies and variations of language, thus established, it is the grammarian's business to submit, not to remonstrate. In pertinaciously opposing the decision of proper authority, and contending for obsolete modes of expression, he may, indeed, display learning and critical sagacity : and, in some degree, obscure points that are sufficiently clear and decided ; but he cannot reasonably hope, either to succeed in his aims, or to assist the learner, in discovering and respecting the true standard and principles of language.

Cases which custom has left dubious, are certainly within the grammarian's province. Here, he may reason and remonstrate on the ground of derivation, analogy, and propriety : and his reasonings may refine and improve the language : but when authority speaks out and decides the point, it were perpetually to unsettle the language, to admit of cavil and debate. Anomalies then, under the limitation mentioned, become the law, as clearly as the plainest analogies.

You will perceive that in the following sentences, the use of the word *mean*, in the old form, has a very uncouth appearance : " By the *mean* of adversity, we are often instructed." " He preserved his health, by *mean* of exercise." " Frugality is one *mean* of acquiring a competency." They should be, " By *means* of adversity," &c. " By *means* of exercise," &c. " Frugality is one *means*," &c.

Good writers do indeed make use of the substantive *mean* in the singular number, and in that number only, to signify mediocrity, middle state, &c. : as, " This is a *mean* between the two extremes." But in the sense of instrumentality, it has been long disused by the best authors, and by almost every writer.

This means and *that means* should be used only when they refer to what is singular ; *these means* and *those means*, when they respect plurals : as, " He lived temperately, and by *this means* preserved his health ;" "The scholars were attentive, industrious, and obedient to their tutors ; and by *these means* acquired knowledge."

2. When two persons or things are spoken of in a sentence, and there is occasion to mention them again for the sake of

distinction, *that* is used in reference to the former, and *this* in reference to the latter : as, " Self-love, which is the spring of action in the soul, is ruled by reason : but for *that*, man would be inactive ; and but for *this*, he would be active to no end."

3. The distributive adjective pronouns, *each, every, either,* agree with nouns, pronouns, and verbs, of the singular number only : as, " The king of Israel, and Jehoshaphat, the king of Judah, sat *each* on *his* throne ;" " *Every* tree *is* known by *its* fruit :" unless the plural noun convey a collective idea : as, " Every six months ;" " Every hundred years."—The following phrases are exceptionable: " Let *each* esteem others better than themselves ;" It ought to be "*himself.*" " It is requisite that the language should be both perspicuous and correct : in proportion as *either* of these two qualities are wanting. the language is imperfect :" it should be, " *is* wanting." " *Every* one of the letters bear regular dates, and contain proofs of attachment :" " *bears a* regular *date*, and *contains.*" " *Every* town and village were burned ; *every* grove and *every* tree were cut down :" " *was* burned. and *was* cut down." " *Every* freeman, and *every* citizen, have a right to give their votes :" " *has* a right to give *his vote.*"

Either is often used improperly, instead of *each :* as, "The king of Israel, and Jehoshaphat the king of Judah, sat *either* of them on his throne ;" " Nadab and Abihu, the sons of Aaron, took *either* of them his censer." *Each* signifies both of them taken distinctly or separately ; *either* properly signifies only the one or the other of them, taken disjunctively.

4. Many persons are apt, in conversation, to use the *personal* pronoun *them*, instead of the *adjective* pronouns *these* and *those :* as, " Give me *them* books," instead of " *those books.*" We also frequently meet with *those* instead of *they*, at the beginning of a sentence, in which there is no particular reference to any preceding word : as, " *Those* that sow in tears, sometimes reap in joy." " *They* that, or *they* who sow," &c. is better.

I will now give you to parse and correct, the following

EXERCISES IN FALSE SYNTAX.

These kind of indulgences soften and injure the mind.

Instead of improving yourselves, you have been playing this two hours.

Those sort of favors did real injury, under the appearance of kindness.

The chasm made by the earthquake was twenty foot broad and one hundred fathom in depth.

How many a sorrow should we avoid, if we were not industrious to make them !

He saw one or more persons enter the garden.

The examples which follow, are suited to the notes and observations under RULE X.

1. Charles was extravagant, and by this mean became poor and despicable.

It was by that ungenerous mean that he obtained his end.

Industry is the mean of obtaining competency.

Though a promising measure, it is a mean which I cannot adopt.

This person embraced every opportunity to display his talents; and by these means rendered himself ridiculous.

Joseph was industrious, frugal, and discreet; and by this means obtained property and reputation.

2. Religion raises men above themselves; irreligion sinks them beneath the brutes: that, binds them down to a poor pitiable speck of perishable earth; this, opens for them a prospect to the skies.

More rain falls in the first two summer months, than in the first two winter ones; but it makes a much greater show upon the earth, in those than in these; because there is a much slower evaporation.

Rex and Tyrannus are of very different characters. The one rules his people by laws to which they consent; the other, by his absolute will and power; this is called freedom, that, tyranny.

3. Each of them, in their turn, receive the benefits to which they are entitled.

My counsel to each of you is, that you should make it your endeavor to come to a friendly agreement.

By discussing what relates to each particular, in their order, we shall better understand the subject.

Every person, whatever be their station, are bound by the duties of morality and religion.

Every leaf, every twig, every drop of water, teem with life.

Every man's heart and temper is productive of much inward joy or bitterness.

Whatever he undertakes, either his pride or his folly disgust us.

Every man and every woman were numbered.

Neither of those men seem to have any idea, that their opinions may be ill-founded.

When benignity and gentleness reign within, we are always least in hazard from without: every person, and every occurrence, are beheld in the most favorable light.

On either side of the river was there the tree of life.

4. Which of them two persons has most distinguished himself?

None more impatiently suffer injuries, than those that are most forward in doing them.

SECTION X.

RULE XI.

Relative pronouns agree with their antecedents in person, number, and gender.

The relative being of the same person that the antecedent is, requires the verb which agrees with it, to be of the same person that it would be to agree with the antecedent: as, "Thou *who lovest* wisdom, walkest uprightly;" "He *who loves* wisdom, walks uprightly;" "I *who love*," &c.

Every relative must have an antecedent to which it refers, either expressed or implied: as, "Who is fatal to others, is so to himself;" that is, "*the man who* is fatal to others."

Who, which, what, and the relative *that,* though in the objective case, are always placed before the verb; as are also their compounds, *whoever, whosoever,* &c.: as, "He whom ye seek;" "This is what you want;" i. e. "*that which* you want, or the thing which, or that which you want;" "Whomsoever you please to appoint."

What is sometimes applied, in a manner which appears to be exceptionable: as, "All fevers, except what are called nervous," &c. It would at least be better to say, "except *those which* are called nervous."

What is very frequently used as the representative of two cases; one the objective after a verb or preposition, and the other, the nominative to a subsequent verb: as, "I heard *what* was said." "He related *what* was seen." "According to *what* was proposed." "We do not constantly love *what* has done us good."—This peculiar construction may be explained, by resolving *what* into *that which:* as, "I heard *that which* was said." &c.

In a few instances, the relative is introduced as the nominative to a verb, *before* the sentence or clause which it represents: as, "There was therefore, *which* is all that we assert, a course of life pursued by them, different from that which they before led." Here, the relative *which* is the representative of the whole of the last part of the sentence; and its natural position is *after* that clause.

Whatever relative is used, in one of a series of clauses relating to the same antecedent, the same relative ought generally to be used in them all. In the following sentence, this rule is violated: "It is remarkable, that Holland, against *which* the war was undertaken, and *that,* in the very beginning, was reduced to the brink of destruction, lost nothing." The clause ought to have been, "and *which* in the very beginning."

20*

The relative frequently refers to a whole clause in the sentence, instead of a particular word in it: as, "The resolution was adopted hastily, and without due consideration, which produced great dissatisfaction;" that is, "which thing," namely, the hasty adoption of the resolution.

1. The pronoun *that* is frequently applied to persons as well as to things; but after an adjective in the superlative degree, and after the pronominal adjective *same*, it is generally used in preference to *who* or *which*: as, "Charles XII. king of Sweden, was one of the greatest madmen *that* the world ever saw;" "Cataline's followers were the most profligate *that* could be found in any city." "He is the same man *that* we saw before." But if, after the word *same*, a preposition should precede the relative, one of the other two pronouns must be employed, the pronoun *that* not admitting a preposition prefixed to it: as, "He is the same man, *with whom* you were acquainted." It is remarkable, however, that, when the arrangement is a little varied, the word *that* admits the preposition: as, "He is the same man, *that* you were acquainted *with*."

There are cases wherein we cannot conveniently dispense with the relative *that*, as applied to persons: as, first, after *who* the interrogative: "Who *that* has any sense of religion, would have argued thus?" Secondly, when persons make but a part of the antecedent; "The woman, and the estate, *that* became his portion, were rewards far beyond his desert." In neither of these examples could any other relative have been used.

2. The pronouns *whichsoever*, *whosoever*, and the like, are elegantly divided by the interposition of the corresponding substantives: thus, "On whichsoever side the king cast his eyes:" would have sounded better, if written, "On which side soever," &c.

3. In some dialects, the word *what* is improperly used for *that*, and sometimes we find it in this sense in writing: "They will never believe but *what* I have been entirely to blame." "I am not satisfied but what," &c. instead of "but *that*." The word *somewhat*, in the following sentence, seems to be used improperly. "These punishments seem to have been exercised in somewhat an arbitrary manner." Sometimes we read, "In somewhat of." The meaning is, "in a manner which is in some respects arbitrary."

4. The pronoun relative *who* is so much appropriated to persons, that there is generally harshness in the application of it, except to the proper names of persons, or the general terms *man*, *woman*, &c. A term which only implies the idea of persons, and expresses them by some circumstance or epithet, will hardly authorize the use of it: as, "That faction in England, *who* most powerfully opposed his arbitrary pretensions." "That faction *which*," would have been bet-

ter ; and the same remark will serve for the following examples : "France, *who* was in alliance with Sweden." "The court, *who*, &c." "The cavalry, *who*," &c. "The cities *who* aspired at liberty." "That party among us *who*," &c. "The family *whom* they consider as usurpers."

In some cases it may be doubtful, whether this pronoun is properly applied or not : "The number of substantial inhabitants with *whom* some cities abound." For when a term directly and necessarily implies persons, it may in many cases claim the personal relative. "None of the company *whom* he most affected, could cure him of the melancholy under which he labored." The word *acquaintance* may have the same construction.

5. We hardly consider little children as persons, because that term gives us the idea of reason and reflection : and therefore the application of the personal relative *who*, in this case, seems to be harsh : "A child *who*." *It*, though neuter, is generally applied, when we speak of an infant or child : as, "*It* is a lovely infant :" "*It* is a healthy child." The personal pronoun is still more improperly applied to animals : "A lake frequented by that fowl, *whom* nature has taught to dip the wing in water."

6. When the name of a person is used merely as a name, and it does not refer to the person, the pronoun *who* ought not to be applied. "It is no wonder if such a man did not shine at the court of Queen Elizabeth, *who* was but another name for prudence and economy." Better thus : "Whose name was but another word for prudence," &c. The word *whose* begins likewise to be restricted to persons ; yet it is not done so generally, but that good writers, even in prose, use it when speaking of things. The construction is not, however, always pleasing, as we may see in the following instances : "Pleasure, *whose* nature," &c. "Call every production *whose* parts and *whose* nature," &c.

In one case, however, custom authorizes us to use *which* with respect to persons ; and that is when we want to distinguish one person of two, or a particular person among a number of others. We should then say, " *Which* of the two," or, " *Which* of them, is he or she ?"

7. As the pronoun relative has no distinction of number, we sometimes find an ambiguity in the use of it : as, when we say, "The disciples of Christ, *whom* we imitate ;" we may mean the imitation either of Christ, or of his disciples. The accuracy and clearness of the sentence, depend very much upon the proper and determinate use of the relative, so that it may readily present its antecedent to the mind of the hearer or reader, without any obscurity or ambiguity.

Now parse and correct the following

EXERCISES IN FALSE SYNTAX.

The exercise of reason appears as little in these sportsmen, as in the beasts whom they sometimes hunt, and by whom they are sometimes hunted.

They which seek wisdom will certainly find her.

The wheel killed another man, which is the sixth which have lost their lives, by this means.

What is the reason that our language is less refined than those of Italy, Spain, or France?

Thou who has been a witness to the fact, can give an account of it.

In religious concerns, or what is conceived to be such, every man must stand or fall by the decision of the Great Judge.

Something like what have been here premised, are the conjectures of Dryden.

> Thou great First Cause, least understood!
>   Who all my sense confin'd
> To know but this, that thou art good,
>   And that myself am blind:
> Yet gave me in this dark estate, &c.

What art thou, speak, that, on designs unknown,
While others sleep, thus range the camp alone?

The following examples are adapted to the notes and observations under RULE XI.

1. Moses was the meekest man whom we read of in the Old Testament.

Humility is one of the most amiable virtues which we can possess.

They are the same persons who assisted us yesterday.

The men and things which he has studied have not improved his morals.

2. Howsoever beautiful they appear, they have no real merit.

In whatsoever light we view him, his conduct will bear inspection.

On whichsoever side they are contemplated, they appear to advantage.

However much he might despise the maxims of the king's administration, he kept a total silence on that subject.

3. He would not be persuaded but what I was greatly in fault.

These commendations of his children, appear to have been made in somewhat an injudicious manner.

4. He instructed and fed the crowds who surrounded him.

Sidney was one of the wisest and most active governors, which Ireland have enjoyed for several years.

He was the ablest minister which James ever possessed.

The court who gives currency to manners, ought to be exemplary.

I am happy in the friend which I have long proved.

5. The child whom we have just seen, is wholesomely fed, and not injured by bandages or clothing.

He is like a beast of prey, who destroys without pity.

6. Having once disgusted him, he could never regain the favour of Nero, who was indeed another name for cruelty.

Flattery, whose nature is to deceive and betray, should be avoided as the poisonous adder.

Who of those men came to his assistance?

7. The king dismissed his minister without any inquiry; who had never before committed so unjust an action.

There are millions of people in the empire of China, whose support is derived almost entirely from rice.

SECTION XI.

RULE XII.

When no nominative comes between the relative and the verb, the relative is the nominative to the verb; but when a nominative does come between the relative and the verb, the relative must be in the possessive case, and governed by the following noun, or in the objective, and governed by the following verb, or by some participle or preposition, in its own member of the sentence: as, He who preserves me, to whom I owe my being, whose I am, and whom I serve, is eternal.

In the several members of the last sentence, the relative performs a different office. In the first member, it marks the agent; in the second, it submits to the government of the preposition; in the third, it represents the possessor; and in the fourth, the object of an action: and, therefore, it must be in the three different cases, correspondent to those offices.

When both the antecedent and the relative become nominatives, each to different verbs, the relative is the nominative to the former, and the antecedent to the latter verb: as, "*True Philosophy, which is* the ornament of our nature, *consists* more in the love of our duty, and the practice of virtue, than in great talents and extensive knowledge."

A few instances of erroneous construction will illustrate both the branches of the rule. The three following refer to the first part. "How can we avoid being grateful to those whom, by repeated kind offices, have proved themselves our real friends?" "These are the men whom you might suppose, were the authors of the work:" "If you were here, you would find three or four, whom you would say passed their time agreeably;" in all these places it should be *who* instead of *whom*. The two latter sentences contain a nominative between the relative and the verb; and, therefore, seem to contravene the rule: but you will reflect, that it is not the nominative of the verb with which the relative is connected. The remaining examples refer to the second part of the rule. "Men of fine talents are not always the persons who we should esteem." "The persons who you dispute with, are precisely of your opinion." "Our tutors are our benefactors, who we owe obedience to, and who we ought to love." In these sentences, *whom* should be used instead of *who*.

1. When the pronoun is of the interrogative kind, the noun or pronoun containing the answer, must be in the same case as that which contains the question: as, "*whose* books are these? They are *John's*." "*Who* gave them to him? *We*." "*Of whom* did you buy them? Of a bookseller; *him* who lives at the Bible and Crown." "*Whom* did you see there? Both *him* and the shopman." You will readily comprehend this rule, by supplying the words which are understood in the answers. Thus, to express the answers at large, we should say, "They are John's books." "We gave them to him." "We bought them of him who lives," &c. "We saw both him and the shopman."

Pronouns are sometimes made to precede the things which they represent: as, "If a man declares in autumn, when he is eating *them*, or in spring, when there are *none*, that he loves *grapes*," &c. But this is a construction which is very seldom allowable.

2. When the relative is preceded by two nominatives of different persons, the relative and verb may agree with either, according to the sense: as, *I* am the man *who command* you;" or, "I am the *man who commands* you."

The form of the first of the two preceding sentences, expresses the meaning rather obscurely. It would be more perspicuous to say; "I who command you, am the man." Perhaps the difference of meaning, produced by referring the relative to different antecedents, will be more evident to you in the following sentences. "I am the general who *gives* the orders to-day;" "I am the general who *give* the orders to-day;" that is, "I who give the orders to-day, am the general."

When the relative and the verb have been determined to agree with either of the preceding nominatives, that agreement must be preserved throughout the sentence; as in the following instance: "I am the Lord that *maketh* all things: and *stretcheth* forth the heavens alone."—*Isaiah*, xliv. 24. Thus far is consistent: The *Lord*, in the third person, is the antecedent, and the verbs agree with the relative in the third person: "I am *the Lord*, which Lord, or he that *maketh* all things." If *I* were made the antecedent, the relative and the verb should agree with it in the first person : as, "*I* am the Lord, *that make* all things, *that stretch* forth the heavens alone." But should it follow ; "*That spreadeth* abroad the earth by myself ;" there would arise a confusion of persons, and a manifest solecism.

Now correct and parse the following

EXERCISES IN FALSE SYNTAX.

We are dependent upon each other's assistance ! whom is there that can subsist by himself?

If he will not hear his best friend, whom shall be sent to admonish him ?

They who much is given to, will have much to answer for.

It is not to be expected that they, whom in early life, have been dark and deceitful, should afterwards become fair and ingenuous.

They who have laboured to make us wise and good, are the persons who we ought to love and respect, and who we ought to be grateful to.

The persons, who conscience and virtue support, may smile at the caprices of fortune.

From the character of those who you associate with, your own will be estimated.

That is the student who I gave the book to, and whom, I am persuaded, deserves it.

1. Of whom were the articles bought ? Of a mercer ; he who resides near the mansion house.

Was any person besides the mercer present ? Yes, both him and the clerk.

Who was the money paid to ? To the mercer and his clerk.

Who counted it ? Both the clerk and him.

2. I acknowledge that I am the teacher, who adopt that sentiment, and maintains the propriety of such measures.

Thou art a friend that hast often relieved me, and that has not deserted me now in the time of peculiar need.

I am the man who approves of wholesome discipline, and who recommend it to others ; but I am not a person who promotes useless severity, or who object to mild and generous treatment.

I perceive that thou art a pupil, who possessess bright parts, but who hast cultivated them but little.

Thou art he who breathest on the earth with the breath of spring, and who covereth it with verdure and beauty.

I am the Lord thy God, who teacheth thee to profit, and who lead thee by the way thou shouldst go.

Thou art the Lord who did choose Abraham, and broughtest him forth out of Ur of the Chaldees.

SECTION XII.

RULE XIII.

Prepositions govern the objective case.

The following are examples of the nominative case being used instead of the objective. "Who servest thou under?" "Who do you speak to?" "We are still much at a loss who civil power belongs to?" "Who do you ask for?" "Associate not with those who none can speak well of." In all these places it ought to be "*whom*."

The prepositions *to* and *for* are often understood, chiefly before the pronouns: as, "Give me the book;" "Get me some paper;" that is, "*to* me.;" "*for* me." "Wo is me;" i. e. "*to* me." "He was banished England;" i. e. "*from* England."

1. The preposition is often separated from the relative which it governs: as, "Whom will you give it to?" instead of, "To *whom* will you give it?" "He is an author whom I am much delighted with;" "The world is too polite to shock their authors with a truth, which generally their booksellers are the first that inform them of." This is an idiom to which our language is strongly inclined; it prevails in common conversation, and suits very well with the familiar style in writing: but the placing of the preposition before the relative is more graceful, as well as more perspicuous, and agrees much better with the solemn and elevated style.

2. Some writers separate the preposition from the noun or pronoun which it governs, in order to connect different prepositions with the same word: as, "To suppose the zodiac and planets to be efficient *of,* and antecedent *to* themselves." This construction, whether in the familiar or the solemn style, is always inelegant, and should generally be avoided. In forms of law, and the like, where fulness and exactness of expression must take place of every other consideration, it may be admitted.

3. Different relations, and different senses must be expressed by different prepositions, though in conjunction with the same verb or adjective. Thus we say, "to converse *with* a person, *upon* a subject, *in* a house," &c. We also say, "We are disappointed *of* a thing," when we cannot get it, "and disappointed *in* it," when we have it, and find it does not answer our expectations. But two different prepositions must be improper in the same construction, and in the same sentence; as, "The combat *between* thirty French, *against* twenty English."

In some cases it is difficult to say, to which of two prepositions the preference is to be given, as both are used promiscuously, and custom has not decided in favor of either of them. We say, "Expert at," and "expert in a thing." "Expert in finding a remedy for his mistakes;" "Expert in deception."

When prepositions are subjoined to nouns, they are generally the same that are subjoined to the verbs from which the nouns are derived : as, "A compliance *with*," "to comply *with* ;" "A disposition to tyranny," disposed *to* tyrannise."

Dr. Priestley observes, that many writers affect to subjoin to any word, the preposition with which it is compounded, or the idea of which, it implies ; in order to point out the relation of the words, in a more distinct and definite manner, and to avoid the more indeterminate prepositions *of* and *to :* but general practice, and the idiom of the English tongue, seem to oppose the innovation. Thus many writers say, " Averse *from* a thing ; " The abhorrence *against* all other sects." But other writers say, "Averse *to* it ;" which seems more truly English : " Averse *to* any advice." *Swift.* An attention to latent metaphor may be pleaded in favor of the former example : and this is a rule of general use, in directing what preposition to subjoin to a word. Thus we say, "devolve *upon* a thing ;" "founded *on* natural resemblance." But this rule would sometimes mislead us, particularly where the figure has become nearly evanescent.

" The words *averse* and *aversion* (says Dr. Campbell) are more properly construed with *to* than with *from*."

4. As an accurate and appropriate use of the preposition is of great importance, we shall select a considerable number of examples of impropriety, in the application of this part of speech.

First—With respect to the preposition OF.

" He is resolved of going to the Persian court ;" "*on* going," &c.

" He was totally dependent of the Papal crown ;" "*on* the Papal," &c.

" To call of a person," and "to wait of him ;" "*on* a person," &c.

" He was eager of recommending it to his fellow citizens ;" "*in* recommending," &c.

Of is sometimes omitted, and sometimes inserted, after *worthy :* as, "It is worthy observation," or, "of observation." But it would have been better omitted in the following sentences. " The emulation, who should serve their country best, no longer subsists among them, but *of* who should obtain the most lucrative command."

" The rain hath been falling *of* a long time ;" " falling a long time."

" It is situation chiefly which decides of the fortune and characters of men :" " decides the fortune," or, " *concerning* the fortune."

21

" He found the greatest difficulty of writing ;" "*in* writing ."

" It might have given me a greater taste of its antiquities." A taste *of* a thing implies actual enjoyment of it ; but a taste *for* it, implies only a capacity of enjoyment.

"This had a much greater share of inciting him, than any regard after his father's commands ;" " share *in* inciting," and " regard *to* his father's," &c.

Second—With respect to the prepositions TO and FOR.

" You have bestowed your favors to the most deserving persons ;" " *upon* the most deserving," &c.

" He accused the ministers for betraying the Dutch ;" " *of* having betrayed."

" His abhorrence to that superstitious figure ;" " *of* that," &c.

" A great change to the better ;" "*for* the better," &c.

" Your prejudice to my cause ;" " *against*."

" The English were very different people then to what they are at present ;" " *from* what," &c.

" In compliance to the declaration ;" " *with*," &c.

" It is more than they thought for ;" " thought *of*."

" There is no need for it ;" " *of* it."

For is superfluous in the phrase, " More than he knows *for*."

" No discouragement for the authors to proceed ;" "*to* the authors," &c.

" It was perfectly in compliance to some persons ;" " *with* some persons."

" The wisest princes need not think it any diminution to their greatness, or derogation to their sufficiency, to rely upon counsel ;" " diminution *of*," and " derogation *from*."

Third—With respect to the prepositions WITH and UPON.

" Reconciling himself with the king."

" Those things which have the greatest resemblance with each other, frequently differ the most."

" That such rejection should be consonant with our common nature." " Conformable with," &c.

" The history of Peter is agreeable with the sacred texts."

In all the above instances, it should be, " *to*," instead o " *with*."

" It is a use that perhaps I should not have thought on ;" " thought *of*."

" A greater quantity may be taken from the heap, without making any sensible alteration upon it ;" " *in* it."

" Intrusted to persons on whom the parliament could confide ;" " *in* whom."

" He was made much on at Argos ;" " much *of*."

" If policy can prevail upon force ;" " *over* force."

" I do likewise dissent with the examiner ;" " *from*."

Fourth—With respect to the prepositions IN, FROM, &c.

" They should be informed in some parts of his character ;" " *about*," or, " *concerning*."

" Upon such occasions as fell into their cognizance ;" "*under*."

" That variety of factions into which we are still engaged;" " *in* which."

" To restore myself into the favor ;" " *to* the favor."

"Could he have profited from repeated experiences;" "*by*." *From* seems to be superfluous after *forbear* : as, " He could not forbear from appointing the pope," &c.

"A strict observance after times and fashions ;" "*of* times." " The character which we may now value ourselves by drawing ;" " *upon* drawing."

" Neither of them shall make me swerve out of the path ;" "*from* the path."

" Ye blind guides, which strain *at* a gnat, and swallow a camel ;" it ought to be " which strain *out* a gnat, or, take a gnat out of the liquor by straining it." The impropriety of the preposition has wholly destroyed the meaning of the phrase.

The verb *to found*, when used literally, is more properly followed by the preposition *on* : as, " The house was *founded on* a rock." But in the metaphorical application, it is often better with *in* ; as in this sentence, "They maintained, that dominion is *founded in* grace." Both the sentences would be badly expressed, if these prepositions were transposed ; though there are perhaps cases in which either of them would be good.

The preposition *among* generally implies a number of things. It cannot be properly used in conjunction with the word *every*, which is in the singular number : as, " Which is found among every species of liberty ;" " The opinion seems to gain ground among every body ;" " *with*."

5. The preposition *to* is made use of before nouns of place, when they follow verbs and participles of motion : as, " I went *to* London ;" " I am going *to* town." But the preposition *at* is generally used after the neuter verb *to be* : as, " I have been *at* London ;" " I was *at* the place appointed ;" " I shall be *at* Paris." We likewise say : " He touched, arrived *at* any place." The preposition *in* is set before countries, cities, and large towns ; " He lives in France, in London, or in Birmingham." But before villages, single houses, and cities which are in distant countries, *at* is used : as, " He lives *at* Hackney ;" " He resides at Montpelier."

It is a matter of indifference with respect to the pronoun *one another*, whether the preposition *of* be placed between the

two parts of it, or before them both. We may say, " They
were jealous of one another ;" or, " They were jealous one of
another :" but perhaps the former is better.

Participles are frequently used as prepositions : as, excepting, respecting, touching, concerning. " They were all in
fault *except* or *excepting* him."

6. The adverb *like*, and the adjectives *worth* and *like*, when
they belong to preceding nouns or pronouns, govern the *objective* case.

Now correct and parse the following

EXERCISES IN FALSE SYNTAX.

We are all accountable creatures, each for hisself.

They willingly, and of theirselves endeavored to make up
the difference.

He laid the suspicion upon somebody, I know not who, in
the company.

I hope it is not I who he is displeased with.

To poor we there is not much hope remaining.

Does that boy know who he speaks to ? Who does he offer
such language to ?

It was not he that they were so angry with.

What concord can subsist between those who commit
crimes and those who abhor them ?

The person who I travelled with, has sold the horse which
he rode on during our journey.

It is not I he is engaged with.

Who did he receive that intelligence from ?

*The following examples are adapted to the notes and observa-
tions under* RULE XIII.

1. To have no one who we heartily wish well to, and who
we are warmly concerned for, is a deplorable state.

He is a friend who I am highly indebted to.

2. On these occasions, the pronoun is governed by, and
consequently agrees with the preceding word.

They were refused entrance into, and forcibly driven from,
the house.

3. We are often disappointed of things, which, before possession, promised much enjoyment.

I have frequently desired their company, but have always
hitherto been disappointed in that pleasure.

4. She finds a difficulty of fixing her mind.

Her sobriety is no derogation to her understanding.

There was no water, and he died for thirst.

We can fully confide on none but the truly good.

I have no occasion of his services.

Many have profited from good advice.

Many ridiculous practices have been brought in vogue.

The error was occasioned by compliance to earnest entreaty.

This is a principle in unison to our nature.

We should entertain no prejudices to simple and rustic persons.

They are at present resolved of doing their duty.

That boy is known under the name of the Idler.

Though conformable with custom, it is not warrantable.

This remark is founded in truth.

His parents think on him, and his improvements, with pleasure and hope.

His excuse was admitted of by his master.

What went ye out for to see?

There appears to have been a million men brought into the field.

His present was accepted of by his friends.

More than a thousand of men were destroyed.

It is my request that he will be particular in speaking to the following points.

The Saxons reduced the greater part of Britain to their own power.

He lives opposite the Royal Exchange.

Their house is situated to the north-east side of the road.

The performance was approved of by all who understood it.

He was accused with having acted unfairly.

She has an abhorrence to all deceitful conduct.

They were some distance from home, when the accident happened.

His deportment was adapted for conciliating regard.

My father writes me very frequently.

Their conduct was agreeable with their profession.

We went leisurely above stairs, and came hastily below.

We shall write up stairs this forenoon, and down stairs in the afternoon.

The politeness of the world has the same resemblance with benevolence, that the shadow has with the substance.

He had a taste of such studies, and pursued them earnestly.

When we have had a true taste for the pleasures of virtue, we can have no relish of those of vice.

How happy is it to know how to live at times by one's self, to leave one's self in regret, to find one's self again with pleasure! The world is then less necessary for us.

Civility makes its way among every kind of persons.

5. I have been to London, after having resided a year at France; and I now live in Islington.

They have just landed in Hull, and are going for Liverpool. They intend to reside some time at Ireland.

6. He writes like she does. . She walks like he does. You behave like they do. You do that just like I do.

21*

SECTION XIII.

RULE XIV.

Nouns and pronouns, connected by conjunctions, must be in the same cases.

RULE XIX.

Verbs, connected by conjunctions, must be in the same mood and tense, and, when in the subjunctive, they must be in the **SAME FORM.**[*]

I find it convenient to consider these two rules together ; and the exercises, which are to be corrected, I shall also give together.

"If thou sincerely *desire*, and earnestly *pursue* virtue, she *will* assuredly *be found* by thee, *and prove* a rich reward ;" "The master taught *her and me* to write ;" "*He and she* were school-fellows."

A few examples of inaccuracy respecting these two rules, may further display their utility. "If he prefer a virtuous life, and is sincere in his professions, he will succeed ;" "if he *prefers*." To deride the miseries of the unhappy, is inhuman ; and wanting compassion towards them, is unchristian ;" "and *to want* compassion." "The parliament addressed the king, and has been prorogued the same day ;" "and *was* prorogued." "His wealth and him bid adieu to each other ;" "and *he*." "He entreated us, my comrade and I, to live harmoniously ;" "comrade and *me*." "My sister and her were on good terms ;" "and *she*." "We often overlook the blessings which are in our possession, and are searching after those which are out of our reach ;" it ought to be, "and *search* after."

1. When the sense requires the verbs to be of *different* moods or tenses, the nominative must be repeated : the conjunctions will, then, connect two members of a compound sentence : as, "*He* cheerfully *supports* his distressed friend, and *he will* certainly be commended for it ;" "They *have rewarded* him liberally, and *they could not do* otherwise ;" "She *was* proud, though she *is* now humble."

When in the progress of a sentence, we pass from the affirmative to the negative form, or from the negative to the affirmative, the subject or nominative is mostly, if not invariably, resumed : as, "He may return, but he will not continue here." "He is rich, but he is not respectable." "He is not rich, but he is respectable." "Though she is high-born, beautiful, and accomplished, yet *she* is mortal, and, occasion-

---

[*] As the neuter verb BE, and passive verbs, have two forms of the subjunctive *imperfect* as well as of the present, this rule applies to the *imperfect* tense of such verbs, as well as to the present.

ally, *she* ought to be admonished of her condition." There appears to be, in general, equal reason for repeating the nominative, and resuming the subject, when the course of the sentence is diverted by a change of the mood or tense. The following sentences may therefore be improved. "Anger glances into the breast of a wise man, but will rest only in the bosom of fools ;" "but *rests* only ;" or, "but *it will* rest only." "Virtue is praised by many, and would be desired also, if her worth were really known ;" " and *she* would." "The world begins to recede, and will soon disappear ;" "and *it* will."

Now correct and parse the following

EXERCISES IN FALSE SYNTAX.

Professing regard, and to act differently, discover a base mind.

Did he not tell me his fault, and entreated me to forgive him ?

My brother and him are tolerable grammarians.

If he understand the subject, and attends to it industriously, he can scarcely fail of success.

You and us enjoy many privileges.

If a man have a hundred sheep, and one of them is gone astray, doth he not leave the ninety and nine, and goeth into the mountains, and seeketh that which is gone astray ?

She and him are very unhappily connected.

To be moderate in our views, and proceeding temperately in the pursuit of them, is the best way to ensure success.

Between him and I there is some disparity of years : but none between him and she.

By forming themselves on fantastic models, and ready to vie with one another in the reigning follies, the young begin with being ridiculous, and end with being vicious and immoral.

The following sentences exemplify the notes and observations under RULES XIV. *and* XIX.

1. We have met with many disappointments; and, if life continue, shall probably meet with many more.

Rank may confer influence, but will not necessarily produce virtue.

He does not want courage, but is defective in sensibility.

These people have indeed acquired great riches, but do not command esteem.

Our season of improvement is short ; and, whether used or not, will soon pass away.

He might have been happy, and is now fully convinced of it.

Learning strengthens the mind ; and, if properly applied, will improve our morals too.

SECTION XIV.

RULE XV.

When two or more nouns, or nouns and pronouns of the singular number, are connected by a COPULATIVE *conjunction, expressed or understood, they must have verbs, nouns and pronouns, in the* PLURAL *number to agree with them; but when they are connected by a* DISJUNCTIVE *conjunction, they must have verbs, nouns and pronouns, of the* SINGULAR *number to agree with them.*

This rule is often violated; some instances of which are annexed. "And so was also James and John, the sons of Zebedee, who were partners with Simon;" "and so *were* also." "All joy, tranquility, and peace, even for ever and ever, doth dwell;" "*dwell* for ever." "By whose power all good and evil is distributed;" "*are* distributed." "Their love, and their hatred, and their envy, is now perished;" "*are* perished." "The thoughtless and intemperate enjoyment of pleasure, the criminal abuse of it, and the forgetfulness of our being accountable creatures, obliterates every serious thought of the proper business of life, and effaces the sense of religion and of God." It ought to be, "*obliterate*," and "*efface.*"

1. When the nouns are nearly related, or scarcely distinguishable in sense, and sometimes even when they are very different, some authors have thought it allowable to put the verbs, nouns, and pronouns, in the singular number: as, "Tranquility and peace dwells there;" "Ignorance and negligence has produced the effect;" "The discomfiture and slaughter was very great." But it is evidently contrary to the first principles of grammar, to consider two distinct ideas as one, however nice may be their shades of difference: and if there is no difference, one of them must be superfluous, and ought to be rejected.

To support the above construction, it is said, that the verb may be understood as applied to each of the preceding terms; as in the following example: "Sand, and salt, and a mass of iron, *is* easier to bear than a man without understanding." But besides the confusion, and the latitude of application, which such a construction would introduce, it appears to be more proper and analogical, in cases where the verb is intended to be applied to any one of the terms, to make use of the disjunctive conjunction, which grammatically refers the verb to one or other of the preceding terms in a separate view. To preserve the distinctive uses of the copulative and disjunctive conjunctions, would render the rules precise, consistent, and intelligible. Dr. Blair observes, that "two or more substantives, joined by a copulative, must *always* require the verb or pronoun to which they refer, to be placed in the plural number :" and this is the general sentiment of English grammarians.

2. In many complex sentences, it is difficult for learners to determine, whether one or more of the clauses are to be considered as the nominative case ; and consequently, whether the verb should be in the singular or the plural number. I will, therefore, set down a number of varied examples of this nature, which may serve as some government to you, with respect to sentences of a similar construction. " Prosperity, with humility, *renders* its possessor truly amiable." " The ship, with all her furniture, *was* destroyed." " Not only his estates, his reputation too *has* suffered by his misconduct." " The general also, in conjunction with the officers, *has* applied for redress." " He cannot be justified ; for it is true, that the prince as well as the people, *was* blame-worthy." " The king, with his life-guard, *has* just passed through the village." " In the mutual influence of body and soul, there *is* a wisdom, a wonderful wisdom, which we cannot fathom." " Virtue, honor, nay, even self-interest, *conspire* to recommend the measure." " Patriotism, morality, every public and private consideration, *demand* our submission to just and lawful government." " Nothing *delights* me so much as the works of nature."

In support of such forms of expression as the following, we see the authority of Hume, Priestley, and other writers ; and I annex them for your consideration. " A long course of time, with a variety of accidents and circumstances, *are* requisite to produce those revolutions." " The king, with the lords and commons, *form* an excellent frame of government." " The side A, with the sides B and C. *compose* the triangle." " The fire communicated itself to the bed, which with the furniture of the room, and a valuable library, *were* all entirely consumed." It is, however, proper to observe, that these modes of expression do not appear to be warranted by the just principles of construction. The words, " A long course of time," " The king," " The side A," and " which," are the true nominatives to the respective verbs. In the last example, the word *all* should be expunged. As the preposition *with* governs the *objective* case, in English ; and if translated into Latin, would govern the *ablative* case, it is manifest, that the clauses following *with*, in the preceding sentences, cannot form any part of the *nominative* case. They cannot be at the same time in the objective and the nominative cases. The following sentence is grammatically formed ; and may serve to explain the others. " The lords and commons are essential branches of the British constitution: the king, with them, *forms* an excellent frame of government."*

The following sentences are variations from the latter part of the rule. "A man may see a metaphor or an allegory in a picture, as well as read them in a description;" "read *it*." "Neither character nor dialogue were yet understood;" "*was* yet." "It must indeed be confessed, that a lampoon or a satire, do not carry in them robbery or murder;" "*does* not carry in *it*." "Death, or some worse misfortune, soon divide them." It ought to be "*divides*."

3. When singular pronouns, or a noun and pronoun, of different persons, are disjunctively connected, the verb must agree with that person which is placed nearest to it: as, "I or thou *art* to blame;" "Thou or I *am* in fault;" "I, or thou, or he, *is* the author of it;" "George or I *am* the person." But it would be better to say; "Either I am to blame, or thou art," &c.

4. When a disjunctive occurs between a singular noun, or pronoun, and a plural one, the verb is made to agree with the plural noun and pronoun: as, "Neither poverty nor riches *were* injurious to him." "I or they *were* offended by it." But in this case, the plural noun or pronoun, when it can conveniently be done, should be placed next to the verb.

You will now correct and parse the following

EXERCISES IN FALSE SYNTAX.

Idleness and ignorance is the parent of many vices.

Wisdom, virtue, happiness, dwells with the golden mediocrity.

In unity consists the welfare and security of every society.

Time and tide waits for no man.

His politeness and good disposition was, on failure of their effect, entirely changed.

Patience and diligence, like faith, removes mountains.

Humility and knowledge, with poor apparel, excels pride and ignorance under costly attire.

The planetary system, boundless space, and the immense ocean, affects the mind with sensations of astonishment.

Humility and love, whatever obscurities may involve religious tenets, constitutes the essence of true religion.

Religion and virtue, our best support and highest honor, confers on the mind principles of noble independence.

What signifies the counsel and care of preceptors, when youth think they have no need of assistance?

Man's happiness, or misery, are, in a great measure, put into his own hands.

---

* Though the construction will not admit of a plural verb, the sentence would certainly stand better thus: "The king, the lords, and the commons, *form* an excellent constitution."

Man is not such a machine as a clock or a watch, which move merely as they are moved.

Despise no infirmity of mind or body, nor any condition of life ; for they are, perhaps, to be your own lot.

Speaking impatiently to servants, or any thing that betrays unkindness or ill-humor, are certainly criminal.

There are many faults in spelling, which neither analogy nor pronunciation justify.

When sickness, infirmity or reverse of fortune, affect us, the sincerity of friendship is proved.

Let it be remembered, that it is not the uttering, or the hearing of certain words, that constitute the worship of the Almighty.

A tart reply, a proneness to rebuke, or a captious and contradictious spirit, are capable of embittering domestic life, and of setting friends at variance.

The examples which follow, are suited to the notes and observations under RULE XV.

1. Much does human pride and self-complacency require correction.

Luxurious living, and high pleasures, begets a langour and satiety that destroys all enjoyment.

Pride and self-sufficiency stifles sentiments of dependence on our Creator : levity and attachment to worldly pleasures, destroys the sense of gratitude to him.

2. Every man and woman were numbered.*

* The copulative conjunction, in this instance, makes no difference with regard to the verb. All the men and women are referred to separately and individually. The verb must therefore have the same construction as it has in the sentence ; " Every one of the men and women *was* numbered." Whatever number of nouns may be connected by a conjunction with the pronoun *every*, this pronoun is as applicable to the whole mass of them, as to any one of the nouns ; and therefore the verb is correctly put in the singular number, and refers to the whole separately and individually considered. In short, this pronoun so entirely coalesces with the nouns, however numerous and united, that it imparts its peculiar nature to them, and makes the whole number correspond together, and require a similar construction.

The subject may be farther illustrated and confirmed, by the following examples. " Every man, woman, and child, *was* preserved from the devouring element ;" " Every good gift, and every perfect gift, *is* from above, and *cometh* down from the Father of lights ;" JAMES i. 17 ; " It is the original cause of every reproach and distress which *has* attended the government ;" JUNIUS ; " To those that have lived long together, every thing heard, and every thing seen, *recalls* some pleasure communicated, or some benefit conferred ; some petty quarrel, or some slight endearment." Dr. JOHNSON.—This construction forms an exception to the fifteenth rule of Syntax ; which was also illustrated in Conversation XIII. Another exception to this rule is, when a copulative conjunction connects two or more nouns, &c. which refer to the same person or thing : as, " That able scholar and critic *has* been eminently useful to the cause of religion."

Good order in our affairs, not mean savings, produce great profits.

The following treatise, together with those that accompany it were written, many years ago, for my own private satisfaction.

The great senator, in concert with several other eminent persons, were the projectors of the revolution.

- The religion of these people, as well as their customs and manners, were strangely misrepresented.

Virtue, joined to knowledge and wealth, confer great influence and respectability. But knowledge, with weal h united, if virtue is wanting, have a very limited influence, and are often despised.

That superficial scholar and critic, like some renowned critics of our own, have furnished most-decisive proofs, that they knew not the characters of the Hebrew language.

The buildings of the institution have been enlarged; the expense of which, added to the increased price of provisions, render it necessary to advance the terms of admission.

One, added to nineteen, make twenty.

What black despair, what horror, fills the mind !

Thou, and the gardener, and the huntsman, must share the blame of this business amongst them.

My sister and I, as well as my brother, are daily employed in their respective occupations.

3. Either thou or I art greatly mistaken, in our judgment on this subject.

I or thou am the person who must undertake the business proposed.

4. Both of the scholars, or one of them at least, was present at the transaction.

Some parts of the ship and cargo were recovered ; but neither the sailors nor the captain, was saved.

Whether one person or more was concerned in the business, does not yet appear.

The cares of this life, or the deceitfulness of riches, has choked the seeds of virtue in many a promising mind.

SECTION XV.

RULE XVI.

Nouns and pronouns in apposition, must be in the same case.

The following are instances of the violation of this rule : which you must correct and parse.

They slew Varus, he that was mentioned before.

I saw John and his sister, they who came to your house.

We must respect the good and the wise, they who endeavor to enlighten us, and make us better.

I sent the book to my brother's house, him whom you saw here.

My two friends gave me this present, them that we visited yesterday.

RULE XVII.

When a direct address is made, the noun or pronoun is in the nominative case independent.

In Conversation XIV, I made all the remarks, respecting this rule, that are necessary.

RULE XVIII.

The passive participle, unconnected with an auxiliary, belongs like an adjective, to some noun or pronoun expressed or understood.

This rule, so far as it respects the syntax of the English language, needs no remark.

RULE XX.

The infinitive mood may be governed by a verb, noun, adjective, or participle

The verbs which require those that follow them in the infinitive mood, to be used without the sign *to*, are make, need, see, bid, dare, feel, hear, let ; and sometimes a few others.

This irregularity, however, extends only to active or neuter verbs ; for all the verbs above mentioned, when made passive, require the *to* to be used before the following verb in the infinitive mood : as, "He was seen to *go* ;" "He was heard *to speak* :" "They were bidden *to* be on their guard."

The infinitive mood has been improperly used in the following sentences : "I am not like other men, *to envy* the talents I cannot reach." It should be, "*who* envy the talents they cannot reach ; or, "I *do* not, like other men, *envy* the talents *I* cannot reach." "Grammarians have denied, or at least doubted, them *to be* genuine ;" "doubted *that they were* genuine." "That all our doings may be ordered by thy governance, *to do* always what is righteous in thy sight ;" "*that we may* always *do*," &c.

When *as* follows *so*, it sometimes governs the infinitive mood : as, "I will endeavor to explain this subject so *as to* make you understand it." But sometimes, when the infinitive mood follows *as*, preceded by *so*, it is governed by another verb understood : as, "He desired nothing so much *as to* see his friends ;" that is, "*as he desired* to see his friends." And it is frequently governed in the same manner, when it follows *than*, after a comparison : as, "He desired nothing more *than to see* his friends ;" that is, "than *he desired* to see," &c.

22

The infinitive mood has much of the nature of a substantive, expressing the action itself which the verb signifies, as the participle has the nature of an adjective. Thus the infinitive mood does the office of a substantive in different cases : in the nominative : as, " To *play* is pleasant :" in the objective : as, " Boys love to *play* ;" " For *to will* is present to me ; but *to perform* that which is good, I find not."

The infinitive mood is often made absolute, or used independently on the rest of the sentence, supplying the place of the conjunction *that* with the potential mood : as, " To confess the truth, I was in fault ;" " To begin with the first ;" " To proceed ;" " To conclude ;" that is, " That I may confess," &c.

The sign *to*, signifying *in order to*, was anciently preceded by *for* : as, " What went he out *for to see* ?" The word *for* before the infinitive, is now, in almost every case, obsolete. It is, however, still used, if the subject of the affirmation intervenes between the preposition and the verb ; as, " *For* holy persons to be humble, is as hard, as *for* a prince *to submit* himself to be guided by tutors."

Now correct and parse the following

EXERCISES IN FALSE SYNTAX.

It is better live on a little, than outlive a great deal.

You ought not walk too hastily.

I wish him not wrestle with his happiness.

I need not to solicit him to do a kind action.

I dare not to proceed so hastily, lest I should give offence.

I have seen some young persons to conduct themselves very discreetly.

It is a great support to virtue, when we see a good mind to maintain its patience and tranquillity, under injuries and affliction, and to cordially forgive its oppressors.

It is the difference of their conduct, which makes us to approve the one, and to reject the other.

We should not be like many persons, to depreciate the virtues we do not possess.

To see young persons who are courted by health and pleasure, to resist all the allurements of vice, and to steadily pursue virtue and knowledge, is cheering and delightful to every good mind.

They acted with so much reserve, that some persons doubted them to be sincere.

And the multitude wondered, when they saw the lame to walk, and the blind to see.

RULE XXI.

Any intransitive, passive, or neuter verb, must have the same case after it as before it, when both words refer to, and signify, the same thing.

If you recollect what I said under this rule in Conversation XX, you can correct and parse the following

EXERCISES IN FALSE SYNTAX.

Well may you be afraid ; it is him indeed.

I would act the same part if I were him, or in his situation.

Search the Scriptures ; for in them ye think ye have eternal life : and they are them which testify of me.

Be composed : it is me : you have no cause for fear.

I cannot tell who has befriended me, unless it is him from whom I have received many benefits.

I know not whether it were them who conducted the business ; but I am certain it was not him.

He so much resembled my brother, that, at first sight, I took it to be he.

After all their professions, is it possible to be them ?

It could not have been her, for she always behaves discreetly.

If it was not him, who do you imagine it to have been ?

Who do you think him to be !

Whom do the people say that we are ?

SECTION XVI.

RULE XXII.

The infinitive mood, or part of a sentence, is sometimes the subject of a verb, and is, therefore, its nominative.

When several phrases, connected by a copulative conjunction, expressed or understood, are made nominatives to a verb, the verb must be plural : as, " To be temperate in eating and drinking, to use exercise in the open air, and to preserve the mind free from tumultuous emotions, *are* the best preservations of health."

But when the whole sentence forms but one nominative, conveying a unity of idea, the verb must be singular : as, " That warm climates should accelerate the growth of the human body, and shorten its duration, *is* very reasonable to believe."

EXERCISES IN FALSE SYNTAX.

To do unto all men, as we would, that they, in similar circumstances, should do unto us, constitute the great principle of virtue.

From a fear of the world's censure, to be ashamed of the practice of precepts, which the heart approves and embraces, mark a feeble and imperfect character.

The erroneous opinions which we form concerning happiness and misery, gives rise to all the mistaken and dangerous passions that embroils our life.

To live soberly, righteously, and piously, are required of all men.

That it is our duty to promote the purity of our minds and bodies, to be just and kind to our fellow-creatures, and to be pious and faithful to Him that made us, admit not of any doubt in a rational and well-informed mind.

To be of a pure and humble mind, to exercise benevolence towards others, to cultivate piety towards God, is the sure means of becoming peaceful and happy.

It is an important truth, that religion, vital religion, the religion of the heart, are the most powerful auxiliaries of reason, in waging war with the passions, and promoting that sweet composure which constitute the peace of God.

The possession of our senses entire, of our limbs uninjured, of our sound understanding, of friends and companions, are often overlooked ; though it would be the ultimate wish of many, who, as far as we can judge, deserves it as much as ourselves.

All that make a figure on the great theatre of the world, the employments of the busy, the enterprises of the ambitious, and the exploits of the warlike ; the virtues which forms the happiness, and the crimes which occasions the misery of mankind ; originates in that silent and secret recess of thought, which are hidden from every human eye.

RULE XXIII.

When a noun or pronoun has no verb to agree with it, but is placed before a participle, independently on the rest of the sentence, it must be in the nominative case *absolute.*

EXERCISES IN FALSE SYNTAX.

Solomon was of this mind ; and I have no doubt he made as wise and true proverbs, as any body has done since : him only excepted, who was a much greater and wiser man than Solomon.

————————Him destroy'd,
Or won to what may work his utter loss,
All this will soon follow.

————————Whose gray top
Shall tremble, him descending.

SECTION XVII.

I have now taken a review of all the rules which I gave in the Conversations, and which are sufficient for the parsing of any sentence, and have made, under each, all the remarks which were necessary to enable you to correct such exercises in *false syntax*, as violate those rules.

There remain yet to be given, a few rules, which you will find useful, and, indeed, necessary, in correcting many bad constructions, to which the rules for parsing merely, do not apply, or are not sufficiently explicit. I will, therefore, proceed to give you the following

SUPPLEMENTARY RULES AND REMARKS,

WITH

APPROPRIATE EXERCISES.

RULE I.

A noun of multitude, or signifying many, may have a verb or pronoun agreeing with it, either of the singular or plural number ; yet not without regard to the import of the word, as conveying unity or plurality of idea : as, " The meeting *was* large ;" " The parliament *is* dissolved ;" " The nation *is* powerful ;" " My people *do* not consider : *they* have not known me ;" " The multitude eagerly *pursue* pleasure, as *their* chief good ;" " The council *were* divided in *their* sentiments."

We ought to consider whether the term immediately suggests the idea of the number it represents, or whether it exhibits to the mind the idea of the whole as one thing. In the former case, the verb ought to be plural ; in the latter, it ought to be singular. Thus, it seems improper to say, " The peasantry *goes* barefoot, and the middle sort *makes* use of wooden shoes." It would be better to say, " The peasantry *go* barefoot, and the middle sort *make* use," &c. ; because the idea in both these cases, is that of a number. On the contrary, there is a harshness in the following sentences, in which nouns of number have verbs plural : because the ideas they represent seem not to be sufficiently divided in the mind. " The court of Rome *were* not without solicitude." " The house of commons *were* of small weight." " The house of lords *were* so much influenced by these reasons." "Stephen's party *were* entirely broken up by the captivity of their leader." " An army of twenty-four thousand *were* assembled." "What reason *have* the church of Rome for proceeding in this manner ?" " There is indeed no constitution so tame and careless of *their* own defence." " All the virtues of mankind are

22*

to be counted upon a few fingers, but *his* follies and vices are innumerable." Is not *mankind* in this place a noun of multitude, and such as requires the pronoun referring to it, to be in the plural number *their?*

When a noun of multitude is preceded by a definitive word, which clearly limits the sense to an aggregate with an idea of unity, it requires a verb and pronoun to agree with it in the singular number: as, "*A* company of troops *was* detached: *a* troop of cavalry *was* raised ; *this* people *is* become a great nation ; *that* assembly *was* numerous ; a great number of men and women *was* collected."

On many occasions, where a noun of multitude is used, it is very difficult to decide, whether the verb should be in the singular, or in the plural number: and this difficulty has induced some grammarians to cut the knot at once, and to assert that every noun of multitude, as it constitutes *one* aggregate of many particulars, must always be considered as conveying the idea of *unity ;* and that consequently, the verb and pronoun agreeing with it, cannot with propriety be ever used *in* the plural number. This opinion appears to be not well considered ; it is contrary to the established practise of the best writers of the language, and against the rules of the most respectable grammarians. Some nouns of multitude certainly convey to the mind an idea of plurality, others, that of a whole as one thing, and others again sometimes that of unity, and sometimes that of plurality. On this ground, it is warrantable, and consistent with the nature of things, to apply a plural verb and pronoun to the one class, and a singular verb and pronoun, to the other. We shall immediately perceive the impropriety of the following constructions : "The clergy *has* withdrawn *itself* from the temporal courts :" "The nobility, exclusive of *its* capacity as hereditary *counsellor* of the crown, *forms* the *pillar* to support the throne :" "The commonalty *is* divided into several degrees :" "The people of England *is* possessed of super-eminent privileges ;" "The multitude *was* clamorous for the object of *its* affections ;" "The assembly *was* divided in *its* opinion ;" "The fleet *was* all dispersed, and some of *it was* taken."—In all these instances, as well as in many others, the plural verb and pronoun should be used : and if the reader will apply them, as he looks over the sentences a second time, he will perceive the propriety and effect of a change in the construction.

EXERCISES IN FALSE SYNTAX.

The people rejoices in that which should give it sorrow.

The flock, and not the fleece, are, or ought to be, the objects of the shepherd's care.

The court have just ended, after having sat through the trial of a very long cause.

The crowd were so great, that the judges with difficulty made their way through them.

The corporation of York consist of a mayor, aldermen, and a common council.

The British parliament are composed of king, lords, and commons.

When the nation complain, the rulers should listen to their voice.

In the days of youth, the multitude eagerly pursues pleasures as its chief good.

The church have no power to inflict corporal punishment.

The fleet were seen sailing up the channel.

The regiment consist of a thousand men.

The meeting have established several salutary regulations.

The council was not unanimous, and it separated without coming to any determination.

The fleet is all arrived and moored in safety.

This people draweth near to me with their mouth, and honoreth me with their lips, but their heart is far from me.

The committee was divided in its sentiments, and it has referred the business to the general meeting.

The committee were very full when this point was decided; and their judgment has not been called in question.

Why do this generation wish for greater evidence, when so much is already given.

The remnant of the people were persecuted with great severity.

Never were any people so much infatuated as the Jewish nation.

The shoal of herrings were of an immense extent.

No society are chargeable with the disapproved misconduct of particular members.

SECTION XVIII.

RULE II.

To determine what case a noun, or pronoun, must be in, when it follows the conjunctions but, than, *and as,* attend well to the sense, and supply the ellipsis : *as,*
"Thou art wiser than I;" that is, "than I am." "They loved him more than me;" i. e. "more than they loved me." "The sentiment is well expressed by Plato, but much better by Solomon than him;" that is, "than it is expressed by him."

The propriety or impropriety of many phrases, in the preceding as well as in some other forms, may be discovered, by supplying the words that are not expressed ; which will be evident from the following instances of erroneous construction. "He can read better than me." "He is as good as her." "Whether I be present or no." "Who did this? Me." By supplying the words understood in each of these phrases, their impropriety and governing rule will appear : as, "Better than I can read ;" "As good as she is ;" "Present or not present ;" "I did it."

1. By not attending to this rule, many errors have been committed : a number of which is subjoined, as a further caution and direction to you. "Thou art a much greater loser than me by his death." "She suffers hourly more than me." "We contributed a third more than the Dutch, who were obliged to the same proportion more than us." "King Charles, and more than him, the duke and the popish faction, were at liberty to form new schemes." "The drift of all his sermons was, to prepare the Jews for the reception of a prophet mightier than him, and whose shoes he was not worthy to bear." "It was not the work of so eminent an author, as him to whom it was first imputed." "A stone is heavy, and the sand is weighty ; but a fool's wrath is heavier than them both." "If the king give us leave, we may perform the office as well as them that do." In these passages it ought to be, "*I, we, he, they*, respectively."

When the relative *who* immediately follows *than*, it must be in the objective case : as, "Alfred, *than whom*, a greater king never reigned," &c. "Beelzebub, *than whom*, Satan excepted, none higher sat," &c. It is remarkable that in such instances, if the personal pronoun were used, it would be in the nominative case : as, "A greater king never reigned *than he*," that is, "*than he was*." "Beelzebub, *than he*," &c.; that is, "*than he sat*." The phrase *than whom*, is, however, avoided by the best modern writers."

The following sentences, "I saw nobody but him ;" "No person but he was present ;" "More persons than they saw the action." "The secret was communicated to more men than him ;" "This trade enriched some people more than them ;" may be explained, on the principle of supplying the ellipsis, in the following manner. In the first, we might say, "I saw nobody, but *I saw* him ;" or, "I saw nobody, but him *I saw* ;" in the second, "None was present, but he *was present* ;" in the third, "More persons than they *were*, saw the action," or, "More than *these persons were*, saw the action ;" in the fourth, "The secret was communicated to more persons than *to* him ;" in the fifth, "This trade enriched some people more than *it enriched* them."—The supply of the ellipsis certainly gives an uncouth appearance to these sentences : but this circumstance forms no solid objection to the truth of the principle.

Now correct and parse the following

EXERCISES IN FALSE SYNTAX.

In some respects, we have had as many advantages as them; but in the article of a good library, they have had a greater privilege than us.

The undertaking was much better executed by his brother than he.

They are much greater gainers than me by this unexpected event.

They know how to write as well as him; but he is a much better grammarian than them.

Though she is not so learned as him, she is as much beloved and respected.

These people, though they possess more shining qualities, are not so proud as him, nor so vain as her.

The following examples are adapted to the notes and observations under RULE IV.

1. Who betrayed her companion? Not me.

Who revealed the secrets he ought to have concealed? Not him.

Who related falsehoods to screen herself, and to bring an odium upon others? Not me; it was her.

There is but one in fault, and that is me.

Whether he will be learned or no, must depend on his application.

Charles XII. of Sweden, than who a more courageous person never lived, appears to have been destitute of the tender sensibilities of nature.

Salmasius (a more learned man than him has seldom appeared) was not happy at the close of life.

SECTION XIX.

The observance of the rule which I am about to give you now, involves an accurate knowledge of all the moods and tenses of the verbs; and before you can understand it thoroughly, you must particularly recollect the appropriate use of all the tenses.

RULE III.

In the use of words and phrases which, in point of time, relate to each other, a due regard to that relation should be observed.

Instead of saying, "The Lord *hath given*, and the Lord *hath taken* away;" we should say, "The Lord *gave*, and the Lord *hath taken* away." Instead of, "I *remember* the family more than twenty years;" it should be, "I *have remembered* the family more than twenty years."

It is not easy, in all cases, to give particular rules, for the management of words and phrases which relate to one another, so that they may be proper and consistent. The best rule that can be given, is this very general one, "To observe what the sense necessarily requires." It may, however, be of use, to exhibit a number of instances, in which the construction is irregular. The following are of this nature.

"I have completed the work more than a week ago;" "I have seen the coronation at Westminster last summer." These sentences should have been; "I *completed* the work," &c.: "I *saw* the coronation," &c.: because the perfect tense extends to a past period, which immediately precedes, or includes, the present time; and it cannot, therefore, apply to the time of *a week ago*, or to *last midsummer*.

"Charles has lately finished the reading of Henry's History of England:" it should be, "Charles *lately finished*," &c.; the word *lately* referring to a time completely past, without any allusion to the present time.

"They have resided in Italy, till a few months ago, for the benefit of their health:" it should be, "they *resided* in Italy," &c.

"This mode of expression has been formerly much admired:" it ought to be, "*was* formerly much admired."

"The business is not done here, in the manner in which it has been done, some years since in Germany:" it should be, "in the manner in which it *was* done," &c.

"I will pay the vows which my lips have uttered, when I was in trouble:" it ought to be, "which my lips *uttered*," &c.

"I have in my youth trifled with health: and old age now prematurely assails me:" it should be, "In my youth I *trifled* with health," &c.

The five examples last mentioned, are corrected on the same principle that the preceding examples are corrected.

"Charles is grown considerably since I have seen him the last time:" this sentence ought to be, "Charles *has* grown considerably, since I *saw* him the last time."

"Payment was, at length made, but no reason assigned for its being so long postponed:" it should be, "for its *having been* so long postponed."

"He became so meek and submissive, that to be in the house as one of the hired servants, was now the utmost of his wishes:" it ought to be, "was *then* the utmost of his wishes."

" They were arrived an hour before we reached the city :"
It ought to be, "They *had arrived.*" &c.; because *arrived*, in
this phrase, denotes an event not only past, but prior to the
time referred to, by the words, " reach the city."

" The workmen will finish the business at midsummer."
According to the meaning, it ought to be, " The workmen
will have finished," &c.

" All the present family have been much indebted to their
great and honorable ancestor :" it should be, " *are* much indebted."

" This curious piece of workmanship was preserved, and
shown to strangers for more than fifty years past :" it ought
to be, " *has been preserved,* and *been shown,*" &c.

" I had rather walk than ride :" it should be, " I *would*
rather walk than ride."

" On the morrow, because he should have known the cer-
tainty wherefore he was accused of the Jews, he loosed him :"
it ought to be, " because he *would know ;*" or rather, " *being
willing to know.*"

" The blind man said unto him, Lord, that I might receive
my sight ;" " If by any means I might attain unto the resur-
rection of the dead :" in both these places, *may* would have
been better than *might.*

" I feared that I should have lost the parcel, before I arrived at the city :" it should be, " I feared that *I should lose,*"
&c.

" It would have afforded me no satisfaction, if I could perform it :" it ought to be, " If I *could have performed* it ;" or,
" It *would afford* me no satisfaction, if I *could perform* it."

To preserve consistency in the time of verbs, and of words
and phrases, we must recollect that, in the subjunctive mood,
the present and the imperfect tenses often carry with them a
future sense ; and that the auxiliaries *should* and *would,* in
the imperfect time, are used to express the present and future,
as well as the past.

1. With regard to verbs in the infinitive mood, the practice
of many writers, and some even of our most respectable writers, appears to be erroneous. They seem not to advert to
the true principles, which influence the different tenses of this
mood. I shall produce some rules on the subject, which, I
presume, will be found perspicuous and accurate. "All verbs
expressive of hope, desire, intention, or command, must invariably be followed by the present, and not the perfect of the
infinitive." " The last week I intended *to have written,*" is a
very common phrase ; the infinitive being in the past time,
as well as the verb which it follows. But it is evidently
wrong : for how long soever it now is since I thought of writing, " to write" was then present to me : and must still be
considered as present, when I bring back that time, and the
thoughts of it. It ought, therefore, to be ; "The last week,
I intended *to write.*"

The following sentence is properly and analogically expressed: " I found him better than I expected to find him." " Expected *to have found him*," is irreconcilable to grammar and to sense. Every person would perceive an error in this expression ; " It is long since I commanded him *to have done it* :" ye , expected to *have found*," is not better. It is as clear that the *finding* must be posterior to the expectation, as that the *obedience* must be posterior to the command.

Some writers on grammar contend, that the sentence, " I intend to have written," is correct and grammatical ;. because it simply denotes, as they assert, the speaker's intention to be hereafter in possession of the finished action of writing. But to this reasoning the following answers may be given : that the phrase, " to have written," is stated, in English grammar, as the established past tense of the infinitive mood ; that it is as incontrovertibly the past tense of the infinitive in English, as *scripsisse* is the past tense of the infinitive in Latin ; that no writers can be warranted in taking such liberties with the language, as to contradict its plainest rules, for the sake of supporting an hypothesis ; that these writers might, on their own principles, and with equal propriety, contend that the phrase, " I intend *having written*," is proper and grammatical ; and that by admitting such violations of established grammatical distinctions, confusion would be introduced, the language would be disorganized, and the most eccentric systems of grammar might be advanced, and plausibly supported.—In short, the phrase, " I intend to have written," appears to involve the following absurdity ; " I intend to produce hereafter an action or event, which has been already completed."

As the verbs *to desire* and *to wish*, are nearly related, you may naturally suppose, from the rule just laid down, that the latter verb, like the former, must invariably be followed by the present of the infinitive. But if you reflect, that the act of *desiring* always refers to the future ; and that the act of *wishing* refers sometimes to the past, as well as sometimes to the future ; you will perceive the distinction between them, and that, consequently, the following modes of expression are strictly justifiable ; " I wished *that I had written* sooner;" " I wished *to have written* sooner :" and you will be perfectly satisfied, that the following phrases must be improper : " I desire that I had written sooner ;" " I desire to have written sooner."*

*In the expression, " I hope that I have done my duty," there appears to be a considerable ellipsis. The sentence at large may very naturally be thus explained : " I hope it will appear, or, I hope to show, or, I hope it is evident, or, I hope you will believe, that I have done my duty." But whether the ellipsis be admitted or rejected, it is indubitable that the infinitive mood cannot be applied on this occasion : to

Having considered and explained the special rule, respecting the government of verbs expressive of hope, desire, intention, or command, I shall proceed to state and elucidate the general rule, on the subject of verbs in the infinitive mood. It is founded on the authority of Harris, Lowth, Campbell, Pickbourn, &c.; and I think too, on the authority of reason and common sense. "When the action or event, signified by a verb in the infinitive mood, is *contemporary* or *future*, with respect to the verb to which it is chiefly related, the present of the infinitive is required: when it is *not* contemporary *nor* future, the perfect of the infinitive is necessary." To comprehend and apply this rule, you have only to consider, whether the infinitive verb refers to a time antecedent, contemporary, or future, with regard to the governing or related verb. When this simple point is ascertained, there will be no doubt in your mind respecting the form which the infinitive verb should have. A few examples may illustrate these positions. If I wish to signify, that I rejoiced at a particular time, in recollecting the sight of a friend, sometime having intervened between the *seeing* and the *rejoicing*, I should express myself thus: "I rejoiced *to have seen* my friend." The *seeing*, in this case, was evidently antecedent to the *rejoicing*; and therefore the verb which expresses the former, must be in the perfect of the infinitive mood. The same meaning may be expressed in a different form: "I rejoiced *that I had seen* my friend;" or, "*in having seen* my friend;" and you may, in general, try the propriety of a doubtful point of this nature, by converting the phrase into these two corresponding forms of expression. When it is convertible into both these equivalent phrases, its legitimacy must be admitted.—If, on the contrary, I wish to signify, that I rejoiced at the sight of my friend, that my joy and his surprise were contemporary, I should say, "I rejoiced *to see* my friend; or, in other words, "I rejoiced *in seeing* my friend." The correctness of this form of the infinitive may also, in most cases, be tried, by converting the phrase into other phrases of a similar import.

The subject may be still further illustrated, by additional examples. In the sentence which follows, the verb is with propriety put in the perfect tense of the infinitive mood: "It would have afforded me great pleasure, as often as I

say, "I hope to have done my duty," is harsh and incorrect. I *hoped* that I *had done* my duty;" that is, "I hoped he would believe, or, I hoped it was evident, that I had done my duty," is a correct and regular mode of expression. But it would not be proper, under any circumstances whatever, to say, "I *hoped to have done* my duty;" it should be, "I *hoped to do* my duty."

reflected upon it, *to have been* the messenger of such intelligence." As the message, in this instance, was antecedent to the pleasure, and not contemporary with it, the verb expressive of the message must denote that antecedence, by being in the perfect of the infinitive. If, on the contrary, the message and the pleasure were referred to as contemporary, the subsequent verb would, with equal propriety, have been put in the present of the infinitive: as, "It would have afforded me great pleasure, *to be* the messenger of such intelligence." In the former instance, the phrase in question is equivalent to these words; "*If I had been* the messenger;" in the latter instance, to this expression; "*Being* the messenger."

For your satisfaction, I shall present you with a variety of false constructions, under the general rule.

"This is a book which proves itself to be written by the person whose name it bears;" it ought to be, "which proves itself *to have been written.*"

"To see him would have afforded me pleasure all my life;" it should be, "*To have seen* him, would have afforded," &c. or, "*To see* him *would afford* me pleasure," &c.

"The arguments were sufficient to have satisfied all who heard them;" "Providence did not permit the reign of Julian to have been long and prosperous:" they should be, "were sufficient *to satisfy*," &c. and, "*to be* long and prosperous."

"It was impossible for those men, by any diligence whatever, to have prevented this accident: every thing that men could have done, was done;" corrected thus; "*to prevent* this accident;" "every thing that men *could do*," &c.

"The respect shown to the candidate would have been greater, if it had been practicable to have afforded repeated opportunities to the freeholders, to have annexed their names to the address:" they should be, "if it had been practicable *to afford*," and "*to annex* their names."

"From his biblical knowledge, he appears to study the Holy Scriptures with great attention:" it ought to be, "he appears *to have studied*," &c.

"I cannot excuse the remissness of those whose business it should have been, as it certainly was their interest, to have interposed their good offices:" "There were two circumstances which made it necessary for them to have lost no time:" "History painters would have found it difficult to have invented such a species of beings." In these three examples, the phrases should have been, *to interpose, to lose, to invent.*

It is proper to remind you, that, in order to express the past time with the defective verb *ought*, the perfect of the infinitive must always be used: as, "He ought *to have* done it." When we use this verb, this is the only possible way to distinguish the past from the present.

In support of the positions advanced under this rule, can be produced the sentiments of the most eminent grammarians. There are, however, some writers on grammar, who strenuously maintain, that the governed verb in the infinitive ought to be in the past tense, when the verb which governs it, is in the past time. Though this cannot be admitted, in the instances which are controverted under this rule, or in any instances of a similar nature, yet there can be no doubt that in many cases, in which the thing referred to, preceded the governing verb, it would be proper and allowable. We may say; " From a conversation I once had with him, he *appeared to have studied* Homer with great care and judgment." It would be proper also to say, " from his conversation, he *appears to have studied* Homer with great care and judg- ment;" " That unhappy man *is supposed to have died* by violence." These examples are not only consistent with our rule, but they confirm and illustrate it. It is the tense of the governing verb only, that marks what is called the abso- late time; the tense of the verb governed, marks solely its relative time with respect to the verb.

To assert, as some writers do, that verbs in the infinitive mood, have no tenses, no relative distinctions of present, past, and future, is inconsistent with just grammatical views of the subject. That these verbs associate with verbs in all the tenses, is no proof of their having no peculiar time of their own. Whatever period the governing verb assumes, whether present, past, or future, the governed verb in the in- finitive always respects that period, and its time is calculated from it. Thus, the time of the infinitive may be before, after, or the same as, the time of the governing verb, accord- ing as the thing signified by the infinitive is supposed to be before, after, or present with, the thing denoted by the gov- erning verb. It is, therefore, with great propriety, that tenses are assigned to verbs of the infinitive mood. The point of time from which they are computed, is of no consequence; since present, past, and future, are completely applicable to them.

It may not be improper to observe, that though it is often correct to use the perfect of the infinitive after the governing verb, yet there are particular cases, in which it would be better to give the expression a different form. Thus, instead of saying, " I wish to have written to him sooner," " I then wished to have written to him sooner," " He will one day wish to have written sooner:" it would be more perspicuous and forcible, as well as more agreeable to the practice of good writers, to say; " I wish that I had written to him sooner," " He will one day wish that he had written sooner."

Should the justness of these strictures be admitted, the past infinitive would not be superseded, though some grammarians have supposed it would: there would still be numerous occasions for the use of it; as we may perceive by a few examples. " It would ever afterwards have been a source of pleasure, to have found him wise and virtuous." " To have deferred his repentance longer, would have disqualified him for repenting at all." " They will then see, that to have faithfully performed their duty, would have been their greatest consolation."

In relating things that were formerly expressed by another person, we often meet with modes of expression similar to the following:

" The travellers who lately came from the south of England, said that the harvest there *was* very abundant:" " I met Charles yesterday, who told me that he *is* very happy :" " The professor asserted, that a resolute adherence to truth *is* an indispensable duty :" " The preacher said very audibly, that whatever *was* useful, *was* good."

In referring to the declarations of this nature, the present tense must be used, if the position is immutably the same at all times, or supposed to be so: as, " The bishop declared, that virtue *is* always advantageous :" not, " *was* always advantageous." But if the assertion referred to something, that is not always the same, or supposed to be so, the past tense must be applied: as, " George said that he *was* very happy :" not, " *is* very happy."

The following sentences will fully exemplify, to the young grammarian, both the parts of this rule. " He declared to us, that he *was* afraid of no man ; because conscious innocence *gives* firmness of mind." " He protested, that he *believed* what *was* said, because it *appeared* to him probable." " Charles asserted that it *was* his opinion that men always *succeed*, when they *use* precaution and pains." " The doctor declared to his audience, that if virtue *suffers* some pains, she *is* amply recompensed by the pleasure which attends her."

Now parse and correct the following

EXERCISES IN FALSE SYNTAX.

The next new year's day, I shall be at school three years.
And he that was dead, sat up, and began to speak.
I should be obliged to him if he will gratify me in that particular.
And the multitude wondered when they saw the dumb to speak, the maimed to be whole, the lame walk, and the blind seeing.
I have compassion on the multitude, because they continue with me now three days.
In the treasury belonging to the Cathedral in this city, is preserved with the greatest veneration, for upwards of six

hundred years, a dish which they pretend to be made of emerald.

The court of Rome gladly laid hold on all the opportunities, which the imprudence, weakness, or necessities of princes afford it, to extend its authority.

Fierce as he mov'd his silver shafts resound.

They maintained that scripture conclusion, that all mankind rise from one head.

John will earn his wages, when his service is completed.

Ye will not come unto me, that ye might have life.

Be that as it will, he cannot justify his conduct.

I have been at London a year, and seen the king last summer.

After we visited London, we returned, content and thankful, to our retired and peaceful habitation.

The following examples are adapted to the notes and observations under RULE III.

1. I purpose to go to London in a few months, and after I shall finish my business there to proceed to America.

These prosecutions of William seem to be the most iniquitous measures pursued by the court, during the time that the use of parliaments was suspended.

From the little conversation I had with him, he appeared to have been a man of letters.

I always intended to have rewarded my son according to his merit.

It would, on reflection, have given me great satisfaction, to relieve him from that distressed situation.

It required so much care, that I thought I should have lost it before I reached home.

We have done no more than it was our duty to have done.

He would have assisted one of his friends, if he could do it without injuring the other; but as that could not have been done, he avoided all interference.

Must it not be expected, that he would have defended an authority, which had been so long exercised without controversy?

These enemies of Christianity were confounded, whilst they were expecting to have found an opportunity to have betrayed its author.

His sea sickness was so great, that I often feared he would have died before our arrival.

If these persons had intended to deceive, they would have taken care to have avoided, what would expose them to the objections of their opponents.

23*

It was a great pleasure to have received his approbation of my labors ; for which I cordially thanked him.

It would have afforded me still greater pleasure, to receive his approbation at an earlier period ; but to receive it at all, reflected credit upon me.

To be censured by him, would soon have proved an insuperable discouragement.

> Him portion'd maids, apprentic'd orphans blest,
> The young who labor, and the old who rest.

The doctor, in his lecture, said, that fever always produced thirst.

SECTION XX.

RULE IV.

Some conjunctions require the indicative, some the subjunctive mood, after them. When something contingent or doubtful is implied, the verb is in the subjunctive mood : as, " *If* he *studies* his lesson well to-day, he may ride to-morrow." " *If* he *study* more, he will learn faster." " He will not be pardoned, *unless* he *repent*."

Conjunctions that are of a positive and absolute nature, require the indicative mood. " *As* virtue advances, *so* vice recedes." " He *is* healthy, because he *is* temperate."

The conjunctions, *if, though, unless, except, whether,* &c. generally require the *second* form of the subjunctive mood *present* tense, and the *second* form of the *imperfect* of the neuter verb *be,* and passive verbs : as, " *If* thou *be* afflicted, repine not ;" " *Though* he *slay* me, yet will I trust in him ;" " He cannot be clean *unless* he *wash* himself ;" " No power, except it *were* given from above ;" " *Whether* it *were* I or they, so we preach." But sometimes they require the *first* form : as, " *If* he *thinks*, as he speaks, he may safely be trusted." " *If* he *is* now disposed to it, I will perform the operation." " He acts uprightly, *unless* he *deceives* me." " *If* he *was* there, we shall know it to-morrow." " *Whether* he *was* deceitful or not, time will determine." But when the sentence does not imply doubt, the verbs following these conjunctions, are in the indicative mood.

1. Almost all the irregularities, in the construction of any language have arisen from the ellipsis of some words, which were originally inserted in the sentence, and made it regular : and it is probable, that this has been generally the case with

respect to the conjunctive form of words, now in use; which will appear from the following examples: "We shall overtake him though he *run*;" that is, "though he *should* run;" "Unless he *act* prudently, he will not accomplish his purpose;" that is, "unless he *shall* act prudently." "If he *succeed* and *obtain* his end, he will not be the happier for it;" that is, "If he *should* succeed, and *should* obtain his end." These remarks and examples are designed to show the original of many of our present conjunctive forms of expression; and to enable you to examine the propriety of using them, by tracing the words in question to their proper origin and ancient connexions. But it is necessary to be more particular on this subject, and therefore I shall add a few observations respecting it.

That part of the verb which I call the second form of the present tense of the subjunctive mood, has a future signification. This is effected by not varying the terminations of the second and third persons singular as the indicative does; as will be evident from the following examples: "If thou *prosper*, thou shouldst be thankful;" "Unless he *study* more closely, he will never be learned." Some writers however would express these sentiments with the personal variations; "If thou *prosperest*," &c. "Unless he *studies*," &c.: and as there is a great diversity of practice in this point, it is proper to offer a few remarks, to assist you in distinguishing the right application of these different forms of expression. It may be considered as a rule, that no changes of termination are necessary, when these two circumstances concur: 1st, When the subject is of a dubious and contingent nature; and 2d, When the verb has a reference to future time. In the following sentences, both these circumstances will be found to unite: "If thou *injure* another, thou wilt hurt thyself;" "He has a hard heart; and if he *continue* impenitent, he must suffer;" "He will maintain his principles, though he *lose* his estate;" "Whether he *succeed* or not, his intention is laudable;" "If he *be* not prosperous, he will not repine." "If a man *smite* his servant, and he *die*," &c. *Exodus* xxi. 20. In all these examples, the things signified by the verbs are uncertain, and refer to future time. These verbs, therefore, are properly used in the *second* form of the subjunctive present.

But in the instances which follow, future time is not referred to; and therefore a different construction takes place: "If thou *livest* virtuously, thou art happy;" "Unless he *means* what he says, he is doubly faithless;" "If he *allows* the excellence of virtue, he does not regard her precepts;" "If thou *believest* with all thy heart, thou mayst," &c. *Acts*, viii. 37. These are properly used in the *first* form of the subjunctive mood present tense.

As there are two forms of the subjunctive imperfect of the neuter verb *be*, and of passive verbs, a rule which will direct you in the proper use of each, may be found useful.   The rule, which will be found generally correct, is, " When the sentence implies doubt, supposition, &c. and the neuter verb *be*, or the passive verb is used with a reference to present or future time, and is either followed, or preceded, by another verb in the *imperfect* of the potential mood, the *second* form of the imperfect must be used : as, " *If* he *were* here, we *should* rejoice together ;" " *Were* she present, she *would* enjoy the scene." " He *might* go, *if* he *were* disposed to." But when there is no reference to present or future time, and it is neither followed nor preceded by the potential imperfect, the *first* form of the imperfect must be used ; as, " *If* he *was* ill, he did not let his friends know it ; *If* he *was* there he did his duty :" " *Whether* he *was* absent or present, is not known."

There are many sentences, introduced by conjunctions, in which neither contingency nor futurity is denoted : as, " Though he *excels* her in knowledge, she far exceeds him in virtue ;" " *Though* he *is* poor, he is contented ;" and then the verbs are in the indicative mood : *were* therefore, in the following sentence, is erroneous. " *Though* he *were* divinely inspired, and spoke therefore as the oracles of God, with supreme authority ; *though* he *were* endued with supernatural powers, and could, therefore, have confirmed the truth of what he uttered, by miracles : yet, in compliance with the way in which human nature and reasonable creatures are usually wrought upon, he reasoned." That our Saviour was divinely inspired, and endued with supernatural powers, are positions that are here taken for granted, as not admitting the least doubt ; therefore the indicative mood, " *Though* he *was* divinely inspired ; *though* he *was* endued with supernatural powers ;" would have been better. The second form of the subjunctive imperfect of the neuter verb *be*, is used in the like improper manner, in the following example : " *Though* he *were* a son, yet learned he obedience, by the things which he suffered." But, in a similar passage, the indicative, with great propriety, is employed to the same purpose : "*Though* he *was* rich, yet for your sakes he became poor."

2. *Lest* and *that*, annexed to a command preceding, necessarily require the following verb to be in the second form of the subjunctive present : as, " Love not sleep, *lest* thou *come* to poverty ;" " Reprove not a scorner, *lest* he *hate* thee ;" " Take heed *that* thou *speak* not to Jacob."

If with *but* following it, when futurity is denoted, requires the second form of the subjunctive present : as, " *If* he *do but* touch the hills, they shall smoke ;" " *If* he *be but* discreet, he will succeed." But the first form ought to be used, on this occasion, when future time is not signified :   as, " *If*, in this expression, he *does but* jest, no offence should be taken ;" " *If* she *is but* sincere, I am happy." The same distinction applies to the following forms of expression : " If he *do* submit, it will be from necessity ;" " If thou *do* not reward this service, he will be discouraged ;" " If thou *dost* heartily forgive him, endeavor to forget the offence."

3. In the following instances, the conjunction *that*, expressed or understood, seems to be improperly accompanied with the subjunctive mood. " So much she dreaded his tyranny, *that* the fate of her friend she *dare* not lament." " He reasoned so artfully that his friends would listen, and think [*that*] he *were* not wrong."

4. The same conjunction followed both by the first and second forms of the subjunctive present, in the same sentence, and in the same circumstances, seems to be a great impropriety ; as in these instances. " *If* there *be* but one body of legislators, it is no better than a tyranny ; *if* there *are* only two, there will want a casting voice." "*If* a man *have* a hundred sheep, and one of them *is* gone astray." &c.

5. On the form of the auxiliaries in the compound tenses of the subjunctive mood, it seems proper to make a few observations. Some writers express themselves in the perfect tense as follows : " If thou *have* determined, we must submit :" " Unless he *have* consented, the writing will be void:" but we believe that few authors of critical sagacity write in this manner. The proper form seems to be, " If thou *hast* determined ; unless he *has* consented," &c. conformably to what we generally meet with in the Bible : " I have surnamed thee, though thou *hast* not known me." *Isaiah* xliv. 4, 4. " What is the hope of the hypocrite, though he *hath* gained," &c. *Job* xxvii. 8. See also *Acts* xxviii. 4.

6. In the pluperfect and future tenses, we sometimes meet with such expressions as these : " If thou *had* applied thyself diligently, thou wouldst have reaped the advantage ; unless thou *shall* speak the whole truth, we cannot determine ;" "If thou *will* undertake the business there is little doubt of success." This mode of expressing the auxiliaries, does not appear to be warranted by the general practice of correct writers. They should be, *hadst, shalt*, and *wilt :* and we find them used in this form, in the sacred Scriptures.

" If thou *hadst* known," &c. *Luke* xix. 47. " If thou *hadst* been here," &c. *John* xi. 21. "If thou *will*, thou canst make me clean." *Matt.* viii. 2. See also, *2 Sam.* ii. 27. *Matt.* xvii. 4.

7. The second person singular of the imperfect tense in the subjunctive mood, is also very frequently used without the personal termination : as, " If thou *loved* him truly, thou wouldst obey him ;" " Though thou *did* conform, thou hast gained nothing by it." This, however, appears to be improp-

er. Our present version of the Scriptures, which are again referred to, as a good grammatical authority in points of this nature, decides against it. "If thou *knewest* the gift," &c. *John* iv. 10. "If thou *didst* receive it, why dost thou glory?" &c. 1 *Cor.* iv. 7. See also *Dan.* v. 22.

8. It may not be superfluous, also to observe, that the auxiliaries of the potential mood, when applied to the subjunctive, retain the termination of the second person singular. We properly say, "If thou *mayst* or *canst* go ;" "Though thou *mightst* live ;" "Unless thou *couldst* read ;" "If thou *wouldst* learn ;" and not, "If thou *may* or *can* go ;" &c. It is sufficient, on this point, to adduce the authorities of Johnson and Lowth : "If thou *shouldst* go ;" *Johnson.* "If thou *mayst, mightst,* or *couldst* love ;" *Lowth.* Some authors think, that when *that* expresses the motive or end, these auxiliaries should not be varied : as, "I advise thee, *that* thou *may* beware ;" "He checked thee, *that* thou *should* not presume :" but there does not appear to be any ground for this exception. If the expression of "condition, doubt, contingency," &c. does not prevent a change in the form of these auxiliaries, why should they not vary, when a motive or end is expressed ? The translators of the Scriptures do not appear to have made the distinction contended for. "Thou buildest the wall, *that* thou *mayst* be their king." *Neh.* vi. 6. "There is forgiveness with thee, *that* thou *mayst* be feared." *Psalms.* CXXX. 4.

9. Some conjunctions have their corresponding conjunctions belonging to them, so that, in the subsequent member of the sentence, the latter answers to the former : as,

1. THOUGH,—YET, NEVERTHELESS : as, "*Though* he was rich, *yet* for our sakes he became poor."
2. WHETHER—OR : as, "*Whether* he will go *or* not, I cannot tell."
3. EITHER—OR : as, "I will *either* send it, *or* bring it myself."
4. NEITHER—NOR : as, "*Neither* thou *nor* I am able to compass it."
5. AS—AS : expressing a comparison of equality : as, "She is *as* amiable *as* her sister."
6. AS—SO : expressing a comparison of equality : "*As* the stars, *so* shall thy seed be."
7. AS—SO : expressing a comparison of quality : as, "*As* the one dieth, *so* dieth the other."
8. SO—AS : with a verb expressing a comparison of quality : as, "To see thy glory, *so as* I have seen thee in the sanctuary."
9. SO—AS : with a negative and an adjective expressing a comparison of quantity : as, "Pompey was not *so* great a man *as* Cæsar."

10. SO—THAT: expressing a consequence: as, "He was so fatigue I, *that* he could scarcely move."

The conjunctions *or* and *nor* may often be used, with nearly equal propriety. "The king, whose character was not sufficiently vigorous, *nor* decisive, assented to the measure." In this sentence, *or* would perhaps have been better: but, in general, *nor* seems to repeat the negation in the former part of the sentence, and therefore gives more emphasis to the expression.

10. Conjunctions are often improperly used, both singly and in pairs. The following are examples of this impropriety. "The relations are so uncertain, as that they require a great deal of examination:" it should be, "*that* they require," &c. "There was no man so sanguine, who did not apprehend some ill consequences:" it ought to be, "So sanguine as not to apprehend," &c.; or, "no man, how sanguine soever, who did not," &c. "To trust in him is no more but to acknowledge his power." "This is no other but the gate of paradise." In both these instances, *but* should be *than*. "We should sufficiently weigh the objects of our hope; whether they are such as we may reasonably expect from them what they propose." &c. It ought to be, "*that* we may reasonably," &c. "The duke had not behaved with that loyalty as he ought to have done;" "*with which* he ought." "In the order as they lie in his preface:" it should be, "in order as they lie;" or "in the order *in which* they lie."

There is a peculiar neatness in a sentence beginning with the conjunctive form of a verb. "*Were* there no difference, there would be no choice."

A double conjunctive, in two correspondent clauses of a sentence, is sometimes made use of: as, "*Had* he done this, he *had* escaped:" "*Had* the limitations on the prerogative been, in his time, quite fixed and certain, his integrity *had* made him regard as sacred, the boundaries of the constitution." The sentence in the common form would have read thus: "If the limitations on the prerogative had been, &c. his integrity would have made him regard," &c.

The particle *as*, when it is connected with the pronoun *such*, has the force of a relative pronoun: as, "Let *such as* presume to advise others, look well to their own conduct;" which is equivalent to, "Let *them who* presume," &c.

"Such sharp replies that cost him his life:" "*as* cost him," &c. "If he were truly that scarecrow, as he is now commonly painted;" "*such* a scarecrow," &c. "I wish I could do that justice to his memory, to oblige the painters," &c.: "do *such* justice *as* would oblige," &c.

In regard that is solemn and antiquated; *because* would do much better in the following sentence. "It cannot be otherwise, in regard that the French prosody differs from that of every other language."

The word *except* is far preferable to *other than*. "It admitted of no effectual cure other than amputation." *Except* is also to be preferred to *all but*. "They were happy all but the stranger."

In the two following phrases, the conjunction *as* is improperly omitted ; "Which nobody presumes, or is so sanguine to hope." "I must, however, be so just to own."

The conjunction *that* is often properly omitted, and understood : as, "I beg you would come to me ;" "See thou do it not :" instead of "that you would," "that thou do." But in the following and many similar phrases this conjunction would be much better inserted : "Yet it is reason the memory of their virtues remain to posterity." It should be, "yet it is *just that* the memory," &c.

Now correct and parse the following

EXERCISES IN FALSE SYNTAX.

If he acquires riches, they will corrupt his mind, and be useless to others.

Though he urges me yet more earnestly, I shall not comply, unless he advances more forcible reasons.

I shall walk in the fields to day, unless it rains.

As the governess were present, the children behaved properly.

She disapproves the measure, because it were very improper.

Though he be high, he hath respect to the lowly.

Though he were her friend, he did not attempt to justify her conduct.

Whether he improve or not, I cannot determine.

Though the fact be extraordinary, it certainly did happen.

Remember what thou wert, and be humble.

O ! that his heart was tender, and susceptible of the woes of others.

> Shall then this verse to future age pretend,
> Thou wert my guide, philosopher, and friend ?

1. Unless he learns faster, he will be no scholar.

Though he falls he shall not be utterly cast down.

On condition that he comes, I will consent to stay.

However that affair terminates, my conduct will be unimpeachable.

If virtue rewards us not so soon as we desire, the payment will be made with interest.

Till repentance composes his mind he will be a stranger to peace.

Whether he confesses, or not, the truth will certainly be discovered.

If thou censurest uncharitably, thou wilt be entitled to no favor.

Though, at times, the ascent of the temple of virtue, appears steep and craggy, be not discouraged. Persevere until thou gainest the summit : there, all is order, beauty, and pleasure.

If Charlotte desire to gain esteem and love, she does not employ the proper means.

Unless the accountant deceive me, my estate is considerably improved.

Though self-government produce some uneasiness, it is light, when compared with the pain of vicious indulgence.

Whether he think as he speaks, time will discover.

If thou censure uncharitably, thou deservest no favor.

Though virtue appear severe, she is truly amiable.

Though success be very doubtful, it is proper that he endeavours to succeed.

The examples which follow, are suited to the notes and observations under RULE IV. ●

2. Despise not any condition, lest it happens to be your own.

Let him that is sanguine, take heed lest he miscarries.

Take care that thou breakest not any of the established rules.

If he does but intimate his desire, it will be sufficient to produce obedience.

At the time of his return, if he is but expert in the business, he will find employment.

If he do but speak to display his abilities, he is unworthy of attention.

If he be but in health, I am content.

If he does promise, he will certainly perform.

Though he do praise her, it is only for her beauty.

If thou dost not forgive, perhaps thou wilt not be forgiven.

If thou do sincerely believe the truths of religion, act accordingly.

3. His confused behaviour made it reasonable to suppose that he were guilty.

He is so conscious of deserving the rebuke, that he dare not make any reply.

His apology was so plausible, that many befriended him, and thought he were innocent.

4. If one man prefer a life of industry, it is because he has an idea of comfort in wealth ; if another prefers a life of gayety, it is from a like idea concerning pleasure.

No one engages in that business, unless he aim at reputation, or hopes for some singular advantage.

Though the design be laudable, and is favorable to our interest, it will involve much anxiety and labour.

5. If thou have promised, be faithful to thy engagement.

Though he have proved his right to submission, he is too generous to exact it.

Unless he have improved, he is unfit for the office.

6. If thou had succeeded, perhaps thou wouldst not be the happier for it.

Unless thou shall see the propriety of the measure, we shall not desire thy support.

Though thou will not acknowledge, thou canst not deny the fact.

7. If thou gave liberally, thou wilt receive a liberal reward.

Though thou did injure him, he harbours no resentment.

It would be well, if the report was only the misrepresentation of her enemies.

Was he ever so great and opulent, this conduct would debase him.

Was I to enumerate all her virtues, it would look like flattery.

Though I was perfect, yet would I not presume.

8. If thou may share in his labours, be thankful and do it cheerfully.

Unless thou can fairly support the cause, give it up honorably.

Though thou might have foreseen the danger, thou couldst not have avoided it.

If thou could convince him, he would not act accordingly.

If thou would improve in knowledge, be diligent.

Unless thou should make a timely retreat, the danger will be unavoidable.

I have laboured and wearied myself that thou may be at ease.

He enlarged on those dangers, that thou should avoid them.

9. Neither the cold or the fervid, but characters uniformly warm, are formed for friendship.

They are both praise-worthy, and one is equally deserving as the other.

He is not as diligent and learned as his brother.

I will present it to him myself, or direct it to be given to him.

Neither despise or oppose what you do not understand.

The house is not as commodious as we expected it would be.

I must, however, be so candid to own I have been mistaken.

There was something so amiable, and yet so piercing in his look, as affected me at once with love and terror.

 ———"I gained a son ;
And such a son, as all men hail'd me happy."

The dog in the manger would not eat the hay himself, nor suffer the ox to eat it.

As far as I am able to judge, the book is well written.

We should faithfully perform the trust committed to us, or ingenuously relinquish the charge.

He is not as eminent, and as much esteemed, as he thinks himself to be.

The work is a dull performance ; and is neither capable of pleasing the understanding, or the imagination.

There is no condition so secure, as cannot admit of change.

This is an event, which nobody presumes upon, or is so sanguine to hope for.

We are generally pleased with any little accomplishments of body or mind.

10. Be ready to succour such persons who need your assistance.

The matter was no sooner proposed, but he privately withdrew to consider it.

He has too much sense and prudence than to become a dupe to such artifices.

It is not sufficient that our conduct, as far as it respects others, appears to be unexceptionable.

The resolution was not the less fixed, that the secret was yet communicated to very few.

He opposed the most remarkable corruptions of the church of Rome, so as that his doctrines were embraced by great numbers.

He gained nothing further by his speech, but only to be commended for his eloquence.

He has little more of the scholar besides the name.

He has little of the scholar than the name.

They had no sooner risen, but they applied themselves to their studies.

From no other institution, besides the admirable one of juries, could so great a benefit be expected.

Those savage people seemed to have no other element but war.

Such men that act treacherously ought to be avoided.

Germany ran the same risk which Italy had done.

No errors are so trivial, but they deserve to be corrected.

SECTION XXI.

RULE V.

All the parts of a sentence should correspond to each other : a regular and dependent construction, throughout, should be carefully preserved. The following sentence is therefore inaccurate ; " He was more beloved, but not so much admired as Cinthio." It should be, " He was more beloved than Cinthio, but not so much admired."

The first example under this rule, presents a most irregular construction, namely, " He was more beloved *as* Cinthio." The words *more*, and *so much*, are very improperly stated as having the same regimen. In correcting such sentences, it is not necessary to supply the latter ellipsis of the corrected sentence by saying, "but not so much admired *as Cinthio was ;*" because the ellipsis cannot lead to any discordant or improper construction, and the supply would often be harsh or inelegant.

As this rule comprehends all the preceding rules, it may, at the first view, appear to be too general to be useful. But by ranging under it a number of sentences peculiarly constructed, we shall perceive, that it is calculated to ascertain the true grammatical construction of many modes of expression, which none of the particular rules can sufficiently explain.

" This dedication may serve for almost any book, that has, is, or shall be published." It ought to be, "that has been, or that shall be published." " He was guided by interests always different, sometimes contrary to, those of the community ;" " different *from ;*" or, " always different from those of the community, and sometimes contrary to them." " Will it be urged that these books are as old, or even older than tradition ?" The words, " as old," and "older," cannot have a common regimen ; it should be " as old as tradition, or even older." " It requires few talents to which most men are not born, or at least may not acquire ;" " or which, at least, they may not acquire." " The court of chancery frequently mitigates and breaks the teeth of the common law." In this construction, the first verb is said, " to mitigate the teeth of the common law," which is an evident solecism. " Mitigates the common law, and breaks the teeth of it," would have been grammatical.

" They presently grow into good humour, and good language towards the crown ;" " grow into good language," is very improper. " There is never wanting a set of evil instruments, who either out of mad zeal, private hatred, or filthy lucre, are always ready," &c. We say properly, " A man acts out of mad zeal," or, " out of private hatred ;" but we cannot say, if we would speak English, " he *acts* out of filthy lucre." " To double her kindness and caresses of me :" the word " kindness" requires to be followed by either *to* or *for*, and cannot be construed with the preposition *of*. " Never was man so teased or suffered half the uneasiness, as I have done this evening ;" the first and third clauses, viz. " Never was man so teased, as I have done this evening," cannot be joined without an impropriety ; and to connect the second and third, the word *that* must be substituted for *as :* " Or suffered half the uneasiness that I have ;" or else, " half so much uneasiness as I have suffered."

The first part of the following sentence abounds with adverbs, and those such as are hardly consistent with one another : " *How much soever* the reformation of this degenerate age is *almost utterly* to be despaired of, we may yet have a more comfortable prospect of future times." The sentence would be more correct in the following form : " *Though* the reformation of this degenerate age is *nearly* to be despaired of," &c.

" Oh ! shut not up my soul with the sinners, nor my life with the blood-thirsty ; in whose hands is wickedness, and *their* right hand is full of gifts." As the passage, introduced by the copulative conjunction *and*, was not intended as a continuation of the principal and independent part of the sentence, but of the dependent part, the relative *whose* should have been used instead of the possessive *their* ; viz. " and *whose* right-hand is full of gifts."

The following sentences, which give the passive verb the regimen of an active verb, are very irregular, and by no means to be imitated. " The bishops and abbots were allowed their seats in the house of lords." " Thrasea was forbidden the presence of the emperor." " He was shown that very story in one of his own books." These sentences should have been ; " The bishops and abbots were allowed to have (or to take) their seats in the house of lords ;" or, " Seats in the house of lords were allowed to the bishops and abbots:" " Thrasea was forbidden to approach the presence of the emperor :" or, " The presence of the emperor was forbidden to

Thrasea :" " That very story was shown to him in one of his own books."

" Eye hath not seen, nor ear heard, neither *have* entered into the heart of man, the things which God hath prepared for them that love him." There seems to be an impropriety in this sentence, in which the same noun serves in a double capacity, performing at the same time the offices both of the nominative and objective cases. " Neither *hath* it entered into the heart of man to conceive the things," &c. would have been regular.

" We have the power of retaining, altering, and compounding those images which we have once received, into all the varieties of picture and vision." It is very proper to say, "altering and compounding those images which we have once received, into all the varieties of picture and vision ;" but we can with no propriety say, " retaining them into all the varieties ;" and yet according to the manner in which the words are ranged, this construction is unavoidable : for, "retaining, altering, and compounding," are participles, each of which equally refers to and governs the subsequent noun, *those images* ; and that noun again is necessarily connected with the following preposition, *into*. The construction might easily have been rectified, by disjoining the participle *retaining* from the other two participles, in this way : " We have the power of retaining those images which we have once received, and of altering and compounding them into all the varieties of picture and vision :" or, perhaps better thus : " We have the power of retaining, altering, and compounding those images which we have once received, and of forming them into all the varieties of picture and vision."

Now correct and parse the following

EXERCISES IN FALSE SYNTAX.

Several alterations and additions have been made to the work.

The first proposal was essentially different, and inferior to the second.

He is more bold and active, but not so wise and studious as his companion.

Thou hearest the sound of the wind, but thou canst not tell whence it cometh, and whither it goeth.

Neither has he, nor any other persons, suspected so much dissimulation.

The court of France or England, was to be the umpire.

In the reign of Henry II. all foreign commodities were plenty in England.

There is no talent so useful towards success in business, or which puts men more out of the reach of accidents, than that quality generally possessed by persons of cool temper, and is in common language called discretion.

The first project was to shorten discourse, by cutting polysyllables into one.

I shall do all I can to persuade others to take the same measures for their cure which I have.

The greatest masters of critical learning differ among one another.

Micaiah said, "If thou certainly return in peace, then hath not the Lord spoken by me."

I do not suppose, that we Britons want a genius, more than the rest of our neighbors.

The deaf man, whose ears were opened, and his tongue loosened, doubtless glorified the great physician.

Groves, fields, and meadows, are, at any season of the year, pleasant to look upon ; but never so much as in the opening of the spring.

The multitude rebuked them, because they should hold their peace

The intentions of some of these philosophers, nay, of many, might and probably were good.

It is an unanswerable argument of a very refined age, the wonderful civilities that have passed between the nation of authors and that of readers.

It was an unsuccessful undertaking ; which, although it has failed, is no objection at all to an enterprise so well concerted.

The reward is his due, and it has already, or will hereafter, be given to him.

By intercourse with wise and experienced persons, who know the world, we may improve and rub off the rust of a private and retired education.

Sincerity is as valuable, and even more valuable, than knowledge.

No person was ever so perplexed, or sustained the mortifications as he has done to-day.

The Romans gave, not only the freedom of the city, but capacity for employments, to several towns, in Gaul, Spain, and Germany.

Such writers have no other standard on which to form themselves, except what chances to be fashionable and popular.

Whatever we do secretly, shall be displayed and heard in the clearest light.

To the happiness of possessing a person of such uncommon merit, Boethius soon had the satisfaction of obtaining the highest honor his country could bestow.

But to the assertions which his intoxicated brain and unbridled phrensy have led him to make, I shall hold him personally responsible.

PUNCTUATION.

PUNCTUATION is the art of dividing a written composition into sentences, or parts of sentences, by points or stops for the purpose of marking the different pauses which the sense, and an accurate pronunciation, require.

The Comma represents the shortest pause; the Semicolon, a pause double that of the comma; the Colon, double that of the semicolon; and the Period, double that of the colon.

The precise quantity or duration of each pause cannot be defined; for it varies with the time of the whole. The same composition may be rehearsed in a quicker or a slower time; but the proportion between the pauses should be ever invariable.

In order more clearly to determine the proper application of the points, we must distinguish between an *imperfect phrase*, a *simple sentence*, and a *compound sentence*.

An imperfect phrase contains no assertion, or does not amount to a proposition or sentence: as, "Therefore; in haste; studious of praise."

A simple sentence has but one subject, and one finite verb, expressed or implied: as, "Temperance preserves health."

A compound sentence has more than one subject, or one finite verb, either expressed or understood; or it consists of two or more simple sentences connected together; as, "Good nature mends and beautifies all objects;" "Virtue refines the affections, but vice debases them."

In a sentence, the subject and the verb, or either of them, may be accompanied with several adjuncts: as, the object, the end, the circumstance of time, place, manner and the like: and the subject or verb may be either immediately connected with them, or mediately; that is, by being connected with something which is connected with some other, and so on: as, "The mind, unoccupied with useful knowledge, becomes a magazine of trifles and follies."

Members of sentences may be divided into simple and compound members.

CHAPTER I.

OF THE COMMA.

The Comma usually separates those parts of a sentence, which, though, very closely connected in sense and construction, require a pause between them.

RULE I.

With respect to a simple sentence, the several words of which it consists have so near a relation to each other, that, in general, no points are requisite, except a full stop at the end of it ; as, "The fear of the Lord is the beginning of wisdom." "Every part of matter swarms with living creatures."

A simple sentence, however, when it is a long one, and the nominative case is accompanied with inseparable adjuncts, may admit of a pause immediately before the verb : as, "The good taste of the present age, has not allowed us to neglect the cultivation of the English language." "To be totally indifferent to praise or censure, is a real defect in character."

RULE II.

When the connexion of the different parts of a simple sentence, is interrupted by an imperfect phrase, a comma is usually introduced before the beginning, and at the end of this phrase : as, "I remember, *with gratitude*, his goodness to me;" "His work is, *in many respects*, very imperfect. It is, *therefore*, not much approved." But when these interruptions are slight and unimportant, the comma is better omitted : as, "Flattery is *certainly* pernicious :" "There is *surely* a pleasure in beneficence."

In the generality of compound sentences, there is frequent occasion for commas. This will appear from the following rules ; some of which apply to simple, as well as to compound sentences.

RULE III.

When two or more nouns occur in the same construction, they are parted by a comma : as, "Reason, virtue, answer one great aim :" "The husband, wife and children, suffered extremely :"* "They took away their furniture, clothes, and stock in trade ;" "He is alternately supported by his father, his uncle, and his elder brother."

---

*As a considerable pause in pronunciation is necessary between the last noun and the verb, a comma should be inserted to denote it. But as no pause is allowable between the last adjective and the noun, under Rule IV. the comma is there properly omitted.—*See Walker's Elements of Elocution.*

From this rule there is mostly an exception, with regard to two nouns closely connected by a conjunction : as, "Virtue *and* vice form a strong contrast to each other :" "Libertines call religion bigotry *or* superstition ;" "There is a natural difference between merit *and* demerit, virtue *and* vice, wisdom *and* folly." But if the parts connected are not short, a comma may be inserted, though the conjunction is expressed : as, "Romances may be said to be miserable rhapsodies, *or* dangerous incentives to evil ;" "Intemperance destroys the strength of our bodies, *and* the vigor of our minds."

RULE IV.

Two or more adjectives belonging to the same substantive, are likewise separated by commas: as, "Plain, honest truth, wants no artificial covering ;" "David was a brave, wise, and pious man :" "A woman, gentle, sensible, well-educated, and religious :" "The most innocent pleasures are the sweetest, the most rational, the most affecting, and the most lasting."

But two adjectives, immediately connected by a conjunction, are not separated by a comma: as, "True worth is modest *and* retired ;" "Truth is fair *and* artless, simple *and* sincere, uniform *and* consistent." "We must be wise *or* foolish ; there is no medium."

RULE V.

Two or more verbs, having the same nominative case, and immediately following one another, are also separated by commas : as, "Virtue supports in adversity, moderates in prosperity :" "In a letter, we may advise, exhort, comfort, request, and discuss."

Two verbs immediately connected by a conjunction, are an exception to the above rule : as, "The study of natural history expands *and* elevates the mind ;" "Whether we eat *or* drink, labor *or* sleep, we should be moderate."

Two or more participles are subject to a similar rule, and exception: as, "A man, fearing, serving, and loving, his Creator ;" "He was happy in being loved, esteemed, and respected ;" "By being admired and flattered, we are often corrupted."

RULE VI.

Two or more adverbs immediately succeeding one another, must be separated by commas: as, "We are fearfully, wonderfully framed ;" "Success generally depends on acting prudently, steadily, and vigorously, in what we undertake."

But when two adverbs are joined by a conjunction, they are not parted by the comma: as, "Some men sin deliberately *and* presumptuously ;" "There is no middle state ; we must live virtuously *or* viciously."

RULE VII.

When participles are followed by something that depends on them, they are generally separated from the rest of the sentence by a comma: as, "The king, *approving the plan*, put it in execution;" "His talents, *formed for great enterprises*, could not fail of rendering him conspicuous:" . "All mankind compose one family, *assembled* under the eye of one common Father."

RULE VIII.

When a conjunction is divided by a phrase or sentence, from the verb to which it belongs, such intervening phrase has usually a comma at each extremity: as, "They set out early, *and*, before the close of the day, arrived at the destined place."

RULE IX.

Expressions in a direct address, are separated from the rest of the sentence by commas: as, "*My son*, give me thy heart;" "I am obliged to you, *my friends*, for your many favors."

RULE X.

The case or nominative absolute, and the infinitive mood absolute, are separated by commas from the body of the sentence: as, "His father dying, he succeeded to the estate;" "At length, their ministry performed, and race well run, they left the world in peace;" "To confess the truth, I was much in fault."

RULE XI.

Nouns in apposition, that is, nouns added to other nouns in the same case, by way of explication or illustration, when accompanied with adjuncts, are set off by commas: as, "Paul, the apostle of the Gentiles, was em   ent for his zeal and knowledge;" "The butterfly, child of the summer, flutters in the sun."

But if such nouns are single, or only form a proper name, they are not divided: as, "Paul, the apostle;" "The emperor Antoninus wrote an excellent book."

RULE XII.

Simple members of sentences connected by comparatives, are, for the most part, distinguished by a comma: as, "*As* the hart panteth after the water brooks, *so* doth my soul pant after thee;" "*Better* is a dinner of herbs with love, *than* a stalled ox and hatred with it."

If the members in comparative sentences are short, the comma is, in general, better omitted: as, "How much *better* is it to get wisdom *than* gold!" "Mankind act *oftener* from caprice *than* reason.

RULE XIII.

When words are placed in opposition to each other, or with some marked variety, they require to be distinguished by a comma, as :

" Though deep, yet clear, though gentle, yet not dull ;
" Strong, without rage ; without o'erflowing, full."

" Good men, in this frail, imperfect state, are often found, not only in union *with*, but in opposition *to*, the views and conduct of one another."

Sometimes, when the word with which the last preposition agrees, is single, it is better to omit the comma before it : as, " Many States were in alliance *with*, and under the pro-tection *of* Rome."

The same rule and restriction must be applied, when two or more nouns refer to the same preposition : as, " He was composed, both under the threatening, and at the approach, *of* a cruel and lingering death ;" " He was not only the king, but the father *of* his people."

RULE XIV.

A remarkable expression, or a short observation, some-what in manner of a quotation, may be properly marked with a comma : as, " It hurts a man's pride to say, I do not know ;" " Plutarch calls lying, the vice of slaves."

RULE XV.

Relative pronouns are connective words, and generally admit a comma before them : as, " He preaches sublimely, *who* lives a sober, righteous, and pious life ;" " There is no charm in the female sex, *which* can supply the place of vir-tue."

But when two members, or phrases, are closely connected by a relative restraining the general notion of the antecedent to a particular sense, the comma should be omitted : as, " Self-denial is the sacrifice which virtue must make ;" " A man who is of a detracting spirit, will misconstrue the most innocent words that can be put together." In the latter ex-ample, the assertion is not of " a man in general," but of " a man who is of a detracting spirit ;" and therefore they should not be separated.

The fifteenth rule applies equally to cases in which the relative is not expressed, but understood : as, " It was from piety, warm and unaffected, that his morals derived strength." " This sentiment, habitual and strong, influenced his whole conduct." In both of these examples, the relative and the verb *which was*, are understood.

RULE XVI.

A simple member of a sentence, contained within another, or following another, must be distinguished by the comma: as, " to improve time, whilst we are blessed with health, will smooth the bed of sickness." " Very often, while we are complaining of the vanity, and the evils of human life, we make that vanity, and we increase those evils."

If, however, the members succeeding each other, are very closely connected, the comma is unnecessary : as, " Revelation tells us how we may attain happiness."

When a verb in the infinitive mood follows its governing verb, with several words between them, those words should generally have a comma at the end of them : as, " It ill becomes good and wise men, to oppose and degrade one another."

Several verbs in the infinitive mood, having a common dependence, and succeeding one another, are also divided by commas : as, " To relieve the indigent, to comfort the afflicted, to protect the innocent, to reward the deserving, are humane and noble employments."

RULE XVII.

When the verb *to be* is followed by a verb in the infinitive mood, which, by transposition, might be made the nominative case to it, the former is generally separated from the latter verb, by a comma: as, " The most obvious remedy is, to withdraw from all associations with bad men." " The first and most obvious remedy against the infection, is, to withdraw from all association with bad men."

RULE XVIII.

When adjuncts or circumstances are of importance, and often when the natural order of them is inverted, they may be set off by commas : as, "Virtue must be formed and supported, not by unfrequent acts, but by daily and repeated exertions." " Vices, like shadows, towards the evening of life, grow great and monstrous." " Our interests are interwoven by threads innumerable ;" " By threads innumerable, our interests are interwoven."

RULE XIX.

Where a verb is understood, a comma may often be properly introduced. This is a general rule, which, besides comprising some of the preceding rules, will apply to many cases not determined by any of them : as, " From law arises security ; from security, curiosity ; from curiosity, knowledge." In this example, the verb "arises" is understood before "curiosity" and "knowledge;" at which words a considerable pause is necessary.

RULE XX.

The words, *any, so, hence, again, first, secondly, formerly, now, lastly, once more, above all, on the contrary, in the next place, in short*, and all other words and phrases of the same kind, must generally be separated from the context by a comma: as, "Remember thy best and first friend; *formerly*, the supporter of thy infancy, and the guide of thy childhood; *now*, the guardian of thy youth, and the hope of thy coming years." "He feared want, *hence*, he over-valued riches." "This conduct may heal the difference, *nay*, it may constantly prevent any in future." "*Finally*, I shall only repeat what has been often justly said." "If the spring put forth no blossoms, in summer there will be no beauty, and in autumn no fruit; *so*, if youth be trifled away without improvement, riper years may be contemptible, and old age miserable."

In many of the foregoing rules and examples, great regard must be paid to the length of the clauses, and the proportion which they bear to one another. An attention to the sense of any passage, and to the clear, easy communication of it, will, it is presumed, with the aid of the preceding rules, enable you to adjust the proper pauses, and the places for inserting the commas.

CHAPTER II.

OF THE SEMICOLON.

The Semicolon is used for dividing a compound sentence into two or more parts, not so closely connected as those which are separated by a comma, nor yet so little dependent on each other, as those which are distinguished by a colon.

The Semicolon is sometimes used, when the preceding member of the sentence does not of itself give a complete sense, but depends on the following clause: and sometimes when the sense of that member would be complete without the concluding one: as in the following instances: "As the desire of approbation, when it works according to reason, improves the amiable part of our species in every thing that is laudable; so nothing is more destructive to them, when it is governed by vanity and folly."

"Experience teaches us, that an entire retreat from worldly affairs, is not what religion requires ; nor does it even enjoin a long retreat from them."

"Straws swim upon the surface ; but pearls lie at the bottom."

"Philosophers assert, that nature is unlimited in her operations ; that she has inexhaustible treasures in reserve ; that knowledge will always be progressive ; and that all future generations will continue to make discoveries, of which we have not the least idea."

"But all subsists by elemental strife ;
"And passions are the elements of life."

CHAPTER III.

OF THE COLON.

The Colon is used to divide a sentence into two or more parts, less connected than those which are separated by a semicolon ; but not so independent as separate distinct sentences.

· The colon may be properly applied in the three following cases.

1. When a member of a sentence is complete in itself, but followed by some supplemental remark, or further illustration of the subject : as, "Nature felt her inability to extricate herself from the consequences of guilt : the gospel reveals the plan of Divine interposition and aid." "Nature confesseth some atonement to be necessary : the gospel discovers that the necessary atonement is made."

"Great works are performed, not by strength, but perseverance : yonder palace was raised by single stones ; yet you see its height and spaciousness."

"In faith and hope the world will disagree ;
"But all mankind's concern is charity :
"All must be false that thwart this one great end ;
"And, all of God, that bless mankind or mend."

2. When a semicolon, or more than one, have preceded, and a still greater pause is necessary, in order to mark the connecting or concluding sentiment : as, "As we perceive the shadow to have moved along the dial, but did not perceive it moving ; and it appears that the grass has grown, though nobody ever saw it grow : so the advances we make in

knowledge, as they consist of such insensible steps, are only perceivable by the distance."

"A Divine Legislator, uttering his voice from heaven ; an almighty governor, stretching forth his arm to punish or reward ; informing us of perpetual rest prepared hereafter for the righteous, and of indignation and wrath awaiting the wicked : these are the considerations which overawe the world, which support integrity, and check guilt.

3. The Colon is commonly used when an example, a quotation, or a speech, is introduced : as, "The Scriptures give us an amiable representation of the Deity, in these words : 'God is love.'" "He was often heard to say : 'I have done with the world, and I am willing to leave it.'"

The propriety of using a colon, or semicolon, is sometimes determined by a conjunction's being expressed, or not expressed : as, "Do not flatter yourselves with the hope of perfect happiness : *for* there is no such thing in the world."

"Where grows ?—where grows it not ? If vain our toil
"We ought to blame the culture, not the soil :
"Fix'd to no spot is happiness sincere ;
"'Tis no where to be found, or ev'ry where."

CHAPTER IV.

OF THE PERIOD.

When a sentence is complete and independent, and not connected in construction with the following sentence, it is marked with a Period.

Some sentences are independent of each other, both in their sense and construction : as, "Fear God. Honor the King. Have charity towards all men." Others are independent only in their grammatical construction : as, "The Supreme Being changes not, either in his desire to promote our happiness, or in the plan of his administration. One light always shines upon us from above. One clear and direct path is always pointed out to man."

A period may sometimes be admitted between two sentences, though they are joined by a disjunctive or copulative conjunction. For the quality of the point does not always depend on the connective particle, but on the sense and structure of sentences : as, "Recreations, though they may be of an innocent kind, require steady government to keep them within a due and limited province. But such as are of an irregular and vicious nature, are not to be governed, but to be banished from every well-regulated mind."

"He who lifts himself up to the observation and notice of the world, is, of all men, the least likely to avoid censure. For he draws upon himself a thousand eyes, that will narrowly inspect him in every part."

The period should be used after every abbreviated word : as, "M. S. P. S. N. B. A. D. O. S. N. S." &c.

CHAPTER V.

OF THE DASH, NOTES of INTERROGATION AND EXCLAMATION, AND THE PARENTHESIS.

SECTION 1.

Of the Dash.

The Dash, though often used improperly by hasty and incoherent writers, may be introduced with propriety, where the sentence breaks off abruptly ; where a significant pause is required ; or where there is no unexpected turn in the sentiment : as, "If thou art he, so much respected once—but, oh ! how fallen ! how degraded !" "If acting conformably to the will of our Creator ;—if promoting the welfare of mankind around us :— securing our own happiness ;—are objects of the highest moment ;—then we are loudly called upon, to cultivate and extend the great interests of religion and virtue." A dash following a stop, denotes that the pause is to be greater than if the stop were alone ; and when used by itself, requires a pause of such a length as the sense alone can determine.

"Here lies the great——False marble, where ?
"Nothing but sordid dust lies here."

"Whatever is, is right.—This world, 'tis true,
"Was made for Cæsar—but for Titus too."

Besides the points which mark the pauses in discourse, there are characters, which denote a different modulation of voice, in correspondence to the sense. These are,

The point of INTERROGATION,   ?
The point of EXCLAMATION,   !
The PARENTHESIS,   ( )

25*

Section 2.

Of the Interrogatory Point.

A note of Interrogation is used at the end of an interrogative sentence ; that is, when a question is asked : as, " Who will accompany me ?"   " Shall we always be friends ?"

Questions which a person asks himself in contemplation, ought to be terminated by points of interrogation : as, " Who adorned the heavens with such exquisite beauty ?"   " At whose command do the planets perform their constant revolutions ?"

"To whom can riches give repute or trust,
" Content or pleasure, but the good and just ?"

A point of interrogation is improper after sentences which are not questions, but only expressions of admiration, or of some other emotion.

" How many instances have we of chastity and excellence in the fair sex !"

" With what prudence does the son of Sirach advise us, in the choice of our companions !"

A note of interrogation should not be employed, in cases where it is only said a question has been asked, and where the words are not used as a question.   " The Cyprians asked me why I wept."   To give this sentence the interrogative form, it should be expressed thus, " The Cyprians said to me, ' Why dost thou weep ?"

Section 3.

Of the Exclamatory Point.

The note of Exclamation is applied to expressions of sudden emotion, surprise, joy, grief, &c. and also to invocations or addresses : as, " My friend ! this conduct amazes me !" ' Bless the Lord, O my soul ! and forget not all his benefits !"

" Oh ! had we both our humble state maintain'd,
" And safe in peace and poverty remain'd !"

" Hear me, O Lord ! for thy loving kindness is great !"

It is difficult in some cases, to distinguish between an interrogative and exclamatory sentence : but a sentence, in which any wonder or admiration is expressed, and no answer either expected or implied, may be always properly terminated by a note of exclamation : as, " How much vanity in the pursuits of men !"   " Who can sufficiently express the goodness of our Creator !"   " What is more amiable than virtue !"

The interrogation and exclamation points are indeterminate as to their quantity or time, and may be equivalent in that respect to a semicolon, a colon, or a period, as the sense may require. They mark an elevation of the voice.

The utility of the points of Interrogation and Exclamation, appears from the following examples, in which the meaning is signified and discriminated solely by the points.

> " What condescension !"
> What condescension ?"

> " How great was the sacrifice !"
> " How great was the sacrifice ?"

SECTION 4.

Of the Parenthesis.

A Parenthesis is a clause containing some necessary information, or useful remark, introduced into the body of a sentence obliquely, and which may be omitted without injuring the grammatical construction : as,

> " Know then this truth, (enough for man to know,)
> " Virtue alone is happiness below."

> " And was the ransom paid ? It was ; and paid
> " (What can exalt his bounty more ?) for thee."

" To gain a posthumous reputation, is to save four or five letters (for what is a name besides ?) from oblivion." "Know ye not, brethren, (for I speak to them that know the law,) how that the law hath dominion over a man as long as he liveth ?"

If the incidental clause is short, or perfectly coincides with the rest of the sentence, it is not proper to use the parenthetical characters. The following instances are therefore proper uses of the parenthesis. " Speak you (who saw) his wonders in the deep." " Every planet (as the Creator has made nothing in vain) is most probably inhabited." " He found them asleep again ; (for their eyes were heavy ;) neither knew they what to answer him."

The parenthesis generally marks a moderate depression of the voice, and may be accompanied with every point which the sense would require, if the parenthetical characters were omitted. It ought to terminate with the same kind of stop which the member has, that precedes it ; and to contain that stop within the parenthetical marks. We must, however, except cases of interrogation and exclamation : as, " While they wish to please, (and why should they not wish it ?) they disdain dishonorable means."   "It was represent ed by an analogy, (Oh, how inadequate!) which was borrow ed from the religion of paganism."

CHAPTER VI.

OF THE APOSTROPHE, CARET, &c.

There are other characters, which are frequently made use of in composition, and which may be explained in this place, viz.

An Apostrophe, marked thus ' is used to abbreviate or shorten a word : as, " *'tis* for *it is* ; *tho'* for *though* ; *e'en* for *even* ; *judg'd* for *judged*." Its chief use is to show the genitive case of nouns : as, " A man's property ; a woman's ornament."

A Caret marked thus ⌃ is placed where some word or letter happens to be left out in writing, and which is inserted over the line. This mark is also called a circumflex, when placed over a particular vowel, to denote a long syllable : as, " Euphrâtes."

A Hyphen, marked thus - is employed in connecting compound words : as, " Lap-dog, tea-pot, pre-existence, self-love, to-morrow, mother-in-law."

It is also used when a word is divided, and the former part is written or printed at the end of one line, and the latter part at the beginning of another. In this case, it is placed at the end of the first line, not at the beginning of the second.

The Acute Accent marked thus ´ : as, " Fáncy." The Grave thus ` : as, " Fàvour."

In English the accental marks are chiefly used in spelling-books and dictionaries, to mark the syllables which require a particular stress of the voice in pronunciation.

The stress is laid on long and short syllables indiscriminately. In order to distinguish the one from the other, some writers of dictionaries have placed the grave on the former, and the acute on the latter, in this manner : "Mìnor, míneral, lìvely líved, rìval, ríver,"

The proper mark to distinguish a long syllable, is this ‾ : as, " Rōsy ;" and a short one this ˘ : as, " Fŏlly." This last mark is called a breve.

A Diæresis, thus marked ¨, consists of two points placed over one of the vowels that would otherwise make a dipthong, and parts them into two syllables : as, " Creätor, coädjutor, aërial."

A Section, marked thus §, is the division of a discourse, or chapter, into less parts or portions.

A Paragraph ¶ denotes the beginning of a new subject, or a sentence not connected with the foregoing. This character is chiefly used in the Old and in the New-Testaments.

A Quotation " ". Two inverted commas are generally placed at the beginning of a phrase or a passage, which is quoted or transcribed from the speaker or author in his own words ; and two commas in their direct position, are placed at the conclusion : as,

" The proper study of mankind is man."

Crotchets or Brackets [ ] serve to enclose a word or sentence, which is to be explained in a note, or the explanation itself, or a word or sentence which is intended to supply some deficiency, or to rectify some mistake.

An Index or Hand ☞ points out a remarkable passage, or something that requires particular attention.

A Brace } is used in poetry at the end of a triplet or three lines, which have the same rhyme.

Braces are also used to connect a number of words with one common term, and are introduced to prevent a repetition in writing or printing.

An Asterisk, or little star, * directs the reader to some note in the margin, or at the bottom of the page. Two or three asterisks generally denote the omission of some letters in a word, or of some bold or indelicate expression, or some defect in the manuscript.

An Ellipsis ———— is also used, when some letters in a word, or some words in a verse, are omitted : as, "The k—g," for " the king."

An Obelisk, which is marked thus †, and Parallels thus ‖, together with the letters of the Alphabet, and figures, are used as references to the margin, or bottom of the page.

CHAPTER VII.

DIRECTIONS RESPECTING THE USE OF CAPITAL LETTERS.

As the commencement of every sentence is distinguished by a capital letter, and as capitals frequently occur in other parts of a sentence ; it is necessary to give you some directions respecting their proper application.

It was formerly the custom to begin every noun with a capital : but as this practice was troublesome, and gave the writing or printing a crowded and confused appearance, it has been discontinued. It is, however, very proper to begin with a capital.

1. The first word of every book, chapter, letter, note, or any other piece of writing.

2. The first word after a period ; and, if the two sentences are *totally independent,* after a note of interrogation or exclamation.

But if a number of interrogative or exclamatory sentences, are thrown into one general group ; or if the construction of the latter sentences depends on the former, all of them, except the first, may begin with a small letter : as, " How long, ye simple ones, will ye love simplicity ? and the scorners delight in their scorning ? and fools hate knowledge ?" " Alas ! how different ! yet how like the same !"

3. The appellations of the Deity : as, " God, Jehovah, the Almighty, the Supreme Being, the Lord, Providence, the Messiah, the Holy Spirit."

4. Proper names of persons, places, streets, mountains, rivers, ships : as, " George, York, the Strand, the Alps, the Thames, the Seahorse."

5. Adjectives derived from the proper names of places : as " Grecian, Roman, English, French, and Italian."

6. The first word of a quotation, introduced after a colon, or when it is in a direct form : as, " Always remember this ancient maxim : ' Know thyself.' " "Our great lawgiver says " Take up thy cross daily and follow me.' " But when a quotation is brought in obliquely after a comma, a capital is unnecessary : as, " Solomon observes, ' that pride goes before destruction."

The first word of an example may also very properly begin with a capital : as, " Temptation proves our virtue."

7. Every substantive and principal word in the titles of books : as, "Johnson's Dictionary of the English Language;" " Thomson's Seasons ;" " Rollin's Ancient History."

8. The first word of every line in poetry.

9. The pronoun *I,* and the interjection *O,* are written in capitals , as, " I write :" " Hear, O earth !"

Other words, besides the preceding, may begin with capitals, when they are remarkably emphatical, or the principal subject of the composition.

———

☞ *For Prosody, and the Figures of Speech, the learner is referred to Conversations on English Grammar, from which this is abridged.*

FINIS.